# Essays in
# German and Comparative Literature

UNIVERSITY OF NORTH CAROLINA
STUDIES IN COMPARATIVE LITERATURE

Lyman A. Cotten
Alfred G. Engstrom
John E. Keller
Albert I. Suskin
Werner P. Friederich, *Chairman and Editor*

THE UNIVERSITY OF NORTH CAROLINA PRESS

# Essays in
# German and Comparative Literature

BY OSKAR SEIDLIN

UNIVERSITY OF NORTH CAROLINA
STUDIES IN COMPARATIVE LITERATURE

Number Thirty                    Chapel Hill, N. C., 1961

Reprinted with the permission of The University of North Carolina Studies in Comparative Literature and The University of North Carolina Press

JOHNSON REPRINT CORPORATION         JOHNSON REPRINT COMPANY LIMITED
111 Fifth Avenue, New York, N.Y. 10003    Berkeley Square House, London, W. 1

Copyright 1961
The University of North Carolina Press

PT
343
.S 45

First reprinting, 1966, Johnson Reprint Corporation
Printed in the United States of America

TABLE OF CONTENTS

The dates in parenthesis indicate the year of the original publication.

*Apologia qua Praefatio* .................................................................... IX

1. Georg Brandes 1842-1927 (1942) .................................................. 1
2. Goethe's *Iphigenia* and the Humane Ideal (1949) ..................... 30
3. Goethe's "Magic Flute" (1943) .................................................... 45
4. Is the "Prelude on the Theatre" a Prelude to *Faust?* (1949) ..... 60
5. Goethe's Vision of a New World ................................................. 70
6. Goethe about Goethe in French (1946) ...................................... 84
7. Schiller: Poet of Politics (1960) ................................................... 92
8. Schiller's "Treacherous Signs" (1959) ......................................... 110
9. Glory and Decline of the *bourgeois:* Schiller and Dumas *fils* (1954) 131
10. Eichendorff's Symbolic Landscape (1957) ................................ 141
11. Picaresque Elements in Thomas Mann's Work (1951) ............. 161
12. Thomas Mann's *Joseph the Provider* and Laurence Sterne's *Tristram Shandy* (1947) ............................................................. 182
13. Hermann Hesse: The Exorcism of the Demon (1953) .............. 203
14. The Shroud of Silence (1953) .................................................... 228
15. The Oresteia Today: A Myth Dehumanized (1959) ................. 237

*To those of my friends and students who wanted to see these miscellanies between the covers of a book*

## APOLOGIA QUA PRAEFATIO

I have long admired the gracious and graceful flourish with which so many of my American colleagues close the prefaces to their book publications: that they alone are to be blamed for whatever shortcomings their work may have, and that none of its insufficiencies is to be charged to their friends, without whose help their book might still have been more grievously wanting in merit. I had hoped that I, as an author of a book, could avail myself of this gentle formula, too, and absolve my friends from the responsibility for all the flaws to be found in the pages following the preface. Yet much as I would like to, I cannot do it. For the simple truth of the matter is that without these devoted friends there would be no book at all, that they have caused it to come into existence, and that, having caused its existence, they must be held responsible for the whole enterprise.

Here, then, is the list of the guilty ones: first of all, the editor of this series, Werner P. Friederich, who conceived and stubbornly promoted the idea of putting these miscellaneous papers between the covers of a book; then the chairman of my department, Dieter Cunz, who egged me on and successfully played on the strain of vanity of which, alas, I am not free; my dear colleague and former student Sigurd Burckhardt, who translated one of the essays (No. 3) from the German original and, by doing so, furnished this volume with its only piece of immaculate English; Mrs. Iris Friederich, who did her best to cleanse my own English of its most obnoxious features; and finally Professor Everett Walters, Dean of the Graduate School of Ohio State University, who, by a generous grant, alleviated the awesome financial burden resting upon the editor of the series. How deeply indebted I am for this overwhelming display of confidence in my modest gifts and achievements, I need not and cannot tell. But with all my gratitude to them, now and forever, I see no way of absolving them from the responsibility for this book.

The fifteen essays, which through the unflagging efforts of these friends are now being presented in this form, were written in the course of almost twenty years. Since some were prepared as public lectures, others as addresses on special commemorative occasions, they lack, probably to their detriment, uniformity of style and approach. It would be dishonest of me and futile to claim that they are imbued and held together by one main theme. I hope, however, that at least some of them will show my endeavor to point up vital problems of the human condition through the interpretation of works of verbal art, and all of them a sincere concern with literature.

With one exception (No. 5), all the articles have been published previously in American periodicals or books, although two of them (Nos. 3 and 6) never before in English. They are being presented here with no, or only very insignificant, changes. It would be very wrong to conclude from this fact that, when rereading and assembling these pieces for book publication, I found such changes unnecessary. Rather the opposite is true: with few exceptions I felt them to be in need of such thorough rewriting, of so complete a re-study of the new secondary literature that I realized the uselessness of minor stop-gap improvements here and there. So I let them stand as they originally appeared in the following publications, whose editors were kind enough to give permission for inclusion in this volume: *Journal of the History of Ideas* (No. 1); *Modern Language Quarterly* (Nos. 2, 11 and 12); *Monatshefte* (No. 3); *Publications of the Modern Language Association, PMLA* (Nos. 4 and 10); *Germanic Review* (Nos. 6 and 14); *A Schiller Symposium* (University of Texas Press, 1960; No. 7); *Schiller 1759/1959* (University of Illinois Press, 1959; No. 8); *Comparative Literature* (No. 9); *Symposium* (No. 13); and *Thought* (No. 15).

Even this long enumeration of names does not at all exhaust the list of those to whom I am greatly indebted. Much more than just professional help, much more precious gifts I owe to the friends in my own department and the other literature departments of the Ohio State University; to the two chairmen under whom I have been working at this institution, Bernhard Blume and Dieter Cunz; and to J. Osborn Fuller, Dean of the Arts and Science College. May they at least, when scanning through this volume, be able to feel that the immeasurable kindness they have shown me, and their efforts to provide me with time for these "extra-curricular" activities have not been altogether wasted.

OSKAR SEIDLIN

Columbus, Ohio
April 1961

# GEORG BRANDES
## 1842-1927

The intellectual climate of Denmark in the sixties of the last century was close and oppressive. The small insular kingdom had retreated into a sulking-corner since, abandoned by its Western-European friends and trustees, it had been pushed aside by the Prussian and Austrian swords. In philosophy, the dominant trend was Hegelianism, which by its bold speculation diverted minds from the narrow realities of the day and surrounded even a reduced existence with the halo of reason; in religion, it was orthodoxy, lacking however Kierkegaard's vehement absoluteness and his passionate feeling of sinfulness; in literature, a tame romanticism, which since the days of Oehlenschläger had lost its inner genuineness while gaining, with the Heibergs and Goldschmidts, informal elegance and subtlety; in politics, a rigid narrow-mindedness, which in euphemistic naïveté called itself "conservatism," though looked at closely it betrayed itself as reaction. Ought one to embrace the ideas of foreigners, of those foreigners who had proved to be either enemies or traitors, who, having destroyed the political foundations of European stability, were now also trying by means of a Mephistophelian philosophy to shake the moral foundations of Europe: religion, the family and the state? Though mutilated as a nation, the people were determined not to sacrifice their inner salvation, for they were, in spite of, or rather because of, their humiliation, "the people of God's heart," as Bishop Grundtvig had so beautifully expressed it.[1] So one locked oneself up in one's four walls and puttied one's window that no draft from outside might enter. At that moment, a man appeared who could not breathe this stifling air, who flung the windows wide open, and forced Denmark back into the stream of the intellectual life of Europe. This man was Georg Brandes.

An intellectual revolution took place in Scandinavia. The barren soil sucked in the waters of the newly dug sources, and proved itself miraculously fertile. Scandinavian letters experienced a flowering which only a decade before no one would have

---

1. *Levned* (Copenhagen, 1905 ff.), III, 354. As far as possible, I have used the English translation of Brandes' works. Where no such translation exists, I have had recourse to and quoted from the Danish or the German editions. In these instances, the title or the place of publication will indicate which edition has been used.

dared to dream of. One man had pierced the wall, had brought the main currents of Europe to Scandinavia. A man had appeared who was to carry in turn the spirit of the new and old Scandinavia to Europe, who was to make the Continent aware of Oehlenschläger and Kierkegaard, Bjoernson and Ibsen, Drachmann and Bang, Strindberg and Jacobsen. This man was Georg Brandes.

Scandinavia was redeemed from her insular existence. But was this enough? Did not the great countries of Europe live side by side without knowing each other? Were not even the major thinkers amazingly unaware of what had happened and what was happening beyond their borders? What was a young Danish critic to think when a man like John Stuart Mill confessed frankly that he had never read a line of Hegel?[2] Europe needed help to understand herself; was it not obvious "that one could do much good by simply studying, confronting and understanding these great minds that fail to understand one another"?[3] Such a mediator was Georg Brandes.

I

"My life, my books may be insignificant in themselves, but if taken symbolically, they are of interest as microcosms."[4] Whatever the immense bulk of Brandes' literary activity may mean to us today, as an illustration of the intellectual movements in the last decades of the nineteenth century it is invaluable. In his writings, the revival of empiricism, the sweep of positivism, celebrate their triumphs; and even the countercurrents rather supplement than distort the picture of the nineteenth century.

His earliest ideas point in the direction of his future development. To be sure, they spring from very different sources. Kierkegaard and Hegel are his first teachers; but the young student is fascinated rather by their "poetic" qualities than by the real substance of their thought.[5] Although in his early

---

2. *Reminiscences of My Childhood and Youth* (= *Levned* I; New York, 1906), 284.
3. "John Stuart Mill," in *Creative Spirits* (London, 1924), 200.
4. *Levned*, III, 1.
5. "I was being initiated into an attempt (Hegel's) to comprehend the universe which was half wisdom, half poetry" (*Reminiscences*, 99); and with reference to Kierkegaard, "his grace and charm, the perfect control of the language" (*Ibid.*, 61).

publications Brandes still followed the speculative method of his great masters, he was mentally prepared for the new tendencies embodied in the works of David Friedrich Strauss and Feuerbach, Comte and Taine, Renan and Mill. He went over to the camp of the positivists; and his personal friendship with Renan, Taine and Mill, formed during his first visits to Paris, only precipitated a result which was inevitable.

Liberation from metaphysics, from speculation, was the new slogan which Brandes now echoed. It was in the world of the exact sciences that the great revolutions of the human spirit took place; here were hidden the sources which nourished all the other forms of human expression.

> Ideas are not begotten by poets. They emerge from the labors of thinkers and inquirers . . . they develop and take form amid scientific investigations.[6]

Whatever cannot hold its own before the tribunal of science is legend and superstition, which arouse our interest solely because from them all the misery of humanity takes its origin.

How, then, was it possible for a modern to profess himself anything but a free-thinker? What, after all, were the scriptures of traditional religion but a collection of fairy tales, whose supernatural elements stood in flagrant contrast to all scientific truth? With the weapons of modern psychological analysis, all of the evil spirit could be driven out. Feuerbach had become one of the great liberators of mankind[7] because, in Brandes' opinion, he had proved God to be a product of the human soul, had turned theology into anthropology, the theological into a psychological problem—and had solved it "in all essentials for all time."[8] It was the spirit of Feuerbach which prompted Brandes, at the beginning of his literary career, to put down in his diary the aphorism:

> When did God become Man? When Nature reached the point in its development at which the first man made his appearance. When Nature became man, then God did.[9]

It goes without saying that because of this attitude Brandes could not possibly understand a religious genius like Kierke-

---

6. "Ibsen," in *Creative Spirits*, 376.
7. *Main Currents of 19th Century Literature*, VI (London, 1906), 353 ff.
8. *Ibid.*, 356.
9. *Reminiscences*, 205.

gaard, in spite of the fact that he admired him profoundly. If such a religious obsession, such a contempt for science, for history and psychology, could be excused at all, it was, Brandes believed, only by assuming that his was a mental case, that here was a man who through a deplorable education had been forced on the wrong track.[10] Throughout his book on Kierkegaard there is a constant struggle going on between the biographer and his hero, except towards the end, when in the passionate fight of Kierkegaard against the present-day representatives of the Protestant church the two seem to have found a common platform; but Brandes overlooks the fact that the crusades of the free-thinker and the intense believer have nothing in common but the outer appearance.

In the light of scientific investigation, the positive religions could not maintain their position. What must take their place was a religion of humanity, a rationalistic moral philosophy, generally binding because freed from all relation to a vague and unexplainable notion of God.[11] He reiterates the argument that Kierkegaard never considered the possibility of a moral philosophy separated from religion.

> He never thought of morality as separate from Christianity, always sought support in some authority . . . Kierkegaard is influenced so little by the progress of modern European science, that morality appears to him as morality only when it is supported by a positive religion.[12]

Provided humanity was in need of salvation—and he himself did not feel this need [13]—it was to be found only within the realm of science, in the study of nature. Just as earlier, in the period of the Renaissance and in the days of Newton, an enthusiastic pantheism turned man's mind toward the science of nature, so Brandes' positivistic attitude originates in an almost religious veneration of nature and her immanent forces. Her imperturbability and her balance, her goodness and her cruelty, her self-sufficiency, which recognizes no law except her own, her incorruptibility, equally great in granting and refusing— these are again and again the mainsprings of his fervent admiration.[14] It is only consistent that, when but a young man, he

---

10. *Kierkegaard* (Leipzig, 1879), 24.
11. *Reminiscences*, 205.
12. *Kierkegaard*, 153.
13. *Reminiscences*, 108.
14. *Ibid.*, 235.

was deeply impressed by Spinoza,[15] that his inmost self was stirred by Goethe's half poetical, half philosophical, hymn *To Nature*.[16] It is true, Spinoza's conception was not entirely his own.

> Naturally Spinoza did not have the conception of life that he would have had, had he known modern chemistry and psychology. For him the universe was only a matter of extension and thought; he never rose to the living and fruitful infinite which history and natural science show as ruling in boundless space. Conceptions such as evolution and progress were foreign to him.[17]

Spinoza had to be supplemented by another who, by means of the concepts of evolution and progress, transformed the dead universe into a living one: Darwin.

Darwin's theory of evolution was in the eyes of Brandes the cornerstone upon which the intellectual edifice of the nineteenth century rested.[18] So axiomatic had this become to him that, in his *Goethe*, he followed up all the connections which lead from the poet to Darwin. It is not surprising that he emphasized in his discussion of the *Metamorphose der Pflanzen* and of Goethe's osteological studies the parallel between Goethe and Darwin, without recognizing how little Goethe's "inneres Gesetz" has in common with Darwin's "survival of the fittest." And again, it is the natural law of evolution which provides the basis for his monumental work *Main Currents of Nineteenth-Century Literature*, the book which made him famous all through Europe, which was hailed by his friends as a revelation,[19] abused by his enemies as heresy. The human mind constituting a unity, in all people and countries essentially the same, must necessarily everywhere obey the same laws of development, must traverse the same stages and find forms of expression whose parallelisms can be demonstrated without great difficulty.[20] What he sets out to present is the "six acts of a great play,"[21] a drama whose hero is the psyche of Europe; he has no doubt that the development as reflected in the literatures of France, Germany, and England must necessarily be a "progressive" one. Thus the division of the acts offers itself auto-

---

15. *Ibid.*, 101.
16. *Goethe* I (New York, 1925), 422.
17. *Ibid.*, 435.
18. *Ibid.*, 421.
19. *Letters of Henrik Ibsen* (New York, 1905), 233 and 266.
20. *Reminiscences*, 258.
21. *Main Currents* I, ix.

matically. First act: the beginning of reaction in the French emigrant literature; second act: beginning and victory of reaction in German Romanticism; third act: the stabilization of reaction in France; fourth act: the rebirth of freedom in English Naturalism; fifth act: the liberal tendencies in French Romanticism; sixth act: the victory of liberal thought in "Young Germany." At that point, the development has come to its close, the "fittest have survived", and a "new species" can originate.

He is permeated with the spirit of the new sciences, and wherever he discovers its essence in poetry, his enthusiasm is awakened. Being modern is Ibsen's foremost title to fame,[22] and the scientifically cool attitude in which Flaubert approaches the phenomena of the outer world and the soul impresses him particularly.[23] Even in Goethe's *Iphigenie* he suspects traces of the doctrine of heredity, and he honestly wonders how it is possible that the model of pure humanity descends from a family of murderers and criminals.[24]

Just as Goethe's characters and problems are confronted by Brandes with the scientific doctrine of heredity, so Taine's theory of environment at times creeps into the discussion of Shakespeare. Richard III, the titan of wickedness, is judged by Taine's categories; and in Brandes' eyes Shakespeare's indifference towards the trinity of heredity, environment and education calls for an excuse.[25]

Whenever Brandes makes any direct statements concerning philosophical and psychological problems, he shows himself a typical empiricist. Kant's doctrine that the categories are the basis of our apperceptions is interpreted in a strictly physiological sense: "that is to say he who has green spectacles sees things green, and he who has red ones sees them red."[26] He follows the same trend of thought in denying, in accordance with the atomistic-empirical psychology, the constitutional unity of the Ego, and in trying to dissolve it into particles of association. Here we find prepared what a few years later was raised into a system by the Empirio-Criticism of Ernst Mach—strangely enough as a part of the discussion of Romantic psychology,

---

22. "Ibsen," in *Creative Spirits*, 392.
23. "Flaubert," *ibid.*, 236.
24. *Goethe* I, 384.
25. *Shakespeare* I (New York 1931), 133.
26. *Main Currents* II, 260.

which would have been not a little at odds with such a conception of the Ego and the soul.

> The Ego is an artificial production, the result of associations of ideas ... Since the Ego is thus not an innate but an acquired conception, founded upon an association of ideas which has to maintain itself against the constant attacks of sleep, dreams, imaginations, hallucinations and mental derangements, it is by its nature exposed to manifold dangers ... It is of this correct psychological theory, originally propounded by Hume that the Romanticists, though they do not define it scientifically, nevertheless had a presentiment.[27]

The spirit of the scientific nineteenth century is a spirit of pragmatism and utilitarianism. It is not by chance that Brandes translated John Stuart Mill's *Utilitarianism* into Danish, nor that he greeted with naïve enthusiasm the technical application of scientific discoveries. The aristocratic purposelessness in which the Romanticists saw the highest goal of life and art aroused only his anger and protest. At great length he argues against Friedrich Schlegel, the prophet of holy indolence. In the midst of the discussion of Schlegel's *Lucinde*, he is overcome by indignation, and against Schlegel's assertion "industry and utility are the angels of death with the flaming swords who stand in the way of man's return to Paradise," he pits his emphatic verdict:

> Yes, that is exactly what they are. Industry and utility bar the way back to all Paradises which lie behind us. Therefore we hold them sacred! Utility is one of the main forms of good; and what is industry but the renunciation of distracting pleasures, the enthusiasm, the power whereby this good is attained?[28]

Since utility is one of the main forms of good, Brandes approves of placing poetry, the highest form of human expression, in the service of a definite cause. It is true, as we have seen, that he objects to having poetry utilized for religious ends. Even Ibsen must be blamed for having in *Brand* abused poetry as a vehicle of religious problems.[29] This however does not imply that Brandes tries to emancipate poetry from all practical tasks. For instance, the greatness of a poet is partly determined by

---

27. *Ibid.*, 172.
28. *Ibid.*, 73.
29. "It is the misfortune of contemporary literature that it fights in the service of a one-sided conception of religion, and frequently so inconsiderately and exclusively that it solemnly opposes all play of fancy as it is mirrored in poetry." (*Das Ibsenbuch*, Dresden, 1923, 39.) See Ibsen's protest against this interpretation of *Brand* (*Letters of H. Ibsen*, 173).

the cause he fights for; and Brandes does not need elaborate arguments to convince himself that Shelley was a far greater poet than the German Romanticist Novalis; for Shelley fought for liberty, Novalis, however, for what Brandes calls reaction.[30]

Utility and industry: it would be hard to find two words which epitomize so briefly and adequately the credo of the late nineteenth century. And it would be equally difficult to find a better illustration of this ethos of industry than the life and work of Georg Brandes. It seems prodigious what a wealth of knowledge this single mind was capable of absorbing, how easily and prolifically he utilized and conveyed his abundant learning. What intensity of industry there must have been in a man who, in his eightieth year, could proudly announce to a friend that in the last seven years he had sent seventeen volumes to the printer's.[31] Activity was for Brandes an article of faith, an end in itself; and it is amusing to notice his disgust when describing the idlers in Rome who concentrate their attention on the creases of their trousers or waste their time in front of the General Delivery boxes waiting for letters from their mistresses.[32] In his literary criticism are manifest also his almost religious reverence for activity and his negation of all those powers which might frustrate the activity of man. Shakespeare's *Hamlet* presents him with a difficult problem; and he does not rest content until he has succeeded in clearing Shakespeare's play of the "reproach" that it depicts the tragedy of inactivity. What he sees in Hamlet is not a tragedy of inactivity, but of disgust with the world, and Hamlet's hesitation is explained as a technical device to fill the five acts of the drama.[33] Yes, Brandes whom one cannot accuse of yielding to compromises, who had chosen as his watchword: "As flexible as possible when it is a question of understanding, as inflexible as possible if it is a question of speaking,"[34] raises his objections

---

30. *Main Currents* II, 206.
31. "In these seven years I had written the four large works: *Goethe, Voltaire, Caesar, Michelangelo*, as well as the collection *Napoleon and Garibaldi* and the two volumes on the World War, and in addition to these eleven volumes published three volumes of *Collected Works* and a fourth volume of *Speeches*. The proof-reading alone of seventeen thick volumes is a task, not to mention the labor of writing them. (Letter to Henri Nathansen). Cf. Henri Nathansen, *Jude oder Europäer Georg Brandes* (Frankfurt a.M., 1931), 218.
32. *Levned* II, 240.
33. *Shakespeare* II, 35.
34. *Reminiscences*, 271.

against Ibsen's rigorism, the passionate absoluteness of a Brand, because the rigid All or Nothing bars the way to action and the gradual realization of the ideal.[35]

Here we have arrived at the crossroad where Brandes takes leave of scientific positivism. This passionate urge for action could arise only upon the basis of a philosophy of will, of an idealism of freedom in Brandes' *Weltanschauung*. In this connection it may suffice to point out that, in spite of being sincerely devoted to the spirit of the natural sciences, he was a fervent opponent of determinism, its legitimate child. So it was but natural that at times the attitude of the ideal scientist, his indifferent objectivity, his dispassionate observing and cool recording of facts, struck him as questionable and dangerous. And when he found in his dearly beloved Renan the following definition of the ideal scholar:

> The savant is a spectator of the universe. He knows the world belongs to him only as an object for study, and even if he could reform it, he would perhaps find it so curious an object that he would lose all desire to do so,

he had but this brief and superior retort: "It is scarcely likely that Renan was altogether in earnest when he uttered these audacious and aristocratic words."[36]

## II

Brandes' belief in the sciences is harmoniously and indissolubly tied up with his belief in reason. Though we shall try later to do justice to the complex and contradictory elements in his attitude, we cannot overlook the rigidly rationalistic traits in his nature. He felt himself a servant of the word which tries to lift the elusive and intangible into the realm of the clear, articulate, and ascertainable. We may be justified in taking in a symbolic sense his confession: "My fatherland is the Danish language." He did not feel himself bound by magic, irrational forces. The only bond he knew was the one to the *logos* which manifests itself in the word.

He was, up to a point, a disciple of the Enlightenment, and his admiration for Voltaire, the apostle of this movement, has something touching in it. He treats hardly any other subject with the same degree of critical benevolence, with the same

---
35. "Ibsen," *Creative Spirits*, 375.
36. "Renan," *ibid.*, 220.

idolizing fondness which tries to excuse or whitewash every dark spot in the character of his hero. He is intoxicated by the clarity of this mind, the conciseness of his analyses, the poignancy of his expressions. And he seems to be blind to the generalizing superficiality of his thoughts, and the questionable traits of character of this "champion of freedom." How sure he is of his victory when confronting Voltaire with Pascal, with what ease does he decide to which of the two the palm belongs:

> Wherever Voltaire opposes his own clear and sane judgment to the paradoxes born of Pascal's dogma-ridden, tortured mind, Voltaire is right. Though theologians may find depth in Pascal's contemplations, a thinker will find them merely moving.[37]

No doubt he lacked the understanding of the "paradoxical"; and even more emphatically than against Pascal he protests against Kierkegaard, who saw in paradox the only road to knowledge, the only attempt at a solution of the problem of human existence.[38] It is in Brandes' view a symptom of Kierkegaard's disease that he so passionately clings to the paradoxical; lyricism and enthusiasm have afflicted his mind and sadly deranged the thought, which has to remain "cool" in order to be "healthy."

He demands clarity and precision in poetry just as in the process of thinking. He was repelled by Hegel's philosophy, which devaluated and dissolved the logical opposites of thesis and antithesis by the superimposition of the synthesis. Like philosophy, poetry also is expected to furnish us with clearcut answers. It is not to be satisfied with just demonstrating the problems but it should work out a satisfactory and convincing solution.[39] If his attitude towards Ibsen vacillates at times, it is because he realizes only too well that the playwright raised questions without intending to offer clear and distinct answers. Planning and organizing reason, which has a firm grip on the various parts and weaves them into a closely knit whole, has a large share in conceiving and executing a work of art. And in connection with Shakespeare, who was the highest idol of all the Romanticists just because of his lack of a distinct plan, of his willful arbitrariness, Brandes asserts:

> The art of dramatic writing consists almost entirely in preparing what is to come.[40]

---

37. *Voltaire* I (New York, 1930), 204.
38. *Kierkegaard*, 103.
39. *Ibsenbuch*, 38.
40. *Shakespeare* I, 157.

At times the rationalistic attitude results in a shallow prosaicness to which the vital and emotional contents of poetry are a closed world. The revolutionary antirationalism of the German Storm and Stress seems ridiculous to him, Maximilian Klinger is "no artist, he lacks that sanity and balance indispensable to the creation of a character that does not act contrary to all principles of reason";[41] and his play, which gave the whole movement its name, is summed up as "world-famous nonsense." But this aversion is not restricted to minor writers; ultimately Brandes is at a loss what to do with Goethe's *Werther*. He fails to grasp the central problem of the novel, the ruin of an individual caused by the superabundance of his emotions, and finds nothing but the story of an unhappy love whose high tension strikes the sober critic as exaggerated and unintelligible.[42]

All poetic symbolism which escapes a healthy verification and analysis has a difficult time against such a prosaic mind. With some slight regret he watches Ibsen's turn toward symbolism;[43] and the way in which he dissects the symbolic elements in Ibsen's work often verges on the grotesque. Even his admission that he is a "prosaic soul" fails to reconcile us to his lack of understanding of the poetic revelation which a symbol is able to achieve. Why did Brand's little son have to die? he asks in all earnestness; the calamity could have been avoided, had he only been sent to a milder climate.[44] What a disheartening philistinism is disclosed in his attempt to blur the moving symbolical meaning of Solness' ascent of the tower by a petty prosaic calculation:

> Let it at once be remarked, that it is by no means a criterion of the artistic greatness of a master-mind whether or not he is seized by vertigo as he climbs to the top of a church steeple, and as a result, the entire mood of the play, its symbolism is lost.[45]

It is but natural that such a "prosaic soul" should have no spontaneous access to the deep enchantment of lyric poetry. It is true, he has tried again and again to capture the spirit of lyrics; and if we may believe the reports of his friends,[46] he was even capable of losing himself in the music and magic

---

41. *Goethe* I, 189.
42. *Ibid.*, 193.
43. *Ibsenbuch*, 151.
44. *Ibid.*, 45.
45. *Ibid.*, 167.
46. Edmund Gosse, *Two Visits to Denmark* (London, 1911), 289.

of a poem with a fervor verging on a trance. But basically he is unmusical, and one will find in his works hardly any reference to music. Where he has to draw the musical element into his discussion, as in the instance of Kierkegaard's audacious *Don Juan*-analysis, one senses the helplessness of the critic who labels Mozart with the attributes "carefree and sparkling."[47] Notwithstanding Brandes' ability to experience poetry intensely, the analyses he puts in writing sound astonishingly flat and uninspired. In so far as he ventures beyond the purely *Weltanschauliche* of a poem, he contents himself with non-committal remarks on the beauty of the language, the audacity and accuracy of the metaphors, the richness of the rhyme. And his extensive quotations from the poems under discussion, particularly conspicuous in the case of Heine,[48] seem to be an indication of his inadequacy and an attempt to unload the task of interpretation onto the shoulders of the reader. However, one must not jump to the conclusion that Brandes lacked a great sensitivity to the shades and potentialities of a language. On the contrary, it is admirable how he, the foreigner, succeeded in feeling his way into the subtleties of German, French, and English styles. Nevertheless, his works hardly contain a profound and creative analysis of lyrical poetry.

His basically rationalistic attitude shows up most conspicuously in his treatment of German Romanticism. The whole volume which he dedicated to this literary movement within the framework of his *Main Currents* is nothing but a protest against and a refutation of a poetic and human conception which he fails to understand, or as far as he does understand it, abhors. Just as in Goethe's *Walpurgisnacht*, under the mask of the Proktophantasmist the enlightened rationalistic Nicolai watches, with disgusted amazement, the uproar of the unchained demons, so Brandes is helpless in the face of a movement which has declared war on sound common sense, has plunged into those abysses of the soul where Ariadne's clue of reason is powerless.

> Taking all this together, one feels as if Romanticism ended in a sort of Witches' Sabbath in which the philosophers played the part of the old crones, amidst the thunders of the obscurantists, the insane yells of the mystics.[49]

---

47. *Kierkegaard*, 123.
48. *Main Currents* VI, 124 ff.
49. *Main Currents* II, 16.

No doubt, he who clung rigidly to the Cartesian conception of the soul as consciousness, as thought, had to see a "Witches' Sabbath" in the Romantic attempt to place the center of man in the unconscious. He saw in "dreams, frenzy, hallucinations, madness . . . the powers which disintegrate the Ego, disconnect its links",[50] while the Romanticists exalted just these very forces as those by which the individual soul partook of the *Allseele*. He looked at the night as "one side of nature",[51] while for the Romanticists it was the medium in which objects and individual souls freed themselves from the curse of individuation and merged with the unconscious unity of the infinite. Not recognizing that for the Romanticists the Middle Ages were a symbol of the great guiltless oneness of mankind, he had nothing better to say than that Romanticism "fell foolishly in love with the past and its childish naïveté."[52] Not once, throughout the whole book, has one the impression that he knew what the Romantic experiment really meant; and he is not even ready to admit that Romanticism had at least helped to conquer new realms of poetic feeling and expression.

> In the matter of language with their intangible imagery, their misuse of words in expressing the strange, weird, and mysterious, their archaisms and their determination to be unintelligible to the ordinary reader, they rather diminished than enriched the poetic vocabulary, rather corrupted than improved literary style.[53]

Romanticism is to him the great corrupting danger, a danger to which unfortunately even Kleist succumbed, whose "clearness and definiteness . . . was disturbed and deranged by the poetic insanity of Romanticism.[54]

Is it then surprising that Rousseau, the father of European Romanticism, gets nothing but poor marks whenever his name is mentioned in Brandes' work? In spite of his own pantheism, he has not the slightest sympathy for this apostle of nature, because in Rousseau's struggle against civilization he sensed only too clearly the frontal attack on the organizing and constructive forces of reason. It goes without saying that in the Voltaire book Rousseau has no chance as the antagonist of the hero, though the weapons Brandes uses against his opponent

---

50. *Ibid.*, 172.
51. *Ibid.*, 151.
52. *Ibid.* VI, 300.
53. *Ibid.* II, 5.
54. *Ibid.*, 258.

can hardly be called fair. What must one think when the apologist for Voltaire, whose firmness of character was more than doubtful, reprimands Rousseau: "The champion of equality accepted the hospitality of a banker's wife"?[55] And one hardly trusts one's eyes when, ten pages later, in referring to Rousseau's refusal to take refuge in a mansion of the Prussian king, one reads the words:

> Rousseau with the pride of the "poor-but-proud" would not accept anything: it would be impossible for him to sleep in a house that had been built by the hand of a King.[56]

But not only when he needs a dark background against which the profile of his hero may stand out all the more advantageously does he paint Rousseau in the blackest colors. So much is Brandes an adherent of civilization, a member of the "City of Man," that to him Rousseau's "Back to Nature" can mean nothing but a relapse into primitive barbarism, which one ought to fight solely with the weapons of ridicule.[57] He who knew German literature more thoroughly than almost any other foreign literary historian blames the young Goethe for having "had . . . the poor taste to prefer, at this period of life, the Swiss Rousseau to native French writers,"[58] as if he did not know how low the level of German literature had been under the influence of the "native French writers," and what an unforgettable share Rousseau and his spirit had had in the development and flowering of German letters.

Is it going too far to credit also his love of the South, manifesting itself so vividly in his autobiography, in his travel-book *Hellas,* to his rationalistic bias? But does it not equally testify to his passion for the clear, the distinct and the unambiguous? Here he witnessed the beauty of balance and form in genuine purity and the simplicity of outline; the clean articulation of shape filled him with a delight similar to that which the great Rationalists felt when dealing with mathematical problems.

### III

We have already pointed out in a different connection how

---
55. *Voltaire* II, 87.
56. *Ibid.,* 97.
57. ". . . a proclamation of reaction. Rousseau desired to return to the state of Nature, when men roamed naked through the pathless forests and lived upon acorns." (*Main Currents* II, 72.)
58. *Goethe* I, 208.

wrong it would be to see in Brandes exclusively the representative of empirical positivism. We shall have to show now to what a strong degree he was dominated by a radical philosophy of the will, by an idealism of freedom, which came constantly into conflict with his scientific deterministic attitude.

All his life long he remained loyal to the sentence which at the age of seventeen he put down in his diary:

> There is only one decisive factor on earth: the will, led by intelligence.[59]

And the older he became, the more this sentence took on the character of his most personal confession. Even Carlyle's hero-worship may at times seem tame compared with the idolization of the great personality, which we encounter at every step in Brandes' work. It struck him like lightning when he read the first lines of Nietzsche: and it is not just chance that he became the first passionate propagandist of Nietzsche, that he was the first, in his lectures on Nietzsche, to call the attention of the European public to the prophet of the "superman," at a time when Nietzsche was still generally decried as a dangerous fool or a ridiculous muddlehead.[60] So thoroughly did he succumb to Nietzsche's influence that he was ready to burn what he had worshipped, to turn against Mill's utilitarianism,[61] and to speak with contempt of those who until then had been his allies.

> People are still busy with the same doctrines, certain theories of heredity, a little Darwinism, a little emancipation of woman, a little morality of happiness, a little free thought, a little worship of democracy.[62]

What has become of his admiration for J. S. Mill and Bentham, of his belief in "the greatest happiness of the greatest number," when he could write:

---
59. *Levned* III, 144.
60. As late as 1895, Hjalmar Boyesen could state in his paper on Brandes (*Essays on Scandinavian Literature*, New York, 1895, 213): "Nowhere has he unmasked so Mephistophelian a countenance as in his essays on Luther and on an obscure German iconoclast Friedrich Nietschke (sic!). It is difficult to understand how a man of well-balanced brain and a logical equipment second to none can take *au sérieux* a mere philosophical savage who dances a war dance amid what he conceives to be the ruins of civilization, swings a reckless tomahawk and knocks down everybody and everything that comes in his way."
61. *Nietzsche* (London, 1914), 24.
62. *Ibid.*, 55.

16  GERMAN AND COMPARATIVE LITERATURE

The answer to the question of culture, how the individual human life may acquire its highest value and its greatest significance, must be by living for the benefit of the rarest and most valuable examples of the human race.[63]

What else is his own life but a permanent endeavor in the service of the "superman," a Pantheon for the rulers of the spirit and the world: Shakespeare, Voltaire, Goethe, Michelangelo, Lassalle, Lord Beaconsfield, Napoleon, Garibaldi, and Caesar? Read his hymns to Caesar, not only in the great book which he devoted to him, but elsewhere, whenever he finds an opportunity for paying homage to the ruler of the world! It is easy to see why he fills so many pages which protestations against Shakespeare's portrait of Caesar, taken over from Plutarch, who extolled the treacherous, ambitious and petty-minded Brutus at the expense of the hero. So much is he impressed by the greatness of a personality that he is even ready to admire when faced with a political or ideological antagonist, provided only that the enemy be great. Although a declared opponent of Prussian militarism, he has even a certain sympathy for Bismarck;[64] and in Paris he falls out with an old friend of his because he defended Moltke against her attacks,[65] the same Moltke who, though a former Danish subject, had been chiefly responsible for the mutilation of Denmark from which Brandes suffered so deeply. However much he loathed the philosophical and political convictions of Joseph de Maistre, he sincerely admired this reckless reactionary, who had the courage of his own odiousness and did not try to disguise his atrocious philosophy.[66] Even the repulsive is beautiful provided it be great; and faced with the alternative of choosing between a good average person and a gigantic monster, he decides for the monster, Richard III.[67]

With Brandes extreme individualism assumed an almost religious form. For this very reason Byron and Shelley signified a turning point in the whole of European literature,[68] because in them forces were set free which made possible the emancipation of the individual from all ties and restrictions. With this deep religious belief in the freedom and emancipation of the

63. *Ibid.*, 15.
64. *Levned* II, 119.
65. *Ibid.*, 344.
66. *Main Currents* III, 111-113; *ibid.*, II, 12; *Levned* II, 151. With reference to Gentz, *Main Currents* VI, 316.
67. *Shakespeare* I, 163.
68. *Main Currents* I, ix.

individual from all external conditions, Brandes was bound soon to come into conflict with Taine and his theory of environment. In spite of all his devotion to the spirit of science, he had to protest against a doctrine which threatened the freedom of the will.

> Did the consistent determinism of modern science, the discovery of an unalterable interdependency in the intellectual as in the physical world, allow scope for actions proceeding otherwise than merely illusorily from the free purposes or determination of the individual?[69]

Individualism is the most precious possession of mankind; and the reason for the cowardly tameness of our culture he attributes to the "disintegration of individuality which the modern order of society involves."[70] And do not also the poisonous invectives launched in his *Shakespeare* against the Baconian theory[71] originate above all in the endeavor to save Shakespeare as an "individuality," and to protect him from the vilification which anonymity would mean from Brandes' point of view?

It is for this reason that the man of antiquity, who in noble harmony gives free rein to his instincts and abilities, and is not yet conscious of the Jewish-Christian "Thou shalt not," becomes the object of his intense admiration, carried over to the Renaissance, which, marked by the revolution of the individual against all restrictions, represents the period of highest human fulfillment. His autobiography, indeed all his works are filled with his allegiance to the Graeco-Pagan ideal of man; his *Michelangelo* is nothing but a hymn to the Renaissance. This Renaissance ideal of free human beings he rejoicingly rediscovers in Shakespeare; and with a biting sharpness he scorns Eduard von Hartmann, the "philosopher of Philistinism," who objected to the character of Juliet because he found in her only "purely sensuous passions."[72]

To this gospel of the great personality, of the superman who does not stop short of full self-realization, corresponds a contempt for the masses which knows no bounds. He never misses an opportunity to expose the stupidity and inertia of the "compact majority"; and in reading his books, one can hardly rid oneself of the painful impression caused by the monotony of

---
69. *Reminiscences*, 230. Another attack on Taine in *Nietzsche*, 11 (note).
70. *Nietzsche*, 17.
71. *Shakespeare* I, 104.
72. *Ibid.*, 102.

his fits of hatred. It is true he himself had to suffer to an incredible extent from reactionary pettiness. For five full years he had to live in voluntary exile because the indignation against him assumed such proportions that he no longer felt safe in Denmark. Reading in his autobiography of the attacks to which he was exposed all through his life—and he fills pages and pages with these anecdotes—we feel ourselves at times confronted with a man suffering from persecution mania. And if we did not possess corroborating statements from others,[73] we would hardly think it possible that a person who fought with such integrity and courage for his convictions could be the object of so much hatred. He was the "enemy of the people";[74] but the unrestrained attacks of the "compact majority" were equalled by Brandes' reactions. Is it understandable that he, the friend of all the great men in Europe, the literary critic whose fame was second to none in the whole world, the man whom the Poles worshipped almost as a national hero, whom the young generation idolized to such a degree that a radical Danish Student Organization put to its new members the question: "Do you believe in God or do you believe in Brandes?"[75]—is it possible that such a man was seized with frenzy when attacked by a local paper of the small Danish town of Aarhus?[76] His hatred of man knew no bounds, and it will not surprise us that his plan to write a book on Shakespeare grew out of his preoccupation with *Timon of Athens*.[77]

However, this *odi profanum vulgus* is again but one aspect of Brandes. The passionate admiration for the great personality, the violent contempt of the mob, are interspersed with an

---

73. One of innumerable examples: Gosse tells us (*op. cit.*, 284) that during his stay in Denmark he did not dare to confess to his host that he knew Brandes and was with him frequently. And when one day Brandes, contrary to their agreement, called on him, his host's sister, who had recognized the visitor, behaved as if Satan in person had appeared to her. Gosse had to ask Brandes explicitly never to repeat this attempt, otherwise he would have lost the friendship of his host.
74. Hermann Weigand (*The Modern Ibsen*, New York, 1925, 102) very rightly dismisses the question whether Brandes was the model of Ibsen's *Enemy of the People* as irrelevant. But in this connection it may be of interest that Ibsen himself told Brandes that he had been thinking of him when writing the play. (*Levned* II, 262.)
75. *Levned* II, 80.
76. Nathansen, *op. cit.*, 143.
77. "But the part alone which I felt passionately urged to work out and wrestled with for five years was the first half of part three, that has its climax in *Timon of Athens* whose emotions and views were then my own." *Levned* III, 301.

incredibly sensitive social conscience, with a bold defense of the rights of the oppressed and those neglected by fate. From his earliest childhood the sight of poverty and human suffering caused him almost physical pain,[78] and it is certain that neither Byron and Shelley nor the authors of Young Germany would have stood so close to his heart had they not been the champions of social justice, of the liberation of the oppressed Poles and Greeks. He was an "enemy of the people," but moved by a deep love for the people, like the prophets of the Bible who chastised men out of concern for their happiness and the salvation of their souls. It is true that this mixture of love and hatred expressed itself in the strangest forms: one day a desperate pessimism, the conviction that everything was futile, that belief in progress was nothing but a vain illusion; and the next a return to the battlefield, which would have been impossible had the outburst of despair really sprung from the depth of his heart. His book on the war is full of these contradictions. On the one hand the belief that nations have been innocent victims of criminally irresponsible diplomats,[79] on the other the conviction that the greed and stupidity of man had automatically to lead to this war.[80] One day the comment: "A pessimist once remarked that humanity is a 'gang of brutes.' He was mistaken. Humanity is divided into a series of different gangs, all fighting each other, and each one trying to beat the others"[81]—and another the disavowel: "But let no one believe that I imply humanity will never rid itself of war."[82]

The same mixture of hatred and love characterizes his relation to Denmark. His outbursts of wrath against his country, against Copenhagen, surpass all reasonable bounds, and yet, when after a voluntary exile of five years, he was invited to return, he jumped at the opportunity without hesitation, though a great future seemed to be waiting for him in Berlin, where even the imperial family had assured him of their favor and interest. He who did not weary of chastising his compatriots for their sins, blamed Theodor Mommsen for overlooking in his criticism of the Danes "the good qualities."[83] And though

---

78. *Reminiscences*, 101.
79. *The World at War* (New York, 1917), 37. Also William Archer, *Shirking the Issue, Open Letter to George Brandes* (London, 1917), 2.
80. *The World at War*, 170.
81. *Ibid.*, 172.
82. *Ibid.*, 177.
83. *Levned* II, 262.

but a guest in a foreign country, he did not miss a single opportunity in his public and private speeches to remind Prussia of the grave injustice she did Denmark in taking North Schleswig from her.

The combination of hatred and love of humanity is also responsible for the inconsistency and elusiveness of his political attitude. He is a confirmed aristocrat, yet all his life an enemy of every brand of conservatism, a fighting protagonist of progressive government. He passionately defends the French Revolution against Nietzsche,[84] and reproaches the same French Revolution harshly for having sent "the best heads,"[85] because of their unmistakably aristocratic imprint, to the guillotine. In a political speech addressed to a leftist group in Denmark, he stresses the point that he does not want to be called a liberal, much less a democrat;[86] nevertheless, what is his whole life but a continuous struggle for liberalism and for the democratic freedom of nations and minds? This incompatability of his political views seems to be drastically expressed in two letters which in a brief space of time he sent to an acquaintance of his in Paris. "J'ai pris part au combat constitutionnel par simple conviction philosophique et par horreur des hommes qui ont brisé la loi et nullement par conviction démocratique," we read in one of his letters; in the other he states clearly and blatantly: "Je suis resté fidèle à la gauche et je le resterai."[87]

However strong his contempt of man may have been in the dark moments of his life, deep down he always believed in the necessity and meaningfulness of the fight for freedom. His pessimism is not of a metaphysical but of a moral nature; it is not the final word of one who is resigned to wisdom, but the passing impulse of an impatient man who is irritated by the slowness of progress. He never doubts that the mission has a meaning, that it has to be realized. It is only consistent that he should have recognized in Ibsen, too, this "indignation—pessimism" which has "its roots in a conviction of the possibility of the realization of the ideal."[88] Though he often believes man-

---
84. *Nietzsche*, 37.
85. *Voltaire* II, 310.
86. *Levned* III, 81.
87. Maurice Bigeon, *Les Révoltés Scandinaves* (Paris, 1894), 23.
88. "Ibsen," *Creative Spirits*, 364. It is true, this essay was written in 1883, when Brandes could not yet have been acquainted with the *Wild Duck*. But in none of his later essays on Ibsen does Brandes refer to the poet's much more melancholy views with regard to the "realization of the ideal."

kind to be hopelessly lost in stupidity and indolence, he undauntedly defends the principle of "compulsory education" against Renan and his friends, and turns a deaf ear to the melancholy question of the skeptics: What good will it do?[89]

But however much he may change his opinions, his passionate belief in the nobleness of the spirit never wavers. In the hierarchy of human possibilities, the artist holds the supreme place. Art to him is not only a beautiful addition to life, but the highest blessing bestowed on mankind. Without any hesitation he calls Shakespeare "one of the greatest benefactors of the human race,"[90] though the term "benefactor" may strike us as strange in this connection. And Ibsen's heart-breaking lament over the lost happiness of life, the melancholy question of *When We Dead Awaken* whether so much resignation in the service of art is not a sin against life, Brandes fails to understand.[91] Since he saw in the spiritual mission the highest bliss of mankind, what but a whim of old age could make Ibsen question it? How can the artist dare to have doubts about himself as king in the world of man, "the truth's ordained priest"?[92]

## IV

We have tried to outline the intellectual and emotional climate of Brandes' world. What remains is to inquire into his approach to the creative genius and the work of art. We shall not be surprised to discover that his was the approach of the positivistic literary critic, a method which, though by no means extinct even today, has become more and more untenable.

We who have been influenced by Croce's aesthetics, by the rigorous art of textual analysis practiced by the New Criticism, no longer believe in the separation of *life* and *work*, which nineteenth-century aesthetics assumed. We see in the self-realization of the genius an indissoluble *Gestalt*, a primary function of life which in its essentials cannot be reduced to biographical dates offered by the external course of a poet's life. From our phenomenological standpoint, the ontological *Wesensschau* has replaced the psychological historical analysis.

To Brandes, however, life and work constitute dual entities, which are only casually related to each other, two different

---
89. "Renan," *Creative Spirits*, 214.
90. *Shakespeare* II, 413.
91. *Ibsenbuch*, 187.
92. *The World at War*, 166.

substances which can be compared to each other, and in this way mutually clarified. He openly adopted Sainte-Beuve's method: "the works illuminating the life, the life supporting and determining the works."[93] Particularly when direct biographical information about the poet is scarce, the work again and again has to furnish the missing data, and the interpretation gives way to guesses as to the "hidden" personal experiences. He explicitly states that it has been the purpose of his *Shakespeare*

> to declare and prove that Shakespeare is not thirty-six plays and a few poems jumbled together but a man who felt and thought, rejoiced and suffered, brooded, dreamed and created,[94]

as though such proof were necessary, as though it helped us in the least to draw closer to the phenomenon Shakespeare. As he believes in the dualism of life and work, the construction of his books is not fundamentally different from the usual pattern of the nineteenth-century literary criticism which used to alternate monotonously one chapter of biography with one chapter of critical analysis. It is true that he arranges his material somewhat more tastefully; but the jumping back and forth from the biographical to the interpretative aspect is only thinly veiled.

To Brandes the world of the creative genius is not a cosmos resting in itself, obeying its own laws, but the everyday reality which he copies with the help of certain formal means, be they of a naturalistic, romantic or idealizing nature. The artist is nothing but a good observer who by a happy accident has also the capacity to give shape to his observations. This conception of the artist is hardly to be stated more explicitly than Brandes states it in his characterization of Flaubert:

> He evidently possessed in an equally high degree the two elements that constitute the being of the artist: the gift of observation and the power of investing with form.[95]

It is for this reason, too, that he hardly ever conceives of a work of art as a self-sufficient creation, a *Gestalt* which has its real center in itself, directly accessible, thus sparing us the detour of historical and psychological detail, but as a more or less arbitrary addition of inner or outer experiences and form. Where do we find the work obeying its own law, resting in it-

---

93. Gosse, *op. cit.*, 289.
94. *Shakespeare* II, 412.
95. "Flaubert," *Creative Spirits*, 241—The same view is expressed in *Main Currents* VI, 37.

self like an organic unity, when Brandes points out the general lines which he followed in producing his collection of essays:

> The mode of treatment in these essays is greatly diversified. In some of them, the individuality of the author portrayed is represented as extensively as possible; in others, an attempt has been made to present the man in actual person before the eyes of the reader; some are purely psychological, others offer a fragment of aesthetics, others again are eminently biographical and historical.[96]

The individuality, the man, the person, psychological, biographical, historical: here we have the whole arsenal of concepts in which the positivist literary critic had made himself at home.

Brandes has hardly any notion of the mysterious wonders of genius, originating in *daimon* and *ananke*. Now and then, it is true, we come across a statement which seems to lead into the very heart of the problem, an intuition which might bar the way to a biographical and psychological interpretation. But how isolated is such an insight as the following:

> The nature of genius is an organically connected whole. Its weakness in one direction is the condition of its strength in another. It is impossible to alter any single particular without disturbing the entire machinery.[97]

And how lacking in consequences is this discovery when Brandes in the same essay compares genius to "a tangled skein ... that we may unravel ... from its coil if we but get hold of the outer end of the thread."[98] How superficial must have been his conception of genius as "an organically connected whole" if ten years later in his book on Kierkegaard he spent pages and pages lamenting that young Kierkegaard had not attended an English college, that he had been exposed to German speculative, instead of to empiric philosophy, that he had inhaled the sticky and bigoted air of his father's house, unlike the young J. S. Mill who, guided by an enlightened natural scientist, had roamed through the open country.[99]

Again and again Brandes applies the principle of causality, the gospel of all natural science, to the process of intellectual creativeness. With a simplicity sometimes bordering on the

---
96. *Eminent Authors of the 19th Century* (New York, 1886), Introduction.
97. "Andersen," *Creative Spirits*, 35.
98. *Ibid.*, 13.
99. *Kierkegaard*, 11, 12, 17, 34.

childish, the great work of art is interpreted as the direct sediment of a concrete experience. So he traces back the religious passion of a Kierkegaard, the arresting struggle of a soul in quest of redemption, to the

> sufferings he underwent at the time of his betrothal [untranslatably phrased by Brandes: "Verlobungs- und Leidensgeschichte"], an experience that forms the basis of his purely aesthetic and dispassionate investigations as well as his strictly religious emotional essay.[100]

So he sees in Kierkegaard's turning to the Passion the result of the campaign by which the Danish humorous magazine *Korsar* tried to ridicule the great philosopher. And he explains the young Heine's longing for death from the biographical fact that the boy Heine at this time was in love with Josepha, the daughter of an executioner.[101] These few examples must suffice to indicate Brandes' fundamentally mechanistic attitude, which in the spiritual world also relates everything to cause and effect. Brandes was never able to free himself from this approach; the urge to "explain" scientifically is ingrained in him and pervades his whole work.

The positivistic aestheticians, obsessed by the idea that the growth of a work of art would be thus "explained" conclusively, had surrendered completely to the notorious hunt for original models, for those sources which they collected with minute accuracy, convinced as they were that they could grasp the secret of a work of art by dissolving it into its various elements like a chemical compound. Compared to the philological zeal with which the nineteenth century ferreted out sources, the work of Brandes signifies a tremendous progress. Still even he relapses at times into the dissection-mania. For Shakespeare's *Tempest* he unearths no less than twelve sources,[102] while, in the course of the discussion of Gretchen's prayer in *Faust*, he reminds us of five Goethean reminiscences which found their way into the poem.[103] It would be unjust to overlook the surprising length to which Brandes had already gone beyond this hunt after sources. But the summative method, reflecting the atomistic mechanistic attitude of the nineteenth century, trying to dissolve the wholeness of a work of art and of life into particles

---
100. *Ibid.*, 73.
101. *Main Currents* VI, 119.
102. *Shakespeare* II, 370.
103. *Goethe* I, 300.

derived from psychological and biographic data, is fundamentally the method of Brandes also. No doubt, it is to his great credit that he kept his mind open to great vistas of ideas, that he had the courage to write a literary history of Europe at a time when literary historiography exhausted itself in collections of philological material, concentrating its interest on minutely detailed inquiries. But the totalities, the great monuments which he tries to construct, show only too blatantly the various single parts from which they have been put together. Thus of the two great works of his old age, his book on Goethe is broken up into 140 small chapters representing almost as many fresh starts, and his *Voltaire* is anything but a well-integrated whole. To be sure, here he strives for a great unity; what he is after is not an isolated portrait but a monumental panorama of the period. Nevertheless, the long chapters which he fills with world history and petty court stories are unconnected with the figure of the hero. Again and again Voltaire disappears completely from the scene, and when we meet him again he seems to us an old acquaintance of whom we had lost sight. And are the *Main Currents*, the work of his mature manhood, essentially different? Do not these six volumes also fall apart into individual portraits, only superficially related to each other, and is the final product the truly comprehensive picture of the European spirit Brandes wanted to draw? Paradoxically, Brandes achieves his purpose only in the part dedicated to German Romanticism, for which he cared little and which he understood less. Here he does not place portrait next to portrait, but tries, by means of a topical arrangement, to do justice to the essential factors of an intellectual movement. The words with which Bjoernson repudiated young Brandes' early critical efforts are certainly unjustified, for they neglect completely the tremendous ethical power which, aside from all "scientism," was ingrained in Brandes' work. But one fundamental trait of his criticism, the mechanistic and atomistic trend of his analyses, is clearly pointed out in Bjoernson's statement:

> It strikes me that if you do choose criticism as your avocation, it should be more strongly in the direction of one educating responsibilities and less as the spyer-out of small things, the dragger together of all and everything which can be brought forward as witness for or against the author . . . [104]

So intimately had positivism related the work of art to chemi-

---
104. *Reminiscences*, 225.

cal and physical phenomena that to assort, to register, and to explain facts, appeared to be the task of the literary critic. With great eloquence, Taine had attempted to raise literary criticism to a science, subject to the same conditions and methods of research as biology, chemistry, and physics. The attitude of the literary "scientist" towards his object was therefore determined. He had to be disinterested, detached and unprejudiced, like the chemist who *sine ira et studio* follows the development of an experiment. He must not be involved, but must look at his problem from the outside, his ideal position being the Archimedean point outside the world. Particularly in his younger years Brandes, too, saw strict detachment as the necessary condition of every critical effort. So he thought the Danish writer Goldschmidt to be in an especially favorable position,

> because the modern Jew in our European civilization has the inestimable advantage as a Semite to be standing on an Archimedean point with a wide perspective outside the congenital limitations of the two Aryan groups when it comes to the contrasts between the Romanic and the Gotho-Germanic cultures.[105]

And he regards himself as particularly well qualified to write a literary history of Europe, because as a foreigner he has the necessary perspective which alone enables the scholar to attain scientific results.[106] In the course of years, however, Brandes more and more abandons this point of view. That in a later edition of his *Aesthetiske Studier* he omits the passage on Goldschmidt quoted above, would still not be conclusive proof. In this case he was probably prompted chiefly by practical concerns, because he himself had been exposed only too often to the spiteful and ridiculous reproach that the spiritual essences of the "gotho-germanic culture" were closed to him as a Jew. But that in his introduction to *Creative Spirits* he vigorously rejects Taine's thesis of "criticism as an applied science," may be taken as valid proof.[107] Here it dawns upon him that the real organ of literary criticism is not a cool observation which tries to maintain rigidly the distance between object and subject, but rather an intuitive process which, in a creative moment, merges object and subject into a real unity.

---
105. Nathansen, *op. cit.*, 78.
106. *Main Currents* II, i.
107. *Creative Spirits*, V.

## V

We have tried to sketch the profile of Brandes. It is, as we have seen, no unified picture, full of lines which may seem to us strange or even bewildering. But how wrong would it be not to be aware of the greatness of this man and his work; for do not even the limitations of his achievement, which we have discussed, reveal a great personality who stamps with his seal whatever he touches? And should the broadness of his horizon not compensate for a certain lack of depth which is, at times, disquieting? Brandes was a conqueror of new worlds; and who could expect from a force striving for expansion the calm of meditative profundity? He was, in terms of the climate of his times, an imperialist, an imperialist of the spirit, who took possession of unknown countries and opened up new horizons. He was a pioneer who tore down boundary lines, a "missionary of culture," as Nietzsche so fittingly characterized him.[108]

His work belongs to the nineteenth century; and however high it may tower above the average, it lacks the touch of the immortal which might make us forget how closely it is tied up with a definite period, how inevitably prone to the destiny of becoming "dated." But the fire that burnt in him, his passion for truth, his enthusiastic willingness to serve the spirit in whatever form it revealed itself, are timeless, and will keep his name alive even if his work should sink into oblivion. His critical conceptions and analyses may be completely outmoded tomorrow; but his instinct for the truly great, his fight for the recognition of the new, will testify for him. That in spite of all his bias he was the first to raise his voice for Kierkegaard, that he made a stand for Ibsen, Nietzsche, Strindberg, at a time when they saw themselves confronted with cold indifference or violent opposition, weighs a hundred times more heavily than the fact that his critical arguments and methods may often fail to convince us. He was a great discoverer, and he had the courage of his discoveries.

When but a young man, he had to experience what it means to profess one's convictions without bowing to public opinion and showing a bigoted reverence for tradition. He wanted to disturb the "sleep of the world" and he did not flinch from the blows with which all those who did not want to be awakened struck

---

108. *Nietzsche,* 64.

him. He was willing to change his opinions, but never to make concessions. When he first met Ibsen, the poet took leave of him, saying: "Irritate the Danes, and I shall irritate the Norwegians."[109] Brandes did more than his share. He not only irritated minds but made them boil with rage, in Denmark and in all Europe as well. Wherever a struggle was taking place against stupidity and for the freedom of the spirit, he was in it. He spoke on matters of literature, religion, philosophy, domestic and foreign policy. At the age of seventy-five, he made his voice heard in the great struggle of the nations. France, which he loved so dearly, Clemenceau, his most intimate friend, called him a traitor because he refused to see in the Germans nothing but a horde of brutes; England wanted to forget his name, because he had the courage to remind her, on the occasion of the storm of moral indignation over Germany's invasion of Belgium, of her policy in Persia; Germany opened the gates of hatred against him, because he, now louder than ever, gave vent to his abhorrence of the imperial policy; Poland decried him, because he called her to account for her treatment of the Jews. But he remained undaunted, for he had the courage to stand by the truth. He was fearless, and he loved fearlessness in others. Even the German Romanticists, who seemed so alien and unhealthy to him, called forth his respect because they had dared to set out on untrodden paths and to pursue them even if they led to defeat and ruin.[110]

He stood unflinchingly by his convictions; but that does not mean that he ever became a slave to his opinions. By this very agility of spirit he irritated not only his enemies, but also his friends. Had he not but recently carried on a passionate campaign for Mill and Taine? Yet he was already welcoming a new star: Nietzsche. Had he not but recently extolled Flaubert as the exemplary novelist? Yet he was already fascinated by a force of a quite different nature: Dostoevsky. He was a Socialist with Lassalle and a Conservative with Beaconsfield, a worshipper of the Renaissance with Shakespeare and Michelangelo and a rigid rationalist with Voltaire, a great democrat with Boerne and Garibaldi and a great autocrat with Caesar and Napoleon. His mind was constantly in motion, and it was as

---

109. *Levned* II, 55. For the relationship of Brandes to Ibsen cf. also A. E. Zucker, *Ibsen* (New York, 1929), 149, 158, 178.
110. "He who discovers a new country may, in the course of his explorations, be stranded on a reef. It is an easy matter to avoid the reef and to leave the country undiscovered." (*Main Currents* II, 10).

though every weak sound trembling in the air gave echo in him so early that it seemed as if the vibration in the atmosphere of the time reached him more quickly and more directly than others. Always out for the discovery of new shores, he was much more than he would have cared to admit to himself in sympathy with Ibsen's confession: "Yes, I may well say the one thing I love in freedom is the struggle for its attainment. Its possession does not greatly concern me."[111]

He was, as he said himself, "the most restless and most impatient of men."[112] Just as he could not bring himself to settle down quietly, so he found it hard to balance his emotions. The shifts from deepest depression to euphoric self-assertion are frightening, the change from satisfaction with his own achievement to despair at his failures uncanny. He was, as he said of his hero Voltaire, "a bundle of nerves, charged with electricity, captivating Europe and enlightening it."[113]

He was so full of intensity, of wild passion that he often believed he would perish of it. "Ma pensée comprimée me tue, exprimée elle me perd," he confessed to his friend Edmund Gosse.[114] It is not by chance that he used, as a motto for the *Main Currents*, Heinse's words: "As for me, I am fire, always and everywhere."

He wanted to be, and he was, a bearer of light. He dispelled darkness, he broadened our horizon, he discovered new stars and dispersed the mist which impaired their brightness. His writings may be forgotten, but not the light which the existence of this man shed over our world. In the last poem of his *Samlede Skrifter*, Brandes has summed up the meaning of his life in a few lines, which at first glance may strike us as melancholy. But he surely has achieved great things who *sub specie aeternitatis* is able to say of his life:

> A shimmer of day
> In the dark of a cave,
> Impalpable spray
> Like foam on the wave,
> Such my life's core,
> Of lightning a ray,
> And hardly more.

---
111. *Letters of Henrik Ibsen*, 205.
112. Nathansen, *op. cit.*, 224.
113. *Voltaire* I, 3.
114. Gosse, *op. cit.*, 157.

# GOETHE'S *IPHIGENIA* AND THE HUMANE IDEAL*

Early in 1802, fully fifteen years after the completion of Goethe's *Iphigenia in Tauris*, the theater of Weimar prepared the play's first performance in the city which, since 1775, had been Goethe's home and, by being Goethe's home, was to become a shrine to the human urge for veneration. Goethe, at that time the artistic head of the ducal theater, showed himself rather uncoöperative and diffident during the preparation of this, one of his greatest plays, for the stage. He left the whole business of scene arrangements, of cutting, and revising in the hands of his trusted friend Schiller, and displayed the attitude of a more or less bored bystander. Indeed, it is quite understandable that, after his long and burdensome experience as the manager of the ducal theater, he was loathe to become too deeply involved in the mechanical matters of play production when one of his own works was placed on the repertoire. Indeed, we know how reluctant he was all through his life to face a past manifestation of his development, a skin which he had shed, to relive the agonies from which an earlier work had sprung; and agonies, the fearful pains of a tormented heart, are the subsoil from which his *Iphigenia* had grown, as they are so often the subsoil of his works which he himself, in his autobiography, called "but fragments of one great confession." Yet in his correspondence with Schiller in which he discusses the forthcoming stage production, he makes hardly any mention of either the technical or the emotionally personal considerations which may have prevented him from playing a more active part in revising his drama for the theater. However, in one of his letters to Schiller (January 19, 1802) we are struck by a rather curious remark. It is here that Goethe calls his *Iphigenia* "ganz verteufelt human" ("quite damnably humane.")

"Quite damnably humane"—what does he mean by that? We can hardly believe that he wanted to repudiate the very basis upon which his *Iphigenia* was built: the extremely noble conception of a humane idealism which nowhere in German letters has found so stirring and so magnificent an expression as in this play. Yet it might be possible that, when using these strange words, he was anticipating the criticism of a new

---
*Public address delivered at the University of Washington, Seattle, within the series of Goethe lectures in 1949.

era leveled against his great play, leveled against the man Goethe altogether, a criticism directed against the loftiness of an ideal which was considered superhuman in its purity,— a criticism against an all too easy belief in man's perfection, in his ability to assume the stature of a god, a criticism against the benign serenity and the unshakable optimism of the eighteenth century; in short, a criticism brought against Goethe by some of his detractors of the nineteenth century, against Goethe, the Olympian, the imperturbable one, unmovable and unmoved by doubts, unassailed by the horror of man's smallness and frailty, so smugly satisfied with what he had reached, and what he had proclaimed to be within the reach of man.[1] Needless to say that there never was a Goethe of this sort. But he must have felt how easy it would be to twist him into the pat picture of a glacial loftiness, to make him a lifeless model of Sunday-school idealism, a preacher of a textbook perfectionism, of starry-eyed goodness; and in the Mephistophelean whimsicality which was so much a part of his being he tagged the words "damnably humane" onto his Iphigenia, as a warning to those who would raise his heroine to the superhuman heights of sanctity, and as a warning to those who would turn away from his heroine because she had been raised so dizzily high.

And indeed to dizzy heights Iphigenia seems to rise. Although Goethe followed rather closely the external course of events of the old Greek legend, he had changed the emphasis, the inner organism of the fable so radically that Schiller was quite right in calling Goethe's Greek drama "astonishingly modern and un-Greek." What Euripides, in his *Iphigenia among the Taurians*, had presented was, as all of Greek tragedy, a ritual festival: man cruelly enmeshed in the inhuman schemes of the gods, thrown at their mercy, driven to crimes because it was so ordained, punished with labors by which alone he can free himself of the curse with which the gods have afflicted him, and finally rescued, not by his own power, but by the interference of the gods who, while lifting man from his desperate plight, lift themselves to everlasting glory.

---

1. It is, of course, this self-reliant and self-assured "humanism" against which so much of twentieth century Goethe criticism (f.i. Ortega y Gasset's and T. S. Eliot's) has reacted more or less violently. About the image of man of German classicism as a noble but dangerous delusion cf. Heinrich Weinstock, *Die Tragödie des Humanismus: Wahrheit und Trug im abendländischen Menschenbild* (Heidelberg, 1953).

So Orestes, who has killed his murderous mother upon Apollo's order, and is from the day of this hideous crime on pursued by the Furies, the goddesses of vengeance, arrives with his friend Pylades on the shores of Tauris. According to Apollo's decree he can rid himself from the frightful pursuers only by bringing back to Greece the statue of Apollo's sister Artemis which, without Orestes' knowing, had for many years been attended to by his own sister, the Artemis priestess Iphigenia. It is a dangerous venture that Orestes is embarking upon, dangerous to carry away the statue, almost impossible to elude the death which awaits every captured foreigner at the hands of the priestess Iphigenia in accordance with the law of the barbarian land. Yet the three Greeks, Iphigenia, Orestes, and Pylades, after recognizing their identities, conspire in a clever plot by which they not only deceive the stupidly credulous barbarian King Thoas and snatch from under his very eyes the holy statue, but make their escapes with Iphigenia in the bargain, who for so many years had been kept an exile in the land of the Taurians. However, to make it quite plain that man's redemption is not man-made, the waves toss the three fugitives back onto the shores of Tauris, deliver them again into the hands of the infuriated King Thaos. Their doom would be sealed if, at the last moment, Pallas Athena were not to descend *ex machina*, impress upon the king the will of the gods and order him to let the three Greeks go free. What a frightful picture of man's forlornness, of his moving under the curse to murder, under the curse to die, under the curse to live, a dark spectacle only dimly lit by the hope that one day the gods may relent their cruel play, only proudly lit by the national feeling of Greek superiority over the uncouth and sluggish slow-wittedness of the barbarians.

Such is the story and the factual material which Goethe, while following it in its outline, actually lifted out of its hinges. The strings that guided the destiny of man from the heights of Mount Olympus have been cut; and the scene is no longer the twilit in-between of the above and the below, but the familiar ground of our earth, the strange and familiar ground of the human heart. No longer a ritual incantation, but a song of man, of his personal plight, his personal hopes, his personal atonement. It is still the matricide Orestes who arrives at the shores of Tauris, but the crime he has committed is his own crime for which no god but he himself is responsible and answerable: the rashness and the wildness of his blood which drove him to the outrage. His terrible fall is man-made, self-made; and therefore his punishment is man-made, and self-made, too. It is no longer the concrete goddesses of revenge that pursue him; he is pursued by the voices of his own heart, by a feeling of guilt and a remorse so bitter that he is actually driven to the verge of madness. Instead of Orestes, the cursed one, the man over whom a terrible fate is suspended, we meet Orestes, the diseased one, the man whose very blood is poisoned. And what is his particular disease? Remorse, feeling of guilt? To be sure, remorse and feeling of guilt torture Orestes most powerfully, but they do not actually represent a disease. His illness is a more frightening one: the will to live is extinguished in Orestes. And perhaps we must reinterpret Orestes' horrible misdeed in terms of modern psychology. Is Goethe really telling the story of the mythological hero Orestes who killed his mother Clytemnestra, or is he not rather telling the story of a sick human heart, of his own sick heart, the story of a man who, in the image of his mother, has killed the source of life, who has lacerated with his own hands the womb which gave him birth, and is now longing for extinction? For it is extinction that Orestes is pining for, deliverance from what he calls "life's fitful fever," the great forgetfulness, the eternal darkness, the realm of the shadows over which the sun, star of the day, never rises. This indeed is the extreme and blissful vision of his diseased mind: the underworld into which he sees himself transported, the nothingness in which the unbearable conflicts of existing, the burden of living have fallen away. This scene, Orestes in the Inferno, which so mistakenly has always been taken only as a poetic hyperbole for his madness, finds at the end of the play an exact counterpart: Orestes, sword in hand, willing and ready to fight against the king who, as he thinks, blocks to him and to his beloved ones the return into life. To be sure, he is mistaken; there is no need for this fight; but that he who once addressed the one who seemed to bring him death with the words

> Ja, schwinge deinen Stahl, verschone nicht,
> Zerreisse diesen Busen und eröffne
> Den Strömen, die hier sieden, einen Weg—

that he can now raise his sword in defense proves that he has been healed, that he has found his way back into the upperworld.

Since man's affliction comes from within, his salvation must come from within, too. The center of the Greek legend, that an external deed, the carrying away of the holy statue, could lift the agony which racks Orestes, was bound to become irrelevant to Goethe. He had to reinterpret this part of the myth, and his reinterpretation makes the humanization of an ancient ritual ceremony complete. In the most magnificent scene of recognition Orestes realizes what Apollo really wanted him to bring home: not the image of the god's sister Artemis, but his own sister Iphigenia, not the object of a religious rite, but the living embodiment of man's salvation, Iphigenia the great healer of man's wounds and ills.

Iphigenia the healer, man's great sister, his own flesh and blood and yet an independent self, as a woman object of love and yet beyond all possessive desires, involved in our fate and yet free to rise above it. In Goethe's Iphigenia the conception of sisterhood seems to have found its tenderest impersonation, as much as, to the emotional consciousness of Occidental man, the Virgin Mary has become the impersonation of the conception of motherhood. Iphigenia is indeed not *a* man's sister, but *the* sister of man. It is surely not by chance that through Goethe's story of the human brother and sister, Orestes and Iphigenia, shines the image of higher brother and sister relationships, of the mythological relationship of Apollo and Artemis, and finally of the cosmic relationship of sun and moon. Goethe's Iphigenia is not by chance the chaste priestess of the moon-goddess Artemis; for the magic power of the moonlight, its soft victory over the frightening darkness of night, its soothing calm that resolves all tensions, its cool and melancholy aloofness from the strain of our daily burdens—all this seems to have taken on human shape in Iphigenia. Of the healing magic of the moon, of the great balm which it sends into man's heart ridden with fear and pain, Goethe has sung again and again, as early as in the first monologue of Faust:

> Ach könnt ich doch auf Berges Höhn
> In deinem lieben Lichte gehn,
> Um Bergeshöhl mit Geistern schweben
> Auf Wiesen in deinem Dämmer weben,
> Von all dem Wissensqualm entladen
> In deinem Tau gesund mich baden—

and never more beautifully than in the first stanzas of his poem "An den Mond":

Füllest wieder Busch und Tal
Still mit Nebelglanz,
Lösest endlich auch einmal
Meine Seele ganz;

Breitest über mein Gefild
Lindernd deinen Blick,
Wie des Freundes Auge mild
Über mein Geschick.

Unless we see Iphigenia as the embodiment of an intimate human relationship, indeed as the human embodiment of well-meaning cosmic forces, we run the risk which the nineteenth century was unable to avoid: to take her as the mouthpiece of a lofty moral gospel. Yet Iphigenia is entirely free of any dogmatic doctrine, no matter from which religious or ethical realm this doctrine may be derived. To be sure, Goethe's *Iphigenia* is the loftiest symbol of the German humane idealism, yet it is an idealism of a specific brand which tries to do away with the nefarious dualism of body and soul, of nature and spirit. The image of man which Goethe has created in his Iphigenia is "the beautiful soul," a conception so dear to his heart because here and here alone the dichotomy of an animalistic and a spiritual part of man is resolved. The law which Iphigenia lives and which triumphs through her is neither the natural law "Thou must," nor the ethical law "Thou shalt," but a miraculous reconciliation in which the "must" and "shall" are one and the same. Following Shaftesbury, Goethe has taken the attribute of such a human attitude, the adjective "beautiful," from the aesthetic sphere; because it is in the work of art that form, the stamp of the spirit, has merged so completely with the material, the given flesh, that an insoluble whole has resulted.

Iphigenia's greatness is exactly this: that she is constitutionally unable to do the ignoble, even if all practical reasoning, even if a specific order of the gods would seem to force upon her the wicked deed. It is not a moral law that prevents her from deceiving the king and from carrying out the plot by which the statue of the goddess Artemis could be spirited away: quite the contrary, the specific order of Apollo would require her collaboration in the dubious scheme. It is her heart which says "no;" not virtue, but instinct, not a noble ethical decision, but her incapability to do wrong. She does not have to weigh the pros and cons; in fact, she is quite unable to do so as she herself states: "I cannot argue, I can only feel." There is in her an immediacy of moral awareness that is in no need of a moral code. The law is not suspended above her but has grown into her, is actually part of her. A heart so unfailingly sure does not need a higher authority to give it direction, and again, as with every aspect of the legend, Goethe has transformed the external into an internal element. For Iphigenia the gods are not external agencies which impose their commands upon man; they exist only in man, in the voice of his heart. This indeed is an utterly un-Greek conception, but it is an un-Christian conception as well, and nothing seems to me more awkward than to make a Christian saint out of Iphigenia. For Goethe the unerring heart is the only guarantor of the existence of God, as he himself has expressed it in one of his most beautiful poems, "Das Göttliche":

> Heil den unbekannten
> Höhern Wesen,
> Die wir ahnen!
> Ihnen gleiche der Mensch;
> Sein Beispiel lehr' uns
> Jene glauben.

For a Christian such lines may verge on the blasphemous: God's existence, our belief in Him made dependent upon the example that man sets. And it is exactly the same sentiment which Iphigenia voices. In the moment of her extreme crisis, when faced with the horrible alternative of shedding her brother's blood on the altar or of plotting against the king, who for so many years has proved generous and kind to her, she cries out to the gods, "Save me, and save your image in my soul!" It is she, man, who sets the standards, the image to which the gods have to live up; by letting her down, by destroying her, the gods would let themselves down, would destroy themselves. In fact, she goes so far as to defy the gods openly. Apollo had ordered Orestes to bring back the statue of Artemis: this is the unmistakable will of the god. Yet what does Iphigenia do? While all the plans are set to spirit away the holy image, she informs the king of the plot which she herself had helped to prepare; she acts to prevent the execution of Apollo's will, because to her it is inconceivable that the gods want a deed carried out which involves deceit, theft, and trickery. And there is almost divine irony in the fact that Apollo seems to endorse, *ex post facto*, Iphigenia's decision, that he, so to speak, takes his cue from her; for what he really wanted, so we hear now, is not the homecoming of an image, the glorification of a holy statue, but the glorification of a human soul which cannot be corrupted even by what may have presented itself as a divine command.

Well, so one may ask at this point, was not Goethe quite right, was not the more realistic nineteenth century quite right in calling this Iphigenia "damnably humane"? Does not this sheer goodness, this infallible righteousness smack of the angelic which we may coolly admire but which cannot really mean anything to us, because it is blind to all the pitfalls, all the gnawing doubts, all the painful anxieties of man's existence? But to argue thus means, so it seems to me, to overlook the orbit in which this Iphigenia moves, the function which she fulfills in this world. As we said before, her greatness is not actually of a moral nature; what she embodies are vital forces in the human heart, the force of light, the force of regeneration, the force of hopefulness. We cannot and should not isolate her, but we must see her in her close relationship to her brother, a relationship so intimate that she herself can say to him, "My fate is bound insolubly to thine." Orestes *and* Iphigenia, the broken heart *and* the unbreakable one, the despair at existing *and* the hope for redemption, the involvement in sin and cruel deeds which life imposes upon us every day *and* the aloofness of a priestly purity: they together constitute man's condition. Neither Orestes nor Iphigenia is a behavioristic human model; rather they represent in polar juxtaposition vital forces in man, the force of self-destruction and the force of regeneration. Exactly as inexplicable as is the working of an energy is the effect which Iphigenia has upon all who surround her. What she works seems magic; she does not manifest herself by action or by preaching, she is, so to speak, an impulse by which the withered and the dead forces in those whom she touches are revitalized. This is true not only in the case of her healing of Orestes who, upon mere contact with her, turns to the road of recovery. It is equally true in the case of King Thoas who, by the mere fact of her being, of her being near him, has developed from a barbarian tyrant into a civilized king. Iphigenia does not stand for values; she *is* the value. She does not set an example for her fellow men, but becomes a part of them, a part that overcomes the sinister forces in man's breast. This indeed may be called magic, or perhaps better, a mystery, the profoundest mystery in which Goethe believed, the inscrutable and irrational power of what he called "die Persönlichkeit," a power against which there is only one means of defense: acceptance. In his novel, *The Elec-*

*tive Affinities,* he has epitomized it in the words: "In the face of the great superiority of another person there is no means of safety but love."

Yet it is not only through association that Iphigenia is involved in the sufferings of man. Her words to Orestes, "My fate is bound insolubly to thine," must be taken quite literally. She lives and she moves under the same frightful shadow which darkens the mind of her brother. It is quite characteristic that Goethe put into her mouth the long recital of crimes and outrages which have exacted their bloody toll from the house of Tantalus, from her house. After she has told the king the grisly story of treachery, rape, and murder, she sees herself as a link in an endless chain of sin and cursedness:

> Dies sind die Ahnherrn deiner Priesterin;
> Und viel unseliges Geschick der Männer,
> Viel Taten des verworrnen Sinnes deckt
> Die Nacht mit schweren Fittichen und lässt
> Uns nur in grauenvolle Dämmrung sehn.

"The slings and arrows of outrageous fortune" which harass Orestes to the point where it seems to him impossible to live on harass Iphigenia no less. In fact, the events she has to go through during the course of the play seem like a diabolically cruel trap from which there is no escape at all. Surely, man's position can hardly be viewed in a more tragic light than the one Goethe spread around Iphigenia. Everything seems to conspire against her, even the tender emotions which she awakens in the hearts of others seem to cause and accelerate her doom. Not only the wrath of the gods, but even the love of men work towards her destruction. For Goethe has added a motif which is completely lacking in the old tradition of the myth, Thoas' love for Iphigenia, the tenderest human feeling which, however, seems to close the trap around her completely. Because she has rejected the wooing of the king, he has, in his resentful anger, revived the barbarian law, already abated by Iphigenia's influence, that every foreigner captured on the shores of Tauris must be sacrificed to the goddess. And the reintroduction of this inhuman rite will now force Iphigenia to kill her own brother and, by doing so, exterminate the house of Tantalus, so sorely tried and pursued by the gods. The ring is closed around her so neatly that there is indeed nothing left but a "peering into frightful gloom."

Can man live? This is the question, not only of Orestes, but of Iphigenia as well, when the cards are so inexorably stacked against him. Is "to be or not to be" really still a question when we are driven, step by step, into deeper entanglement with nowhere a door left into freedom and liberation? Is not complete loss of consciousness indeed the "consummation devoutly to be wished," since our whole life is nothing but a painful sickness unto death, spared to no one, the innocent one no less than the evil-doer? Are we not lost before we have started? Is Iphigenia not lost? Indeed, is she not dead before she is even put to the test of living?

At this point, it seems to me, Goethe's play takes on its deepest meaning. The land of the shadows to which Orestes turns as the last hope since life has so cruelly beaten him,—Iphigenia has lived in it for years. Once, in Aulis, she was marked to die in order to appease the angry goddess. But before the sword fell upon her neck, the goddess carried her away to a distant and remote country. It is an island, which means it is separated from the rest of the world, not only isolated by the waters, but isolated by the cruel law that everyone who sets foot on these shores must die. It is the underworld, the place beyond space, the place beyond time. For time stood still when Iphigenia arrived, and no messenger ever brought her news of the world, of her world. Both Orestes and Iphigenia are moving under the shadow of death; Orestes sees the underworld in his most exalted vision, Iphigenia has for many years lived in the kingdom of death. Yet the direction of their desires is opposite: Iphigenia, her spirits undaunted by the lure of death, wants to return, return home, return to life. Orestes, his spirits broken by the onslaught of life, wants to cross the border whence no traveler returns. Iphigenia remembers and wants to make her memories reality again. Orestes does not want to remember, but wants to flee into eternal forgetfulness. It seems quite significant to me that Iphigenia's first word, indeed the first word of the whole play, is "heraus" (out of); while Orestes' first words at the beginning of the second act are: "It is the path of death that now we tread"—both of them indicating motion, but motion in opposite directions: Iphigenia's direction—the road out of deadness, Orestes' direction—the road into the night.

Indeed, "frightful gloom" envelops Iphigenia no less than Orestes. But the word that counts in the quotation above is the word "to peer." Iphigenia's eyes are open, and they remain open although nothing that can be seen seems to present itself. She is willing to face even utter darkness, and this willingness to face it makes her great, not superhumanly great, but humanly great. That she does not turn away when Pylades unlocks before her eyes the horrible deed which her own mother perpetrated against her father, that she does not turn away when Orestes unlocks before her eyes the horror which is raging in his breast, that she keeps on "peering" even though there is nothing to be seen but "frightful gloom"—this is the final test of her humaneness. There is none of the righteous shudder of the angel, there is none of the benign aloofness of the saint; this is simply a human heart not willing to shut itself even if the most abominable sins, the vipers of the abyss are arrayed against it. In the words of T. S. Eliot's "Gerontion" Iphigenia could well call out: "After such knowledge, what forgiveness?" But Iphigenia knows the answer that Gerontion does not know: the forgiveness is hope.

Goethe's *Iphigenia* is not an easy message of hope, and not a message of easy hope. It is hope wrung from the deepest despair. Even the noble and brave heart trembles lest all be in vain. The moment comes when she, too, has reached the bottom of the pit, when the word "heraus" seems to her a pious and mocking delusion. At the end of the fourth act, in the poem which we usually refer to as "Das Parzenlied," it dawns upon Iphigenia that everything may be futile, that no hope and no faith can exact a friendly answer from the gods, that only silence or Olympian laughter answers the cries of the human heart:

> Sie aber, sie bleiben
> In ewigen Festen
> An goldenen Tischen.
> Sie schreiten vom Berge
> Zu Bergen hinüber;
> Aus Schlünden der Tiefe
> Dampft ihnen der Atem
> Erstickter Titanen
> Gleich Opfergerüchen,
> Ein leichtes Gewölke.
>
> Es wenden die Herrscher
> Ihr segnendes Auge
> Von ganzen Geschlechtern
> Und meiden, im Enkel
> Die ehmals geliebten,
> Still redenden Züge
> Des Ahnherrn zu sehn.

Even Iphigenia, the hopeful one, the hope of man, is not spared the most heart-rending doubts. Yet it seems that this very doubt, the journey through the hell of despair, gives her the strength to do the liberating deed. That man could be forever lost, that all his fortitude and striving should end with the triumphant laughter of the forces of evil, this was indeed inconceivable to Goethe. Man may be entangled, may entangle himself in error, sin, and crime, he may have to travel through a dark world and the darkness of his own heart, but that he was meant to perish without any chance of resurrection, this was simply unthinkable to Goethe. He could not deliver his Faust into the hands of the devil, he could not leave Iphigenia in the "fathomless chasms," because the admittance of such a possibility would undo the Creation, would make life itself a farcical game, utterly meaningless and shallow.

A message of hope, and yet no message of easy hope. Bound to a fate which we cannot escape, forced by practical necessities, driven by our own selfish desires, living in a world in which goodness is by no means a guarantee for survival—how can we do the free deed which alone can extricate us from the entanglements in which life involves us daily? This exactly is Iphigenia's question. How can she act as a free agent, obedient only to the voice of her heart, when she is assailed from all sides by forces of necessity which allow no room for a free decision? It is almost a test case with which we are confronted here: is action at all possible to a creature so thoroughly conditioned, confined, and bound as man is? Subject to the immutable laws of nature, subject to the inscrutable will of higher forces, is man not indeed doomed forever, reduced to the level of animal existence? Is reason, the gift by which he thinks he can lift himself above the dictates of his own confinement and temporality, not a senseless mirage which makes him only more miserable since it teases him with a conception of freedom which he cannot possibly attain? Is not Mephistopheles right when, talking to the Lord about man, he characterizes him with these contemptuous words:

> Ich sehe nur, wie sich die Menschen plagen.
> Der kleine Gott der Welt bleibt stets vom gleichen Schlag,
> Und ist so wunderlich als wie am ersten Tag.
> Ein wenig besser würd' er leben,
> Hättst du ihm nicht den Schein des Himmelslichts gegeben;
> Er nennt's Vernunft und braucht's allein,

> Nur tierischer als jedes Tier zu sein.
> Er scheint mir, mit Verlaub von Euer Gnaden,
> Wie eine der langbeinigen Zikaden,
> Die immer fliegt und fliegend springt
> Und gleich im Gras ihr altes Liedchen singt;
> Und läg er nur noch immer in dem Grase!
> In jeden Quark begräbt er seine Nase.

Can man ever avoid the hopping and flitting and dancing, can he ever stand upright? Is not Iphigenia caught in a dilemma to which there is no solution? Conditions are such that in order to save her brother, in order to save herself, she can do either of two things. She can appease the king and accept his wooing and, by doing so, become unfaithful to herself, to her mission in life which, she knows, awaits her in Greece. Or she can carry out the scheme, collaborate in the theft of the statue and, by doing so, become unfaithful to the king who has trusted her as he has trusted no one else. The trap is so neatly set that only one of these two decisions is possible. Yet Iphigenia decides— for the impossible, for the thing that, in a determined and conditioned world, cannot be done, for a free, a gratuitous deed. Against necessity, against everything and everyone, including the command of the gods, she pits what her heart tells her is the right thing to do. There is nothing reckless and nothing superhuman in Iphigenia's action when she faces the king and tells him the truth, when she gives away the plot which is already successfully under way. She is shaken by doubts, she is shaken by fear because she knows very well what an enormous risk she is taking. If she fails, and fail she may very easily, everything is lost, her brother, she herself, and with her man's faith in the victory of life over death, of light over darkness. Yet the challenge must be met, because only by the free deed, by rising above his own condition, by thrusting himself into absolute insecurity, can man prove that he is man, the paradoxical being, immersed in the flux of temporality and yet capable of penetrating to the eternal by apprehending timeless existence within time and above it. And only this free deed can be a liberating deed, can break the chain from which we all are smarting, can, in the midst of misery, helplessness, and forlornness which, indeed, are our share, reëstablish the dignity of man.

Man, the paradoxical being who in Goethe's own words "can do the impossible," mercilessly bound by an unalterable fate and yet capable of a free decision, of the gratuitous deed by which he can shape his own destiny. But paradoxical in a still higher sense. For the deed born from the most intimately personal crisis, from man's need for his own personal redemption, is at the same time the deed that can shape the destiny of all mankind, alter the face of the world. For this indeed is Iphigenia's greatest glory: by saving her soul she not only decides her own future and that of her house, but blasts a path into a vast and unknown future. Out of her deed rises a new millenium. It is in her farewell to Thoas that the full meaning of her act of liberation becomes evident:

> Nicht so, mein König! Ohne Segen,
> In Widerwillen scheid' ich nicht von dir.
> Verbann' uns nicht! Ein freundlich Gastrecht walte
> Von dir zu uns . . .

Through Iphigenia, a world, separated by hatred and suspicion, has become united. The horror of man's loneliness is overcome in her last vision: Tauris, the island, separated from the inhabited world by the unsafe element, the water, and isolated by the cruel law against all foreigners, Tauris has been joined to the continent of the living, has become part of the *oikumene*. There is now no longer a Greek world and a barbarian world set against each other in atavistic and eternal enmity. There is, from now on, *one* world held together by love and understanding. The last words of Iphigenia, some of the most beautiful poetry in the German language, sound like a complete revocation of Iphigenia's first monologue. At the beginning there was the atmosphere of the prison: man caught by a merciless fate, banished to the deadly island where no messenger ever appears. Now the walls have fallen. It is not by chance that in Iphigenia's last speech the messenger plays such an important part, the man who goes back and forth to relate and to keep alive interrelationships:

> Bringt der Geringste deines Volkes je
> Den Ton der Stimme mir ins Ohr zurück,
> Den ich an euch gewöhnt zu hören bin,
> Und seh ich an dem Ärmsten eure Tracht:
> Empfangen will ich ihn wie einen Gott,
> Ich will ihm selbst ein Lager zubereiten,
> Auf einen Stuhl ihn an das Feuer laden
> Und nur nach dir und deinem Schicksal fragen.

This indeed is man's paradoxical condition that the deed done for the sake of his own personal redemption harbors in its folds the future destiny of the whole world.

This then is Goethe's humane idealism. It has nothing whatsoever to do with an easy belief in man's perfection, with shutting one's eyes to the smallness and the frailty of man's existence. It takes full stock of the destructive forces that act upon man from within and without, of the cruel necessities of life, of the doubts, the despair, the murderous passions in our heart. In Goethe's *Iphigenia* there are, muffled by a deceptive serenity, the cries from the Inferno, the sighs from the Purgatorio, but there is, at the same time, the conviction that the gates to the Paradiso cannot be forever closed.

In an American author, Nathaniel Hawthorne, I recently found a phrase which could fittingly stand as a motto over Goethe's *Iphigenia,* as a pithy condensation of Goethe's view of man's fate. It reads: "at once all shadow and all splendor." Indeed, *Iphigenia* is not "all splendor," not "damnably humane," but it is not all shadow, either. A gulf separates it from the easy optimism of the eighteenth century, and a gulf separates it from the philosophy of despair which has taken hold of so many a contemporary thinker and poet. One of them, one of the greatest German writers of the twentieth century, Franz Kafka, who at this point comes to mind because he loved Goethe more dearly than any other writer he knew—Franz Kafka once wrote the aphorism: "There is hope, perhaps plenty of hope, but not for us." Goethe, had he heard this statement, would have angrily shaken his head. He might have pointed to his *Iphigenia* and to Iphigenia's message: there is hope, perhaps very little hope. But the little there is, is for us.

## GOETHE'S MAGIC FLUTE

Among the mass of outlines, fragments and sketches which accumulated during Goethe's incomparably productive life, there is a plan for a sequel to Mozart's *Magic Flute*. Besides an almost fully worked-out first act, we have an outline of scenes and a considerable number of paralipomena, from which we can form a fairly clear picture of what the whole was to be like. The fragment, overshadowed by the splendid perfection of Goethe's finished works, has failed to attract much attention. The educated lay public is generally not even aware of its existence, and Goethe scholars have labelled it "incidental" and put it aside. Biedermann, for example, treats the libretto as a typically *ad hoc* production, occasioned by Goethe's wish to fill out the meagre repertory of the Weimar theatre, of which he was the director.[1] Max Morris does not bring us much closer to a genuine understanding; with the dogged curiosity of much nineteenth-century biographical criticism, he sets himself to tracking down the real-life model from which Goethe supposedly drew the Queen of Night and after strenuous detective work arrives at the conclusion that it must have been Frau von Stein.[2] Even the short monograph which Victor Junk devotes to the fragment is unsatisfactory—almost more so because at times it does move toward the heart of the matter, only to retreat again without even a sign of regret.[3]

It would be extravagant, of course, to claim that the "Magic Flute" is one of Goethe's major works. Admittedly it is a *Gelegenheitswerk*, which Goethe conceived and began for a quite practical reason: to enrich the Weimar repertory by a stage-worthy musical entertainment—and also, let us note in passing, to enrich his own purse by one hundred guineas. But a protest needs to be entered against the foolish and corrupting romantic notion that it is not really worthy of a great author to write under the compulsion and in the service of a concrete task. Goethe, the last *homo universalis* of our Western culture, would have opposed such a notion most determinedly. For what we

---

1. Woldemar von Biedermann, "Dramatische Entwürfe Goethe's," in *Goethe-Forschungen*, Leipzig 1899.
2. Max Morris, "Frau von Stein und die Königin der Nacht," in *Goethe-Studien* I, Berlin 1902.
3. Victor Junk, *Goethes Fortsetzung der Mozartschen Zauberflöte* (Forschungen zur neueren Literaturgeschichte, ed. Franz Muncker), Berlin 1900.

are in the habit of calling an artist's life was for Goethe wholly of a piece with his art; his work and his life were informed by, indeed *were,* the same instinct, the identical force—so much so that the seemingly random coils and knottings of his life had to turn for him into the organically interwoven tapestry of *Dichtung und Wahrheit.* In his "Maximen und Reflexionen" Goethe answers the question: What is man's highest duty? with the words: "Die Forderung des Tages." To meet this demand with the whole of his being—a poet's being—seemed to him just as natural, and just as noble, as it was for Johann Sebastian Bach to compose his weekly chorale for the next Sunday's service in the Thomaskirche. Only after we have cleansed the word *Gelegenheitswerk* of all demeaning connotations do we have the right to apply it to any of Goethe's works—and once we have so cleansed it, we can go so far as to follow Goethe in calling *all* his works by this term. This means that even when we deal with one of his "left-handed" compositions, we must focus, not on its ephemeral and incidental aspects, but on its inner law and inevitability, on the immutable Goethean substance which forms the core of even his most minor works.

Goethe was serious in all he did; that the plan to write a sequel to the *Magic Flute* was no passing fancy is proved by the span of years during which it engaged his attention. Mozart's opera had had its first Weimar production in 1794. It deeply impressed Goethe—so deeply that he worked an unmistakable allusion to it and its popularity into the second canto of *Hermann und Dorothea,* while in his direct comments on it he praised the art of the librettist, Schikaneder, for knowing "durch Kontraste zu wirken und grosse theatralische Effekte herbeizuführen." Thus he defended Schikaneder against the many critics who, then as now, saw nothing in the libretto but a conglomeration of nonsense unsuccessfully trying to sound profound by talking through the mask of Masonic symbolism. (How the Masonic elements in particular impressed and stimulated Goethe will be considered below.) As early as 1795 Goethe began work on his plan for a sequel; in 1796 he wrote to Wranitzky, the musical director of the Vienna Hoftheater, whom he tried to win for the plan by explaining that the public would be delighted to see the well-remembered figures on stage once more, and that, moreover, there would be a substantial saving in production costs, since the old sets and costumes could be re-used. However, these economies were not to be carried so far as to affect the librettist's fee; for his labors the author demanded a full hundred guineas—which Wranitzky thought decidedly too much, on the amusing grounds that even authors as popular as Kotzebue and Iffland were satisfied with twenty-five guineas. Well, Goethe was not, and the negotiations came to nothing.

In 1798, under the stimulus of a guest performance by Iffland in Weimar, Goethe took up the plan once again, rather to the annoyance of Schiller, who reminded him of the *Hauptsache* (surely the labor, resumed that year, on *Faust*). We do not know if Goethe heeded Schiller's admonition and stopped working on the "Magic Flute." But we may doubt it, for there is in it so much genuine Goethean substance, such a wealth of his core symbols, such an abundance of his favorite ideas, that a hint from Schiller—who possibly took for a frivolous diversion something which for Goethe was a serious undertaking—would hardly have been enough to recall him to his "duty." If nevertheless he put the libretto aside once more, it was most probably because all his efforts to find a composer for it proved fruitless. Since from the start he had been determined that this work was to clarify and put into effect his ideas about the opera as an art form, he found it impossible to go on as long as the decisive question of the musical embodiment remained wholly unanswered. In 1800 Goethe appears to have given up hope for a completion of the libretto; when the Bremen publisher Wilmans asked him for a contribution to his almanac, Goethe offered him the "Magic Flute" fragment, which duly appeared in the 1802 almanac, though it contained only about half of the text as we have it today.[4] It was a surrender of high hopes, finding its aptly material counterpart in Goethe's satisfied acknowledgment of Wilmans' honorarium: two small cases of good wine instead of a hundred guineas.

But even now Goethe did not completely abandon the project; he worked on it intermittently and finally thought he had found the long-sought composer: his friend Zelter. Repeatedly he tried to arouse Zelter's interest; in 1803, finally, he asked the straight question: "Wie steht's um die Musik des 2. Teils der Zauberflöte?" But Zelter, who evidently had never seriously considered the idea of composing the music to Goethe's operatic venture,

---

4. "Der Zauberflöte zweiter Teil," in Wilmans' *Taschenbuch auf das Jahr 1802*. "Der Liebe und Freundschaft gewidmet."

completely misunderstood the question, thinking that it referred to another *Magic Flute* sequel, which was just then being performed in Berlin. However, spurned love has its revenges: eleven years later, realizing too late what he had lost by his coldness, Zelter came to Goethe begging him to finish the fragment, because he, Zelter, would like to write the music to it. Now it was Goethe who was non-committal and reserved. The "Magic Flute" was dead, had to be dead; for what he had meant to say in it he had by now said in other works. Its symbols and ideas had found their firm places in the cosmos of his poetry—places they could not be dislodged from. The shoot of the "Magic Flute" had been stifled by other growths, in which the vital energies had found full scope.

As I turn now to the substance of Goethe's libretto, I shall follow Victor Junk's reconstruction of the unfinished portions, which I find generally convincing. The Queen of Night, her hatred unappeased, has sent her faithful servant Monostatos to rob the royal pair, Tamino and Pamina, of the child Pamina is about to bear. Monostatos and his men have made their way to the palace undiscovered; at the moment of birth they envelop the palace in a darkness which emanates from the golden casket in which the newborn child is to be abducted. The black scheme seems successful: Monostatos gains possession of the child, puts it in the casket and hurries to make his escape. But Sarastro's magic spells frustrate the plan. The casket grows so heavy that the abductors have to abandon it—but not before they have sealed it with the Queen of Night's seal. The seal not only locks the casket forever; it also carries the curse that the child must die if it ever sees its parents, and that the parents themselves will be struck with melancholy if they behold each other. Sarastro, the High Priest of the beneficent Order, appears powerless against this curse. All he can do is soften it: after the abductors have fled, the casket grows light again, and its precious inmate can be kept alive as long as the golden prison is carried about and kept in constant motion. Unluckily, Sarastro, the noble prince of wisdom and sole succor of his friends, is removed from them at this very moment, for the lot by which one member of the Order is chosen every year to go forth into the world and spread the holy message has fallen on him.

The moving and tragic story of the sorrows of the great is followed, in comic variation, by the unhappiness of Papageno and Papagena, the tender bird-couple. They also, in their chirping way, are aggrieved, for their expectation of having a brood of little Papagenos and Papagenas has until now remained unfulfilled. But for them there is an easy remedy. Thanks to the magic power of Sarastro—who happens to arrive just then in the course of his wanderings—three lovely little child fledglings break out of three multicolored eggs which have suddenly appeared in Papageno's nest. By way of compensation for his aid, Sarastro demands that the bird family proceed to the palace and assuage, through the merry notes of the magic flute, the grief of Pamina and Tamino.

Meanwhile the despair at court has deepened. Pamina has wanted to dedicate the golden casket to the sun, but at the moment of the sacred ceremony the machinations of the Queen of Night cause the casket to fall into the underworld, where it is watched over by wild beasts and two guards, creatures of the heartless Queen. But Papageno's flute-playing re-animates Tamino and Pamina; they begin the search for their child. In heroic devotion they walk through barriers of fire and water to the infernal regions, make their way into the tomb where the casket is hidden, approach the child—when the Queen of Night, trembling with rage, blocks their way. But the parents' readiness for self-sacrifice has broken the evil spell. The child, now called "Genius," breaks forth from the casket and rises into the air . . . Here the fragment ends, but the remainder—the capturing of Genius—can easily be reconstructed. The much tried parents and the child are reunited through the aid of Sarastro and of Papageno's offspring. The happiness is short-lived: Genius escapes once more and falls into the hands of Monostatos and the Queen of Night. The Queen is triumphant; darkness seems the final victor. But the last word is still not spoken; there is one more great battle, in which Pamina and Tamino are victorious. The last scene unites the forces of light, Sarastro, the priests and the royal family, who celebrate their triumph over the dark plots of the nocturnal Queen and her cohorts.

All this may strike us, at first glance, as the stuff of a wildly rambling fairy-tale got up for a conventional fairy-tale opera. Still, these motifs—though apparently strung together with more fancy than care—have so Goethean a quality that they are surely worth a closer look. Even a casual reader cannot help noticing that what prompted Goethe's imagination to continue Schikaneder's story was its Masonic elements. These

Goethe eagerly took up and carried further; through them he made contact with the whole subject—as the subject made contact with him—and was able to shape it into a work of his own, intimately related to his *Wilhelm Meister* and to the poetic fragment "Die Geheimnisse." Is not Sarastro's Order, so evidently imagined as a kind of Masonic lodge, almost identical with the "Society of the Tower" which in its mysterious wisdom guides Wilhelm Meister's steps until he has attained the maturity necessary to be accepted into the community of "brothers?" Thus the "Magic Flute" takes its organic place among Goethe's Masonic writings; the reason for its conception is not the merely external one that Goethe had, since 1780, been a member of the Weimar lodge "Amalia," but the more profound motives behind his becoming a Mason in the first place. In the community of brothers, he discovered, traits of his own philosophy of life and art had found visible expression; so it was inevitable that he should give them visible expression in his work.

There were several affinities between Freemasonry and Goethe's innermost being. There was, first of all, the language of symbols, which the Masons had worked out with almost pedantic precision and which Goethe joyfully seized upon—so joyfully that he was able to overlook the sterile hocus-pocus in it. Making visible the invisible, naming the nameless—this was, for Goethe, the fundamental and truly sacral function of art; all his creative energies were directed toward the creation of symbols. In the symbol, the formless assumes form and still does not lose its connection with the unencompassable divine source from which all art flows. Thus we read in the "Sprüche in Prosa" : "Das ist die wahre Symbolik, wo das Besondere das Allgemeine repräsentiert, nicht als Traum und Schatten, sondern als lebendig augenblickliche Offenbarung des Unerforschlichen." In "Kunst und Altertum" Goethe tried to define the magical essence of the sign still more precisely: "Die Symbolik verwandelt die Erscheinung in Idee, die Idee in ein Bild, und so, dass die Idee im Bild immer unendlich wirksam und unerreichbar bleibt, und, selbst in allen Sprachen ausgesprochen, doch unaussprechlich bliebe." For him, then, the symbol language of Freemasonry was not conventional mystification, but the attempt to point to the inexplicable by means of the image, to capture the eternal in the visible without violating its unfathomable infinitude; and the attempt was fully in harmony with the law which governed his own existence: to create art. We can never take too seriously Goethe's love of the symbol, which in external matters sometimes manifested itself in an almost pedantic ritualism; it would be a grave mistake to pass over his fascination with Masonic symbolism as a somewhat comical vagary.

But the symbolism was not the only, perhaps not even the decisive affinity; another look at the *Magic Flute* directs us to the determining element. For there we see an order, a congregation of priests, a religious institution, which is not bound to a positive dogma, but finds fulfillment in an ethic embracing all humanity and professing, as the highest article of its faith: "Recht zu handeln, grad zu wandeln, sei des edlen Mannes Wahl." A distinction must here be kept in view: The highest realization of humanity is seen from the outset as being achieved within an organized structure. It is no accident that Sarastro's first entrance shows him in the circle of priests, nor that the brotherhood of the wise men is shown in close proximity to Tamino and Pamina, who as rulers represent the sphere of secular organization. True, as an embodiment of the highest form of humanity, Sarastro is of a kind with Iphigenia; but the difference is that now the humane takes its place and finds its fulfillment in a collective; it manifests itself no longer as an individual redemption, but as a transcending of the individual, an acceptance of and into the group—as that ultimate kind of "Bildung" which Wilhelm Meister also achieves only after he has ceased to be merely a private person and has become a member of the Society of the Tower.

The tie between the religious order and the secular power is so close that Goethe implies that Sarastro himself handed the crown over to Tamino upon being sent forth as a missionary:

> Die Krone gab ich meinem lieben,
> Ich gab sie schon dem werten Mann.

This closeness accurately reflects the determination of Freemasonry (fully affirmed by Goethe) to be more than a charitable club, to become a representative, influential organization capable of wielding power. Goethe dreamed of a league of initiates, branching beyond all national boundaries, since the realization of true *humanitas* could not be achieved by an association pledged to particular national or racial interests. Also, the secrecy surrounding the league harmonized with Goethe's mistrust of all that was too public, his inclination toward a certain aristocratic exclusiveness. An organization such as the Society in *Wilhelm Meister*, which had the function of guarding and guiding human destiny by wise planning, had to work in secrecy, in semi-darkness. The community of brothers, thus organized, was dedicated to an intense activism; *Wilhelm Meister's* "Hier oder nirgends ist Amerika" echoes in the "Magic Flute." Effective, competent activity, in which Goethe, as he grew old, was to see "der Weisheit letzten Schluss," is the principle of our libretto as it is that of the *Wanderjahre* and of *Faust II*. The motif of wandering, which was to enter into the very title of Wilhelm Meister's later story, is here anticipated in the sacred rule of the order by which, each year, one of the brothers is sent abroad. Goethe could not conceive of vital being except in the image of unceasing motion; wherever the divine in its vital aspect demands expression in his work, it appears in symbols of motion and change. And does not Sarastro's beneficent magic, by which the child is kept alive as long as it is kept in steady motion, is unceasingly carried about in its casket, prefigure the profound "Stirb und werde," the burden of the most beautiful poem in the *West-östliche Diwan?*

I have gone, I realize, beyond the limits of the Masonic element in the strict sense. The ethic of practical action is so essential a part of the later Goethe's nature and message that it cannot well be ascribed to the credo of a specific organization, however close Goethe may have felt to it. But since the purpose of this explication is the pointing up of the permanent Goethean substance even in a work apparently so *ad hoc* as the "Magic Flute," it is surely proper to show how the poet was bound to be attracted and engaged by ideas so similar to his own. This holds even more clearly for the basic figure which permeates the entire libretto: the symbolic struggle of light and darkness. This struggle, archetypal in Goethe's thought, is also part of the symbolism of Freemasonry. The very name "Queen of Night" was bound to set off in Goethe's mind a chain of associations which he was strongly predisposed to pursue. I think it idle to ask, with Max Morris, whether Goethe saw the dark queen as an image of Charlotte von Stein, who persecuted him with petty vengefulness and contemptible hatred when he began living with Christiane. Such merely personal motives prove distressingly confining if we measure them against the fact that in Goethe's thinking light and darkness are coextensive with good and evil, that the images of night and day embody the eternal powers which struggle for man's soul. Schiller need not have worried that the work on the "Magic Flute" would divert Goethe from the *Hauptsache,* from *Faust.* The symbolic confrontation of light and darkness proves that Goethe's imagination was pregnant with those poetic archetypes which later found full incarnation in the still unwritten sections of *Faust I.* May we not see in the Queen of Night, with her hatred of "das sanfte Wandeln deines Tags," the majestic sister of Mephistopheles? May we not imagine her uttering the dark cosmogony which the Evil One recites to Faust at their first meeting:

> Ich bin ein Teil des Teils, der anfangs alles war,
> Ein Teil der Finsternis, die sich das Licht gebar,
> Das stolze Licht, das nun der Mutter Nacht
> Den alten Rang, den Raum ihr streitig macht.

Mephisto's "Mutter Nacht" sounds almost like the cue for the entrance of the dark queen, who—to be quite precise—as Pamina's mother, did give birth to light. However, this is rather a reminiscence of Mozart's *Magic Flute* than strictly part of an interpretation of Goethe's libretto. For Goethe, who wanted the Queen to represent the principle of absolute evil, severed all family ties between her and Pamina; nowhere does he hint that her diabolic scheming is the vengefulness of a deserted mother. He meant to set forth the pure principle, the essentially evil against the essentially good; the mother-daughter relation of Mozart's *Magic Flute* could only have lessened the metaphysical absoluteness of the conflict. This was the reason for his eliminating from the final version the only passage which could have suggested a personal relationship between the opponents. From the Queen's opening song he struck these lines:

> Wer wagt es, ohne Grauen
> Das Angesicht der Königin zu schauen,
> Die tiefen Schmerz in ihrem Busen trägt.

Rid of all human bonds, the Queen becomes the symbol of night and darkness, the cruelly destructive power which spreads the blanket of annihilation over all things living.

The affinity to *Faust* is audible in the compelling cadences of the Queen's first great song, which sounds like the cosmic master plan of the Mother Night to whose power Mephisto bore witness:

> Woget ihr Wolken hin,
> Decket die Erde,
> Dass es noch düsterer,
> Finsterer werde!
> Schrecken und Schauer,

> Klagen und Trauer,
> Leise verhalle bang,
> Ende den Nachtgesang
> Schweigen und Tod.

In the final line—doubly awful and compelling because it stands as a rhymeless supernumerary within the stanza—the Queen reveals her true nature, for she is the queen not only of night but also of eternal silence and death, the principle not only of darkness but also of non-being, the quintessence of all life-denying forces. This is how we must see the "Magic Flute," if we want to discover the profound meaning beneath the fairy-tale plot. What at first glance might appear as a lighthearted exercise of fancy is in truth something quite different: in the wild spells and enchantments, in the rape and recovery of the child we recognize the struggle of the powers of death against budding new life, the frost of eternal silence broken at the last moment by the blessed spell of rebirth. Thus the libretto enacts the futile battle of nothingness against life, of the universal void against the procreant power of organic nature. Again we are reminded of Mephisto's stating the program of a metaphysical nihilism:

> Ich bin der Geist, der stets verneint!
> Und das mit Recht, denn alles, was entsteht,
> Ist wert, dass es zugrunde geht,
> Drum besser wär's, dass nichts entstünde.

In fact, Goethe worked this struggle even into the comic subplot, the humorous episodes about Papageno and Papagena. Childlessness is the amusing bird-couple's strident grievance; and to them also Sarastro appears as the bearer of the life principle: by his friendly spell three lively, fluttering creatures burst from the eggs. This struggling for fertility and battling against silence and death is at the very core of the fragment.

It befits this complex of motifs that the Queen of Night exists and schemes in icy solitude. These are her first words:

> Wer ruft mich an?
> Wer wagt's mit mir zu sprechen?
> Wer diese Stille kühn zu unterbrechen?
> Ich höre nichts—so bin ich denn allein!
> Die Welt verstummt um mich, so soll es sein.

Being alone is the tragic curse which stifles life; again and again Goethe invokes the terror of solitude, beneath which life freezes into the rigor of a deadly paralysis. We recall the Harfner's song from *Wilhelm Meister*; there, as perhaps nowhere else, we are moved by the moan of the outcast, the de-parted (*Abgeschiedenen*) in the full and heartrending double sense of the German word, which combines solitude and death in a true identity:

> Wer sich der Einsamkeit ergibt,
> Ach, der ist bald allein,
> Ein jeder lebt, ein jeder liebt
> Und lässt ihn seiner Pein.

Being alone is death; this is the deeper meaning also of the Queen's curse upon Tamino and Pamina that they must fall into melancholy if they lay eyes on each other. Not only the child is hunted by death; the parents are cast into that state of *Abgeschiedenheit* which the mistress of non-being has chosen as her proper sphere. And again it is Sarastro who brings help: the sounds of the magic flute dispel the paralysing melancholy. There can be little doubt that here the flute itself assumes symbolic significance. The wonder-working music which issues from this instrument stands as a symbolic abbreviation for all art, as an emblem of that healing power which will lift us beyond life's harsh grip and at the same time immerse us in life's creative current—in the sense of the aphorism from Ottilie's diary in the *Wahlverwandtschaften*: "Man weicht der Welt nicht sicherer aus als durch die Kunst, und man verknüpft sich nicht sicherer mit ihr als durch die Kunst."

In the attempt to find a way through the rich growth of fairy-tale matter to the Goethean substance we have discovered basic motifs which place the "Magic Flute" in close proximity to *Wilhelm Meister* and *Faust I*. But as yet we have not touched upon a layer of poetic visions which point from the libretto into the future and will find a richly beautiful development only in the second part of *Faust*. There is good reason to think that the figure of Genius and the improbable constellations of which he is a part contain the germs of the later Euphorion, one of the central figures in the Helena episode. Both figures show the grievous impermanence of creative genius, imaged in the motif of flying and flight—the impossibility of capturing it and assigning it a fixed place in our ordered terrestrial world. Just as Euphorion, heedless of Faust's and Helena's warning shouts, rises higher and higher into the air and finally destroys himself in a last dare-devil leap, so Genius is freed from the casket only to fly away and to repeat this enchantingly dangerous, airy game even after he has been caught and reunited with his parents. In the "Magic Flute" as in *Faust II*, the genius of art demonstrates that his kingdom is not of this world. We do not know where he has his home, but we do know that he has a dangerous and fateful affinity to death. He is at home in the realm of shadows; he lives in a golden coffin and rises from the nether world into which the Queen of Night has made him sink. Goethe was familiar with those dark depths, with that dangerous chasm of death in which beauty has her dwelling; and although he did not, like Schopenhauer and Mann, continually point to the mark of death on beauty's brow, he knew as much as anyone of the intimate tie between death and art. Even if we had no other testimony—as in *Tasso* and *Faust II*—Genius' song as he breaks out of his casket would be testimony enough:

> Hier bin ich, ihr Lieben,
> Und bin ich nicht schön?
> Wer wird sich betrüben,
> Sein Söhnchen zu sehn?
> In Nächten geboren
> Im herrlichen Haus,
> Und wieder verloren
> In Nächten und Graus?

Pamina and Tamino must descend into the underworld to free the captive from his coffin—very much as Faust has to go down into the realm of the Mothers, the underworld, in order to bring first Helena's image and then her embodied self into our world. Could not Helena, beauty incarnate, also say of herself:

> In Nächten geboren
> Im herrlichen Haus,
> Und wieder verloren
> In Nächten und Graus?

Does not this recurrent joining of visions of art and death clearly reveal the fearful awe which seized Goethe before the mysterious power of beauty, the force which governed his own existence? The likeness of Euphorion and Genius, the similarity between the inner meanings of the two visions, seems conclusive. And surely we may see a startling parallel even in poetic images defining the habitations from which beauty ascends into our world: the cave of the "Magic Flute" and the realm of the Mothers in *Faust II*. True, we do not actually see the latter; Goethe shrank from putting on the stage these regions of awesome gloom. But Mephisto circumscribes in mysterious words the nothingness in which the Mothers have their ghostly being: "Um sie kein Ort, noch weniger eine Zeit," and then: "Kein Weg! Ins Unbetretene Nicht zu Betretende; ein Weg ans Unerbetene Nicht zu Erbittende." This tone of shuddering mystery, of vague groping, which seeks to describe the place beyond all space and to fix the time beyond all time—this tone we hear also in the "Magic Flute," in that magnificently meaningless antiphone of the two guards who watch over the golden casket in the underworld:

>Bruder, wachst Du?—
>Ich höre.—
>Sind wir allein?—
>Wer weiss?—
>Wird es Tag?—
>Vielleicht ja.—
>Kommt die Nacht?—
>Sie ist da.—
>Die Zeit vergeht.—
>Aber wie?—
>Schlägt die Stunde wohl?—
>Uns nie.—

The place beyond space and time is the dwelling of beauty and art, in the "Magic Flute" as in *Faust II*; in this magic opera Goethe poetically explored the equivocal love affair between "Geist" and death, very much as, in our day, Mann explores it in the mighty fiction he entitled—by a significant coincidence, surely—*The Magic Mountain*.

I hope I have shown how intimate the connection is between the "occasional" operatic fragment and *Faust II*. Even the seemingly unimportant constellation Genius-gold—it is a golden casket in which the child is imprisoned—will recur in *Faust*. We will encounter Genius once more in the great masquerade at the imperial court; this time he is called "Knabe Wagenlenker," and Goethe marks him unmistakably as a precursor of the later Euphorion. And the carriage the boy drives is the costly one of Pluto, prince of the underworld and of gold, who in this masquerade distributes his glittering gifts among the populace. In this alliance between the boy and Pluto we recognize once more the uncanny familiarity of genius with death to which the "Magic Flute" bears such unambiguous testimony.

I have tried to interpret the symbols which point from the "Magic Flute" forward to *Faust II*. But the affinity is closer still; it lies, above all, in the *art form* which Goethe sought, still somewhat tentatively, to discover in the libretto and which then found full and splendid development in *Faust II*: the form of great opera. For *Faust II* is a fairy opera quite as much as the

"Magic Flute" is; it was no accident that Goethe subtitled the Helena-episode (the first section to be executed) a "klassisch-romantische Phantasmagorie," nor that, after completing the great work, he called *Faust II* "ein inneres Märchen."[5] It was in his labors on the "Magic Flute" that Goethe fully discovered the possibilities of opera as the highest and last art form to engage his energies.

Space does not permit a full discussion of the elements of fairy opera; I must confine myself to pointing out how the libretto is Goethe's first decisive step toward the majestic *Gesamtkunstwerk* which found so exemplary an embodiment in *Faust II*. Goethe wanted to revive the truly theatrical—that comprehensive union of grand-style stage magic and musical and pantomime masque which does not limit itself to purely literary effects but combines all the elements of theatrical art: music, dance, illusion (*féerie*) and the spoken word. What Goethe had in mind was "unchained theatre" (if so ultra-modern a term is admissible here)—the art form which allows the poetic imagination the greatest latitude and the fullest possible range of effects, and which enlists all technical means in the service of the grandly festive occasion. The theatre director's advice in the "Vorspiel" to *Faust* is to the purpose here:

> Ihr wisst, auf unseren deutschen Bühnen
> Probiert ein jeder, was er mag;
> Drum schonet mir an diesem Tag
> Prospekte nicht und nicht Maschinen.
> Gebraucht das gross' und kleine Himmelslicht,
> Die Sterne dürfet ihr verschwenden;
> An Wasser, Feuer, Felsenwänden,
> An Tier und Vögeln fehl' es nicht.

These words about stars, water, fire, towering rocks, animals and birds, sound exactly as though Goethe, in writing them, had been thinking specifically of the "Magic Flute." But however that may be, he was assuredly thinking of the form of the fairy opera, the unconstrained, festive stage-play—with profounder meaning. What he dreamed of was the combination of intoxicating popular entertainment and highest poetry—the great synthesis which would release the European theatre from its isolating bondage to the purely literary, and restore to it the popular and celebratory rôle which it had had in ancient Greece. The only

---

5. Letter to Hermann Meyer, July 20, 1831.

form available for this purpose was opera, the *Zauberposse* for example, which in Vienna (birthplace of Mozart's *Magic Flute*) made the theatre into an institution of genuinely and inclusively popular entertainment. Opera as poetry, poetry as opera—that was Goethe's aim; that was what he strove to accomplish in his supreme work, *Faust*: a colorful, direct, festive, dramatic spectacle, which made its impact by purely visual effect and at the same time gave the initiates access to the highest regions of poetry and philosophy. Fragmentary though it is, the "Magic Flute" represents the first major realization of that union of colorful fairy-tale play and the creation of a profound poetic symbolism. In its fabulous and carefree appearance a final and richly wrought wisdom becomes manifest; we may apply to it what Goethe hopefully wrote of *Faust II*: "Da steht es nun, wie es auch geraten sei. Und wenn es noch Probleme genug enthält, keineswegs jede Aufklärung darbietet, so wird es doch denjenigen erfreuen, der sich auf Miene, Wink und leise Hindeutung versteht. Er wird sogar mehr finden, als ich geben konnte."[6]

---

6. Letter to Sulpiz Boisserée, September 8, 1831.

# IS THE "PRELUDE IN THE THEATRE" A PRELUDE TO *FAUST*?

Everyone knows that "The Prelude in the Theatre" belongs to *Faust*; that it has introduced the so-called First Part of the tragedy ever since the earliest publication of the great play in 1808; that nowhere in Goethe's written or oral statements can the slightest indication be detected from which we may infer that this prelude had not been from the very beginning in the very spot where it is found today.[1] All this is unquestionably true; and yet, without any claim to final conclusiveness, I should like to consider the possibility whether or not, within the organic structure of Goethe's works, the Prelude in the Theatre may have grown on a branch which was not the one that produced *Faust*.

Our first suspicion is aroused by the complete uncertainty concerning the date of the Prelude's origin—quite a serious reason for suspicion, we must admit, if we consider how carefully Goethe has recorded and kept track of the gradual growth of his *magnum opus*. Almost all *Faust*-scholars take it for granted that the Prelude was written in the summer or early autumn of 1797.[2] Only Hans Gerhard Gräf, who knows more thoroughly than anyone else all of Goethe's utterances about his own productions and who is aware of the total lack of any support for an unequivocal dating of the Prelude, thinks it possible that 1798 may have been the year of origin.[3] He cannot proffer any proofs for either date; because nowhere, either in Goethe's diaries, or in his letters, or in his conversations is the slightest hint as to the conception and writing of the Prelude to be found. This fact alone should make us suspicious. For we are indeed well informed about the other passages which Goethe in the summer

---

1. Goethe undoubtedly considered the "Prelude" an integral part of his *Faust*. When, with the active help of the poet, the actor Pius Alexander Wolff drew up plans to perform the tragedy's First Part on the stage of Weimar, the "Prelude" was actually considered for stage-presentation. These plans, taken up by Wolff again and again between 1810 and 1816, did not materialize. For over a century it has been a generally accepted custom to omit the "Prelude" when *Faust* is being performed. Cf. Julius Petersen, *Goethes Faust auf der deutschen Bühne* (Leipzig, 1929), p. 9.
2. The only dissenting opinion I find is Karl Heinemann's in his notes to *Faust—Goethes Werke* (Leipzig: Bibliographisches Institut, 1900), v, 519. He gives without any indication as to his source August 9, 1799, as the exact date of the completion of the Prelude.
3. *Goethe über seine Dichtungen* (Frankfurt, 1904), II, 2. Teil, 63.

of 1797 added when he resumed work on the long neglected fragment. The diary of June 24, 1797, records the drafting of the "Zueignung"; the "Chronologie" handed down by Riemer and Eckermann mentions the "Prolog im Himmel"[4]—but not a word about the Prelude in the Theatre. Should we really believe that in all his diary entries and conversations Goethe had completely forgotten the charming little sketch which, moreover, is so well rounded as to present an entity in itself? Or is it not possible that within the frame of the *Faust*-chronology no mention of the Prelude is made because it did not belong originally in this frame and must be fitted into a different chronological context?

Speculation of this sort would be utterly idle if in mood or content a clear connection between the Prelude and the Tragedy's First Part could be discovered. But all *Faust*-commentators realize only too well that such a link is missing, even though they try with great ingenuity and trickish juggling to establish such a connection. For it is all too obvious that no road leads from the wittily satiric tone of the Prelude to the majestic serenity of the Archangels' dithyrambs—and quite apart from the tone, could any possible link be found between the mocking *lever de rideau* and the great drama of humanity? In whatever way one may turn and twist it, the play for which we are being prepared in the Prelude is not *Faust*, or if it is *Faust*, the poet in the Prelude has played a nasty trick on his colleagues, the theatre manager and the lustige Person. For the play which the theatre manager orders from his poet, the play in which the lustige Person is already anxiously waiting to act, is certainly not the Tragedy's First Part. To be sure, all the *Faust*-interpreters who never entertained any doubts as to the appositeness of this *Faust* prelude have tried very hard to make the unintelligible seem intelligible. Had not the first germ of the great drama grown from the soil of the puppet-theatre, the fairground amusements, the *Plundersweilerei*—and is not the introductory burlesque therefore quite in order? Maybe so, if Goethe had written

---

4. *Goethes poetische und prosaische Werke* (Stuttgart 1836, II, 2. Teil, 660. The entry for 1797 reads: "Das Schema zum *Faust* vervollständigt, sowie 'Oberons und Titanias goldene Hochzeit,' die 'Zueignung' und den 'Prolog' geschrieben." Gräf, in his disappointment at the total lack of any supporting evidence for the origin of the Prelude, suggests (*op. cit.*, p. 66) that the word "Prolog" could be construed to mean both the "Prolog im Himmel" and the Prelude. This suggestion is psychologically understandable, but factually untenable and unconvincing. "Prolog" means "Prolog im Himmel" and nothing else.

it in 1773, but certainly not in 1797 when the puppet-play atmosphere had long vanished. (Or could anybody who reads the "Zueignung" get the idea that the "schwankende Gestalten" which waver before and press against the poet's heart are runaways from the shabby planks of the amusement fair?) To remind us here and now of the punch-and-judy show could only occur to the philologist who is so well informed about the where and how of the Faust-legend, but hardly to the poet in whose mind the puppet-play had broadened to a drama of humanity. And even if we accepted the contention of the many *Faust*-scholars that the lustige Person takes over the part of Mephistopheles in the announced play,[5] this again would be a reasonable supposition only if we were thinking of the Mephisto in the puppet-play (or possibly still of the Mephisto of the *Urfaust*), but never of the devil in the Tragedy's First Part. Yet even in the rôle of a puppet-play Mephisto the merry and sensible lustige Person would be badly miscast. He calls himself explicitly a "braven Knaben," and the cheerful jests with which he plans to elicit the laughter of the crowd hardly belong to the repertory of a Mephistophelian Punch. No doubt, the theatre manager and the lustige Person will find themselves sorrily led by the nose and thoroughly left out in the cold if the play which they announce in the Prelude is really *Faust*.

But still, do not the final words of the theatre manager, the announcement of a drama "vom Himmel durch die Welt zur Hölle," point to the following tragedy? Indeed, they offer a hint, but hardly a conclusive one. For the stages of the *Faust*-action are only insufficiently indicated by these cues, even if we are willing to concede that Goethe, as early as 1797, had a clear conception of the general course of action of the Second Part and that he may already have thought of the yawning hell which transitorily opens its jaws in the fifth act, shortly before Faust's apotheosis. Whatever plans with regard to Faust's end Goethe may have entertained at this period, the words of the theatre manager are so ambiguous that one of the more recent *Faust*-commentators, Heinrich Rickert,[6] wants them to be taken

---

5. Among many others Georg von Loeper, *Faust* (Berlin, 1879), p. 11, and Erich Schmidt *Goethes Werke* (Jub. Ausg.), XIII, 265.
6. *Goethes Faust* (Tübingen, 1932), p. 54. How difficult it is to arrive at a clear interpretation of the concluding line of the Prelude, becomes evident if one follows the long drawn-out dispute between Kuno Fischer and Friedrich Theodor Vischer about the meaning of these last words. (Cf. Friedrich Th. Vischer, *Altes und Neues*, Stuttgart

in a generally symbolic sense only, so as to mean that in the play under preparation God, Man, and Devil will meet and reveal their respective positions. Yet Rickert does not seem to be aware of the fact that his suggestion runs counter to the words of Goethe, who, in a conversation with Eckermann (May 6, 1827), explicitly protested against an interpretation which tries to find the "idea" of *Faust* in the words "vom Himmel durch die Welt zur Hölle." They circumscribe only the "course of action," so Goethe maintains—this, however, in so fragmentary and inconclusive a manner that we cannot count heavily on this as a link of connection between the Prelude and *Faust*. To add to the confusion: how awkward and unconvincing would the program of a cosmic drama of damnation and redemption sound in the mouth of the theatre manager, who up to this point has insisted so sternly on undiluted entertainment.

There remains then as the only, and indeed most likely, link of connection between the Prelude and *Faust* a stylistic one: the fact, namely, that the poet in the Prelude seems to take up in his first speeches the ottava rima of the "Zueignung." Yet this evidence, too, is by no means conclusive. Goethe's poetic work, both before and after 1797, is rich in ottava rima, and an infallible coordination of the two pieces on the grounds of their metrical similarity is therefore quite impossible. One might say that the ottava rima has a specific function within Goethe's poetic productions. This form seems to suggest itself to him whenever he feels the need to evoke the *daimon*, be it the *daimon* of personality as in "Gewiss, ich wäre schon so fern, so ferne" and in "Urworte. Orphisch"; be it the *daimon* of creative productiveness as in "Zueignung" ("Der Morgen kam") and in the "Epilog zu Schillers Glocke"; or be it, in his later years, the majestic in general ("Einer hohen Reisenden," "Der Kaiserin Platz," "Ihro des Kaisers von Oesterreich Majestät," "Ihre der Kaiserin von Oesterreich Majestät," "Ihre der Kaiserin von Frankreich Majestät"). Perhaps we are justified in calling the ottava rima, especially of the middle-aged Goethe, an Orphic tone, a Tasso-tone; as such it would come naturally enough to the poet of the Prelude as well as to the poet of the "Zueignung." This would seem logical without the necessity of deducing a closer relation-

---

1881, Heft II, 42 ff). Friedrich Th. Vischer who was not given to drop a fight before his opponent was defeated ends the argument on a note of helpless resignation: "Lassen wir den Knoten ungelöst liegen, wie er liegt" (p. 44).

ship between the two pieces from the similarity of their poetic forms.

Yet the Prelude in the Theatre does contain a clear hint about the play which is to follow; this play, however, is not *Faust*. The theatre manager submits to his poet a detailed list of sets and accessories which he can and should make use of:

> Drum schonet mir an diesem Tag
> Prospekte nicht und nicht Maschinen.
> Gebraucht das gross' und kleine Himmelslicht,
> Die Sterne dürfet ihr verschwenden,
> An Wasser, Feuer, Felsenwänden,
> An Tier und Vögeln fehl' es nicht.

Even if it could be proved that all these accessories and animals actually appear in *Faust*,[7] the type of play which the theatre manager presents here is an entirely different one. It is the type of the great decorative *revue* in which these accessories are not only "present" but in the action of which they take, so to speak, a decisive part. In short, it is the *Zauberposse*, and again it is a quite specific *Zauberposse, Die Zauberflöte*, in which each accessory, enumerated above, appears, and not only in the incidental manner of being present, but in a genuinely constitutive and type-establishing manner. This "coincidence" has, of course, not escaped the attention of the *Faust*-scholars; most of them have pointed out that Goethe, while writing his prelude to *Faust*, was thinking of the stage-apparatus of the *Zauberflöte*,[8] which had been first performed in the theatre of Weimar in January 1794. And how would it be if we took this half-hearted concession seriously? Not while writing a prelude to *Faust* did Goethe perchance think of the settings of Mozart's *Zauberflöte*, but he thought of them while writing a prelude to the *Zauberflöte*—and not to Mozart's but to his own. To his own opera-libretto, *Der Zauberflöte zweiter Teil*, this Prelude in the Theatre would fit very well indeed.

If we once assume that the Prelude belongs to the *Zauberflöte* and not to *Faust*, then all the elements which seemed confusing

---

7. The *Faust*-commentators do their utmost to prove it, although in some cases, as in the instance of the "Vögeln," they have to anticipate the Klassische Walpurgisnacht in the Second Part. Cf. for instance Erich Schmidt, *op. cit.*, p. 269, who assures us "wirklich kommt alles im *Faust* vor."
8. Oswald Marbach, *Goethes Faust* (Stuttgart, 1881), p. 31; Heinrich Düntzer, *Goethes Faust* (Leipzig, 1882), p. 73; K. J. Schröer, *Faust von Goethe* (Heilbronn 1886), I, 20; G.v. Loeper, *op. cit.*, p. 12; Georg Witkowski, *Goethes Faust* (Leipzig, 1906), II, 195; *et al.*

and out of tune take on a perfectly sensible meaning. We know all of a sudden where the lustige Person belongs: it is Papageno, whose impersonator can claim with full justification that he is a "braver Knabe." If we add the paralipomena, i.e., those verses which Goethe struck from the final version of the Prelude, Papageno suddenly stands bodily before us:

> Seht mir nur ab, wie man vor Leute tritt.
> Ich komme lustig angezogen,
> So ist mir jedes Herz gewogen.
> Ich lache, jeder lachet mit.
> Ihr müsst, wie ich, nur auf euch selbst vertrauen,
> Und denken, dass hier was zu wagen ist.
> Denn es verzeihen selbst gelegentlich die Frauen,
> Wenn man—mit Anstand—den Respekt vergisst.
> Nicht Wünschelrute, nicht Alraune,
> Die beste Zauberei liegt in der guten Laune.

Does anybody seriously believe Goethe could have put these words into the mouth of the actor who was about to don the devil's costume? Every single word would be a parody on his rôle in *Faust*, and therefore it is easily understandable that we no longer find these charming verses in the text of the Prelude in the Theatre but in the paralipomena. They point so unmistakably to Papageno that Goethe could not possibly retain them in a prelude which he finally hitched onto *Faust*.[9] In the part of Papageno the lustige Person will indeed get his due, as will the theatre manager, who can be quite satisfied with this *Zauberflöte* which the poet is about to write for him. It is to be a "stark Getränke" which will delight the gaping crowds anxiously awaited by the theatre manager in front of his wooden planks. It is to be a play with plenty of action, worth watching, and worth laughing at, a play in which everything will be "gefällig mit Bedeutung." And if we may point to another paralipomenon, undoubtedly to be ascribed to the theatre manager—

> Nur heute schränkt den weiten Blick mir ein,
> Nur heute lasst die Strenge mir nicht walten,
> Lasst unser Stück nur reich an Fülle sein,
> Dann mag der Zufall selbst als Geist der Einheit walten

—as an address to the author of *Faust* these words would be

---

9. There is, of course, a possibility that Goethe may have added verses which the Prelude did not contain originally, after he had once decided to use the little one-act play for *Faust*. However, if asked, I could not point out a single verse in the Prelude which would fulfill the function to establish *a posteriori* such a connection between Prelude and *Faust*.

pure nonsense (for this reason they are today to be found among the paralipomena), but as an address to the author of the *Zauberflöte*-continuation they would stand at their proper place in the Prelude.

A fairytale-like folk-amusement, with deeper meaning, this is exactly what Goethe wanted to offer in his *Zauberflöte*,[10] and this is exactly the synthesis of the three radical positions which the characters of the Prelude in the Theatre present. Such a synthesis must be achieved if the Prelude is to be followed by a *ludum* at all. With his *Zauberflöte* Goethe wanted to show which elements were required by a play that would equally satisfy the entrepreneur (theatre manager), the actor (lustige Person), the audience, and last, but by no means least, the poet himself. Goethe, as the author of the *Zauberflöte*, actually thought on the three different levels which he presents in his Prelude: as a theatre manager, as the director of his actors, and as the poet he was. Goethe, as the author of *Faust*, never did anything of the sort. Only a grave misunderstanding could lead to the conclusion that Goethe identifies himself with the poet in the Prelude; this would be a relapse into an extreme Tasso-mood which Goethe in the middle or late nineties would certainly no longer profess as his own. The poet's program in the Prelude is not Goethe's program: Goethe's program is a synthesis of three centrifugal positions, and this program he tried to carry out in his *Zauberflöte*. When, with his letter of January 24, 1796, he attempted to sell his opera libretto to the conductor of the Vienna Court Theatre, Wranitzky, he wrote explicitly that his *Zauberflöte* intended "den Schauspielern und Direktoren die Aufführung eines neuen Stükes zu erleichtern," and to give to the audience what the audience had a good right to expect in a theatre.

To these direct proofs,[11] which in themselves may be already sufficient, we can add some circumstantial evidence that seems to me irrefutable. Goethe sensed—more than that, he knew from his acquaintance with Goldoni, Gozzi, and the Roman folk-

---

10. Cf. for this and the following the preceding essay on Goethe's *Magic Flute*.
11. I point only parenthetically to the very interesting fact that the cryptic words of the theatre manager, "vom Himmel durch die Welt zur Hölle," epitomize exactly the action which Goethe has unfolded in his *Zauberflöte*-fragment: from the seat of the Queen of the Night above the clouds and stars through Tamino's palace and Papageno's hut into the underworld where Tamino's and Pamina's child is kept in captivity by the somber queen.

comedy—very well where the *Zauberoper* has its origin: in the *commedia dell' arte*.[12] To the style of the *commedia dell' arte* the disputation between theatre manager, actor and poet fits extremely well, while as an opening for the great drama of humanity it is definitely "out of tune." Here in the *commedia dell' arte* lies the common germ of the Prelude and the *Zauberflöte*, and since they grow out of the same germ, they belong together in tone and style.

However, still more decisive is the spiritual and artistic neighborhood into which the Prelude is transplanted if we sever it from *Faust* and tie it up with the *Zauberflöte*. Then it becomes a contemporary of *Wilhelm Meister*, with which the opera libretto is intimately connected, as I tried to show in my article on the *Zauberflöte*. All of a sudden, the voice of the theatre manager which has no legitimacy and no function in the *Faust*-complex sounds very familiar to us; for what he expounds here in the Prelude is—at many places literally—an exact echo of

---

12. After I had read this paper before the German III group at the 63rd annual meeting of the Modern Language Association in New York, Professor Richard Alewyn was kind enough to draw my attention to the fact that only the Papageno-scenes contain genuine *commedia dell' arte* elements. The *Zauberoper* itself has a different family-tree: it represents a late popularized stage of the great mythologic-heroic Baroque opera. (Details about its history in Moritz Enziger *Die Entwicklung des Wiener Theaters vom 16. zum 19. Jahrhundert*, XXVIII. Bd. der Schriften der Gesellschaft für Theatergeschichte, 1918/19).—Since the days of Heine, all *Faust*-commentators have repeated his contention that the Prelude in the Theatre was suggested to Goethe by the *Sakuntala*. There is no need to discuss this theory here. Since the *Sakuntala*-translation was published in 1791, it could very well have served as a model even if one accepts my dating of the Prelude. I personally believe with Alewyn that the Prelude springs from the spirit of the *ex tempore* comedy and the Opera Buffo, for which preludes of this sort are almost obligatory.

It may be worth pointing in this connection to a letter written by Goethe to Eduard Jerrmann, dated July 22, 1825 (*Weimarer Ausgabe*, Abtl. iv, xxxix, 257 f·). Jerrman had asked Goethe's permission to use the Prelude as a curtain-raiser for a performance of *Iphigenie* (of all things!). Goethe gently refused, pointing out that the Prelude in its present form ("trotzig und unfreundlich") was not fit for performance and would have to be changed for such a purpose to become "höflich und artig und einnehmend." Then it might be a suitable *lever de rideau*, yet only for a "recht heiteres und lustiges, personen- und abwechslungsreiches Stück." I do not want to press the point, inasmuch as this letter was written almost thirty years after the Prelude. Yet it is interesting that, at least in his old age, Goethe associated the Prelude with something "merry and gay," with a good-natured entertainment which would indeed be a far cry from the tragedy's First Part.

what theatre manager Serlo expresses in *Wilhelm Meister*.[13] And almost verbatim we find in Wilhelm Meister's great outburst in the second chapter of the second book the poet's complaints about his being manhandled by the public as well as his dithyrambs on his exalted mission. In the *Wilhelm Meister* period the problems of the theatre were a profound living concern to, and a concrete daily demand on, Goethe. In the *Zauberflöte*, which originates at just that time, he tried to answer these demands practically; in the prelude (to the *Zauberflöte*) he mastered them theoretically and poetically, as a little *commedia dell' arte*, i.e., in a style congenial to the *Zauberflöte*.

Still another association results if we group the Prelude with the *Zauberflöte*: the association with the *Zahme Xenien*, which are equally a product of the years 1795 and 1796. Do we not clearly hear in the somewhat irritated and unfriendly criticism of the German public that satirical voice which we know so well from the *Xenien*? And would we not swear to it that, apart from their metric form, the following verses found among the paralipomena to the Prelude are part of the great settling of accounts which the *Xenien* represent?

> Und wenn ihr schreiet, wenn ihr klagt,
> Dass ich zu grob mit euch verfahre—
> Und wer euch heut recht derb die Wahrheit sagt,
> Der sagt sie euch auf tausend Jahre.

What reference to *Faust* could these lines possibly have? Yet in the *Zauberflöte*-period, which is the *Xenien*-period as well, they would find their natural place.

This, then, is my thesis: the prelude to *Faust* was originally planned as a prelude to the *Zauberflöte*. As such it was probably conceived and written toward the end of 1795 or early in 1796.[14] Only when Goethe realized that his opera libretto was a stillborn child, he hitched the charming and meaningful little play onto *Faust*, and eliminated the passages which would have pointed too clearly to the *Zauberflöte*. He could do that so much more easily since he recognized very clearly that many elements which

---

13. Previous *Faust*-research has, of course, pointed to parallel passages, partly even literal correspondences, in the speeches of the theatre manager and Serlo—above all Erich Schmidt, *op. cit.*, p. 265 ff. and Witkowski, *op. cit.*, p. 190. Yet no consequences have been drawn from this astounding fact.
14. It would be possible to earmark 1798 as the year of origin, in which year Goethe, very much to Schiller's annoyance, returned to the *Zauberflöte*-plan. However, the interrelationship with *Wilhelm Meister* and the *Xenien* speaks most definitely for the years 1795/96.

had their original place in the *Zauberflöte* entered into *Faust* from 1797 on. For his opera libretto, which is so closely related to *Wilhelm Meister*, is equally closely connected with the Mephisto scenes which, since 1797, were being added to *Faust*. The *Zauberflöte* is the watershed from which the currents are streaming backward into *Wilhelm Meister*, forward into the Tragedy's First Part. And how closely the *Zauberflöte*, representing the type of the great *Zauberoper*, is connected with the second part of *Faust*, Goethe himself testified, when he said to Eckermann and Soret: "Wenn es [he talks of the Helena-act] nur so ist, dass die Menge der Zuschauer Freude an der Erscheinung hat! Dem Eingeweihten wird zugleich der höhere Sinn nicht entgehen, wie es ja auch bei der *Zauberflöte* . . . der Fall ist."[15]

Thus it was possible that, without serious inner constraint and contortion, a poetic production, originally meant as a prelude to the *Zauberflöte*, came into the world as the Prelude in the Theatre, as the curtain-raiser to *Faust*.

---

15. W. v. Biedermann, *Goethes Gespräche* (Berlin, 1890), v, 38.

# GOETHE'S VISION OF A NEW WORLD

The aphorisms which Ottilie, the heroine of Goethe's *Elective Affinities,* jots down in her diary in the second part of the novel, are hardly the fruit of her own insight and wisdom. It is quite frankly her creator, the poet himself, who speaks through her, nowhere more undisguised than at the point when he makes Ottilie proclaim: "We may turn any way we wish, we shall always conceive of ourselves as seeing creatures. Perhaps man even dreams only so that he does not have to stop seeing." For to Goethe, who has enriched our world by a wealth of things seen, living and seeing were almost the same, and the older he grew the more fervently he developed a piously religious veneration for the human eye, the precious door through which the images of the living universe enter our soul.

We cannot help seeing images; and therefore a clearly defined, concrete picture should provide a focus to our eyes when we are in danger of losing ourselves in the vast and limitless panorama which Goethe's life and work present to the viewer, and of which a modest reflection at least ought to be conveyed by a commemorative address.* Let us then fasten our eyes to a small radius of visibility: the tiny room upstairs in the spacious and almost manorial house on the Frauenplan in Weimar, furnished with a plain desk and a few simple book cases, a monk's cell rather than the study of a writer whom all of Europe reveres as the uncrowned ruler over the realm of the spirit. At this desk he is at work now, a very old man, over eighty years of age, holding himself quite erect, under a thin crown of white hair and a majestically high forehead a pair of dark eyes whose clarity, firmness and power have struck so many of his visitors as supranatural. He knows that death already awaits him at the threshold, that he has traversed almost to the end a life richer than that of any other mortal in experiences and in productive responses to these experiences. But he has yet to finish his greatest work, the dramatic poem of *Faust,* which has accompanied him through all his life. For he was an impetuous and

---

*Given in commemoration of Goethe's two-hundredth anniversary (1949) at the University of the South, Johns Hopkins University, the Groton School, and the Goethe Society of Washington, D. C. The translations of some of the "Sprüche in Versen" in the text are B. Q. Morgan's and Isidor Schneider's from *The Permanent Goethe,* ed. Thomas Mann (New York, 1948).

rebellious youngster of hardly more than twenty when the image of Faust first appeared before his mind; and now, sixty years later, he still lies chained to this poem of his. Faust has traveled with him through all the avenues of life, has partaken of his experiences: the passionate search for truth, the bliss of love, the agonies of suffering, error and sin, fulfillment and failure, loud worldly splendor and the serene devotion to beauty. For sixty years this creation of his has been at his side; and now the moment has come when, in the great poem, Faust's final hour has struck. And while the wingbeat of death already touches his own shoulder, Goethe, the old man in his eighties, takes leave of Faust, the old man of 100. Yet before the poet lowers the last curtain over Faust's earthly existence, he grants this child of his imagination a last vision. Once more Faust sees, no longer with his physical eyes whose light old age and worry have extinguished; but before his inner eye a sight opens which transforms the moment of his death into the moment of highest triumph:

> A marsh extends along the mountain chain
> That poisons what so far I've been achieving:
> Could I that noisome pool now drain,
> 'Twould be the highest, last achieving.
> Thus space to many millions I will give
> Where, though not safe, yet free and active they may live.
> Green fertile fields where straightway from their birth
> Both men and beast live happy on the newest earth,
> Settled forthwith along the mighty hill
> Raised by a daring, busy people's will.
> Within: a land like paradise, outside:
> Up to the brink may rage the mighty tide,
> And where it gnaws and would burst through and sap
> A common impulse hastes to close the gap.
> Yes, to this thought I hold unswerving,
> To wisdom's final fruit, profoundly true:
> Of freedom and of life he only is deserving
> Who every day must conquer them anew.
> That there, by danger girt, the active day
> Of childhood, manhood, age will pass away.
> Aye, such a throng I fain would see,
> Stand on free soil, among a people free.
> Then I might say, that moment seeing:
> Oh linger on, thou art so fair!
> The traces of my earthly being,
> Can perish not in aeons—they are there.
> That lofty moment I now feel in this:
> I now enjoy the highest moment's bliss.

A new world, Faust's last vision, Goethe's last vision: not a peacefully sweet Utopia, but a world fought for, a world to be defended every day, soil won from the bottomless, destructive element, the water; not ready-made land into which we just have to move, but earth created by our own hands, made fertile by the rhythm of our work and life. Free people on free soil: free not by virtue of brief and seal, but free because this land is created out of the nothingness, and because these people are creating it.

A man whose life has been filled with work, a poet crowned with fame as no other in centuries, a human being who suffered more intensely than any other man—and now when the lights grow dim, there is no gloating over great achievements, there is no bitterness over great disappointments, there is a vision of new living things, an echo of the words which, at about the same time, at the age of eighty-one, he spoke when he was told that his only son, his hope for the future, had died: "Over graves—onward!" And it might be that the example of the old man in his stately house in the city of Weimar holds a promise and a hope for all humanity, especially for a world which has stood before so many graves, and a time which has become paralyzed by smugness or by fear and doubt.

We need not strain our eyes too much in order to recognize the rough outlines of Faust's envisaged new world, in order to give it an at least approximately correct name: a frontier and frontiersmen, land to be wrung from the hold of the unknown and dangerous, bulwarks built by the communal efforts of a new nation,—who, and who in this country, could fail to call these people on free soil by their proper name? Indeed, ever since the beginning of the nineteenth century, Goethe was fascinated by the experiment whose name was America: and if we may dismiss as a whimsical jest the remark of the septuagenarian that he, were he only twenty years younger, would like to set sail and settle in this new world, there are indications aplenty that the older he became, the more attentively and curiously he watched this young nation which was growing up under his eyes. In the great novel of his old age, *Wilhelm Meister, Journeyman,* America, now called by its proper name, appears again as the vision of a new life and a new society, and we know how eagerly he listened to those young men who came to visit him from Massachusetts and Maryland, when they gave him information pertaining to their country. There is warmth in his voice whenever he speaks of America, a cordial and paternal "good luck to you", a joyful feeling as if these faraway people who may never have heard of him, were his true children, going the way he wanted the new generation to go:

> America, you're better off
> Than our continent, the old.
> You have no castles which are fallen,
> No basalt to behold.
> You are not disturbed in your inmost being,
> In the very pulsation of life
> By useless remembering
> And unrewarding strife.
> Use well the present—and good luck to you!
> And when your children begin writing poetry,
> Let them guard well, in all they do,
> Against knight-, robber-, and ghost-story.

If we listen closely enough to this little congratulatory poem, we may be inclined to think that it contains a slightly left-handed compliment. For what he finds so enviable and fortunate about this new country is not that it has things others don't have, but that it does not have things others, unfortunately, have. America has no memories, no spectres rising out of the twilight zone of the human heart and human history, no ghosts which haunt the living and make their hands tremble. Geologist that he is, he even believes (and we know that he was quite wrong in that) that the very earth upon which this new nation has grown holds no memories of violent volcanic outbursts by which old and hidden formations of the soil are vehemently thrown onto the surface, that the basalt, witness of such explosions, is lacking in the make-up of this "newest earth." The hour that strikes over this country is always morning, its illumination the light of early day. Newly opened spaces where expansive and active motion is still possible, newly born time not yet overshadowed by the broodings and memories of yesteryears—this is the bright vision for which Goethe found the name: America.

It would be wrong and much too simple to explain Goethe's love for a youthful country, for youth altogether, as the yearning for freshness and vitality of one who knew himself to be— and very proudly at that—the focal point of traditions amassed and handed down through centuries, and who, at times, may have felt heavily burdened by the very riches which he represented for the entire world. His devotion to youth had nothing nostalgic at all: it was a salute to his own vitality, his pride in an inexhaustible fertility, which made the man of sixty-five call out like a youngster who sees his whole life still ahead of him:

>My heritage, how splendid, rich and grand,
>My property is time, and time my harvest land!

Time was a magic word for him, and that he was granted so much of it, eighty-three years of it, filled him with an exultant and charmingly naïve delight. His harvest land—the ground on which he stood, the beloved medium in which things come to pass, the medium beloved because in it always new things may come to pass.

That things were in permanent flux, always beginning anew, and every end only the starting point for more and richer life,— that was his profoundest conviction, and it was, the older he grew, the source of all his happiness. *Stirb und werde*, (Die and grow!)—this is the formula by which he expressed the secret of his own life, by which he tried to express the secret of life itself. And it was the very principle of stagnation which he embodied in the character of his devil Mephistopheles, the "bastard, half hellfire and half dung," who raises his cold fist against the eternally creative power. Goethe may, at times, have been annoyed when the young generation turned against him, the great colossus, who, in the eyes of some, stood in the way of new principles and new forms of life. Yet again and again he acknowledged the right of those who traveled on roads alien to him, because they were the roads of a new era:

>An aged man is always like King Lear.
>Who shared your doings, hand in hand,
>Long since went down the highway;
>Who loved and grieved at your command
>Is courting in another byway.
>Just for its own sake youth is with us here;
>It would be folly to demand:
>Come, grow a little old with me, my dear.

Indeed, it would be folly—and worse. It would be an attempt to interfere with the organic rhythm of birth, growth, decay and re-birth which he not only worshipped in nature but which he observed and enjoyed in every single individual, in all manifestations of man's activities. It would be the most objectionable violation of what he recognized as man's highest duty. "And what is your duty?" he asks; and he answers himself: "The demand of the day!" The demand of the day, the challenge of the hour!

When he was thinking of a new world, he thought of a humanity which listened obediently to what every hour expected of them and answered the call of the hour by an active response—by work. His devotion to work, to purposeful, practical activity, became with him more and more a religious credo, and it is not by chance that he wrote into the album of his grandson, then a little fellow hardly seven years old:

> The hour has sixty minutes in store,
> The day a thousand and more.
> Now figure out, my little son,
> All the things that can be done.

Only through work can man become real: only in his work can he recognize himself and become recognizable to others. What Goethe found at the bottom of nature, of art, was a secret creative force which knew only one end: to become visible in an innumerable variety of manifestations. This pattern man had to follow if he was not to miss his real vocation: to become visible, to press and to express all his potentialities in manifest symbols, to crystalize the dark and impalpable whirl of his energies into durable objects which would bear witness of his existence in the light of day. Without this work, man was for him an amorphous mass, something without contours, floundering in a twilight which is the twilight before the creation. A form—and a formless thing was for him a non-existent thing—a form man could find only in the work he did. It fulfilled the function every form has to fulfill: to free and to limit at the same time. To free: because through form alone inner impulses and forces can manifest themselves; and to limit: because form narrows down the vagueness of infinite possibilities to the one finite and distinguishable phenomenon. Work, then, the concrete answer to the concrete demands of every day prevents man from being engulfed by the two extreme dangers: to atrophy in mute unexpressiveness, or to dissolve himself in the innumerable but shapeless potentialities of the infinite.

> This solves the great interrogation
> As to our second fatherland.
> For our work here, if it has duration,
> Insures that we eternally shall stand.

Perhaps we can now distinguish more clearly the outline of the new horizons which open before Faust's inner eye at the moment of his death: a milling throng of people following the eternal rhythm of life, childhood, manhood, age—working, and by working, lifting the concrete, the formed land, out of the chaotic shapelessness of the waters, fighting for it daily so that it will not slip back into the deadly silence of the unformed. If we asked under which form of government this new world would stand, Goethe would answer with a skeptical smile. The thing that really mattered to him was what he called the communal effort: the daily work of the common people for their common good. He did not believe in political slogans, no matter in which camp they had been formulated; he was highly suspicious of general principles, of grandiose ideas which, in spite of their solemn ring, could only divert man from his sole and primary duty: the demand of the hour. He had no use for missionaries who preached the salvation of man through a magic formula, be it even so bewitching a formula as "liberty, equality, fraternity." Not that he objected to these ideals, but he feared that the passionate fight for these principles, for any principles as a matter of fact, allowed man only to play hooky, to run behind the school, to neglect, while searching in the clouds, the concrete tasks with which our daily existence confronts us. "Grand ideas and great conceit," he remarked, "are always geared to bring about fearful misfortune."

We know what he meant by this fearful misfortune: it was the French Revolution whose sight frightened and upset him. When opposing the French Revolution, he did not defend any privileges, and certainly not the many which he himself considered unjust. What he feared was the dissolution of order, of form and shape in the socio-political field, the unleashing of chaotic forces which would burst through the dams and destroy—not only the guilty ones, but the innocent, plain, hardworking people as well. He anticipated—and he anticipated correctly—the Reign of Terror, the endless chain of Napoleonic Wars, an upheaval which would not only bury under its weight the "old regime" for which he held no particular brief, but which would endanger and obstruct the slow and laborious progress of mankind which was to be achieved only step by step, by a devoted application to the exigencies of each day, and not by running amuck under the spell of abstract ideas, no matter how noble they sounded.

It is quite revealing that in the little well-wishing poem to America there is not even a hint at a new political or social order, at representative government or majority rule or the like. What he saw was a country which would make good use of the present moment, without being blinded by the luring stars of a far-away eternity, a country which is not disturbed in the very pulsation of life by unrewarding quarrels, and whose very earth does not exhibit the scars and remnants of violent volcanic outbursts. In another document, however, he does make mention of the American form of government, and we cannot help being amused at the perspective in which he views it. In 1819, at the age of seventy, he sent upon request of his New England friends a set of his collected works to the Harvard library. And this copy he dedicated "to the magnificent country which draws the eyes of the whole world upon herself by a solemnly lawful state of affairs which promotes a growth hampered by no bounds." Aren't we slightly startled by his calling our democratic government a "solemnly lawful state of affairs"? Be that as it may, he approved of it; and not because it rested on a set of political ideas which he may or may not have preferred to others—and to be quite frank, he hardly did—but because it promoted growth, and whatever promoted growth was good in his eyes. Only order, only a concrete visible organization capable of warding off the onslaught of unruly impulses, of chaotic and shapeless elemental forces, can promote growth. What mattered in a new world as he saw it in his vision, was to permit the communal effort to come into play, to see to it that every individual could become real by being allowed to do his work, that everybody could stand firm on his own place, no matter how modest. Then indeed the body politic as a whole could not help being sound and healthy.

The communal effort—that is what counted in his eyes, the common fight against the dangers which threaten the community of men. And this community was for him indivisible and all-embracing. Every barrier which tried to harm this indivisibility was to him a dangerous and meaningless abstraction. A farm where people and things are growing had a meaning to him, the word fatherland, so he said, hardly any; and he openly stated that he considered the pillaging of a farm a more sinister calamity than what people pompously called "the destruction of the fatherland." The idea of different fatherlands became to him more and more a nebulous superstructure erected over the palpable, concrete life and activities of the individual and the community. The only citizenship he proudly claimed was that of a citizen of the world, and it was in his eighty-first year, at a time when Europe entered a phase of violent nationalism and imperialism, that he made a statement whose benevolent wisdom mankind has not yet learned a hundred and twenty years later: "All in all, it is a strange thing with national hatred. On the lowest level of culture you will always find it most strongly and violently. But there is a level where it disappears entirely, and where the good or bad fortune of one's fellow-nation is felt as keenly as if it had befallen your own. This level of culture corresponded to my own nature, and I had entrenched myself firmly on this level before I had reached my sixtieth year."

Indeed, Goethe does well to use the word "entrench", a word connoting labor and persistence. He knows only too well that steady and steadfast practice is required. It would not come easily to anybody, and it certainly did not come easily to him. More than anybody else he was threatened by the extremes which undermine the communal effort; on the one hand, a wild and reckless tendency toward self-assertion which destroys the *communal* spirit, on the other hand a longing for flight from reality, for the great and absolute calm in which no practical effort, no effort at all, can assert itself. He was exposed, and exposed until his very old age, to the passionate and storming beat of his insatiable heart which could not stop short of extreme self-fulfillment regardless of the ravages it might work. But he was equally exposed to the deadening lure of complete withdrawal, of losing himself in the irresponsible bliss of dreaming and forgetting, exposed to the yearning of for-ever-turning-away from what Orestes in his *Iphigenia* calls "life's fitful fever." The greatest achievement, the greatest glory of this man is not his poetry, his artistic and scientific endeavors, but the mainspring of his life, his refusal to go to pieces under the strain of conflicting tendencies, his perseverance in finding a balance on the razor's edge, his discipline—and what a severe discipline it was!—in training himself for the communal effort, for the great reconciliation which embraces at the same time self-limitation in service to and for others, and self-expression through free, personal creation.

Better than anybody else Goethe knew—or rather: more painfully than anybody else Goethe had experienced within himself, that it takes a long and laborious training to develop the attitude without which a new world cannot be born, an attitude which succeeds in balancing harmoniously man's rightful claim to independence and society's rightful claim to man's submission. The level must be found where man can save his own face, that individual face which Goethe loved so dearly, and still become a part of a larger whole, a community without whose shelter man destroys himself and his surroundings. It is, indeed, a most timely problem, and Goethe, citizen of a much less shaken world than ours, saw it in all its mercilessness and inevitability. Long before others, he was afraid of the rise of a mass civilization, of an anonymous uniformity in which the individual would lose his unmistakable face, and he knew very well that this danger could arise under any form of government, a democratic no less than an autocratic one. Yet he knew equally well the destructive results of a reckless individualism which would not only destroy all order, but would, at the same time, isolate man, transport him into a frigid loneliness in which the individual himself could not survive. To be sure, he did not care for the masses, this shapeless monster which blurred and gobbled up the distinguishing features of each individual; but he cared even less for those who believed that the only thing that mattered was to release and to realize their unbridled urge for personal freedom.

To achieve this balance where man does not abdicate before the demands of society, and where society is not ripped apart by man's rightful claim to self-realization—that is the task we have to fulfill if we want to bring about a new world. Goethe knew that it would never do to find an easy but superficial compromise between the two conflicting tendencies, a grudging give-and-take where, more often than not, the right hand does not know what the left hand is doing. A basic attitude had to be found, not a composite of two or more, but just one basic attitude which would at the same time comprise self-preservation and self-abandonment. This attitude was to be made the cornerstone upon which the education of a new man for a new world was to rest. He found it, and in the great novel of his old age, in *Wilhelm Meister, Journeyman,* he describes the school in which the generation of the future is educated for the future. He leads us in this novel into his "pedagogical province," one of the most inspiring pedagogical utopias ever developed by Western man. But before he introduces us to the concrete curriculum of the school, he shows us the pupils' training in the basic attitude without which no curriculum and no program would be of any avail. And what is this attitude? Goethe calls it reverence, a reverence extending to three spheres: the reverence for that which is above us, the reverence for that which is around us, and the reverence for that which is underneath us. When speaking of "above, around and below" he does not only refer to the human and social structure, although in the case of the reverence for that which is underneath us, he takes pains to point specifically to the human level, to those who through suffering, social inequality, lack of strength, are being held in the lower regions. With his "above, around and below" Goethe wants to draw a much wider circle: he wants to point to all possible directions of the universe. Below: that is the very earth upon which we stand, the solid soil from which we and all nature derive our daily food, the forces under the surface which feed all vegetative life. Around: this is human level, the sphere of man, man as our neighbor and equal. And above: this is the world of the spirit, of the stars into which our destiny is inscribed, the world of the spirit's Highest: of God. This is what the disciples of the pedagogical province learn as their first and basic lesson: that they owe reverence to the whole cosmos, the suprahuman, the human, and the subhuman.

Reverence, then, appears to Goethe as the basic attitude of a new man in a new world, for it is the human sentiment in which man's insistence on his independence and his recognition of his dependence on other powers are blended. It does not obliterate man's face, for reverence has nothing whatsoever to do with slavish submission, yet it does, at the same time, give proper due to everything which is outside our own ego, be it "above, around or below." The German word, the German equivalent for reverence which Goethe uses here, seems to define the attitude of which we are speaking much more clearly. The word is *Ehrfurcht,* a compound of two words: *Ehre,* meaning honor, and *Furcht,* meaning fear, or awe. *Ehrfurcht,* then, is the human sentiment which permits man to show awe without losing his honor. This is exactly the way Goethe defines the word: "If man lets himself be governed by *Ehrfurcht,* he can keep his honor while rendering honor." In this sentiment, and in this sentiment alone, pride and modesty have become one and the same; it makes us great and small at the same time; it keeps us aware of the fact that we are faced with powers which determine us, but that we have the right and the duty to face these powers as free men. Not to be blindly overcome by the forces that are above, around and below us, nor on the other hand, to burst into a reckless freedom which tries to break down all the barriers that are set to man—this is the problem we have to solve, and only reverence, only *Ehrfurcht*, will enable us to solve it.

Not to be overcome by fear, not to abdicate, not to feel that we are only playthings in the hands of outside forces—could there be a more timely lesson? And do we not remember in this connection a word of an American statesman which, quite unconsciously to be sure, sounds like an echo of Goethe's wisdom even if it is, more likely, the echo of a Thoreauean dictum: "The only thing we have to fear is fear itself." Yet this is only half the truth as Goethe saw it. Being wiser than the statesman in question, he would have continued: and the next worst thing we have to fear is absolute fearlessness, the denial of our limitations, the arrogant emancipation from the awe which we owe to the above, the around and the below. There is a sort of freedom, a rebellious blindness against everything that limits us, which is as disastrous as fear. Fear gives the powers outside ourselves complete control over our own existence, but recklessness makes us lose control over ourselves, transforms us into helpless puppets—not in the hands of others, but in our own hands. And who, in our days, in the days of the atom bomb, in the days of a perniciously unfettered self-confidence and self-righteousness would not have to ponder Goethe's words: "Everything that liberates our mind without giving us control over ourselves is ruinous."

Liberty and control, being free and being bound at the same time—this in Goethe's eyes is the position man has to find. And therefore the disciples of the "pedagogical province," after having acquired the three forms of reverence, have yet to learn the highest type of reverence: reverence for oneself. Not to violate our own honor to which we, as human beings, are entitled, nor, on the other hand, to violate the limitations and conditions of our nature; not to become subject to the dark and instinctive drives in our soul, nor to hurt and suppress our innate, God-given constitution. This, then, would be wisdom's final fruit: to be true to self, yet never to become a slave of self.

This is Goethe's lesson, the lesson that is taught in the "pedagogical province." And who would deny that this lesson may have a meaning for our own lives and our own days, no matter how much the conditions of Goethe's world and ours may differ? A poet never tries to give answers which will hold good under all circumstances, and certainly no such attempt was made by Goethe who, more fervently than anybody else, believed that every day has its own demands, and that, obviously, the demands of today cannot be met with the answers of yesterday. Nothing would have appalled him more than the sight of a humanity which would cling to a ready-made formula, even if it were his own. After all, it was he who addressed his contemporaries, all those who were so smugly satisfied with their own cleverness and who had found a permanent niche from which they did not care even to peep out:

> Get wise to yourself, now trot
> Out of this mucky groove,
> There is more to earth than this spot,
> Move! — —

and he would have been the first one to protest if anyone had tried to elevate his own answers and his own intuitions to the status of canonical laws, valid for all eternity. Yet he knew equally well that man's basic problems are always the same, and that we cannot do more than re-formulate the principle attitudes so that they will furnish us with a definite answer in a definite situation. "All intelligent thoughts," he said, "have already been thought; what is necessary is only to try to think them again." He tried—and he tried as sincerely and honestly as any man can. Once, when he was a very old man, a Frenchman came to see him, and, after looking into this venerable face, furrowed by wisdom and sorrow, exclaimed: "Voilà un homme qui a eu de grands chagrins." Goethe liked these words and translated them, somewhat arbitrarily and incorrectly, as you will not fail to notice, by the words: "There is a man who has taken life seriously." Indeed, he had the right to confess that he never played with life, that he never shut himself against the sufferings, the doubts and arduous tasks which are man's lot. He accepted all of it, beauty and despair, joy and misery.

He knew the dangers, dangers in his own heart, and dangers approaching him from outside, yet he never lost hope that somehow he—and we—would pull through. One of his most beautiful poems he ends with the words: "We bid you hope;" and the old man of eighty stood in his little study, and while his life was drawing to a close, he put into the mouth of his dying Faust the hymn to a new life, to a new world. And this, indeed, Goethe would have wished the coming generations to learn from him: the hope and the faith that man's endeavors are not lost, that the vision of a new world can and must remain alive, even if darkness is closing in on us. He did not want to offer ready-made answers on how to do things tomorrow. But he hoped and wished that his whole life's work, the sum total of his existence, would strengthen future generations in their belief that there will *be* a tomorrow, and that our own daily work will bring it about. His whole existence, not this or that work of his, was to hold out hope for the future. And we cannot do him greater honor than by just repeating the little song of gratitude which he addressed to a fellow-poet, to Schah Sedschaa, an old Persian sage and singer of the thirteenth century:

> And fear will seize us never
> While living with your song!
> Your life, may it last long,
> Your kingdom—ever!

# GOETHE ABOUT GOETHE IN FRENCH

When, on a winter evening of the year 1830, Eckermann found Goethe reading Gérard de Nerval's *Faust* adaptation, he used the opportunity to elicit from the poet some general remarks concerning the mood of the first part of the tragedy, and some specific comments on the efforts of the young French translator.[1] On this occasion, Goethe made the astonishing confession that he no longer cared very much to read the great *oeuvre* of his earlier years in the German original, but that in the French version everything impressed him again as "thoroughly fresh, new and full of *esprit*".[2] To the octogenarian, the echo of his work reaching him from beyond the Rhine sounded so welcome and pleasant that he gladly heard his own voice drowned out by it and gently fade away.

It had not always been that way. Till the middle of the twenties, his letters, conversations, and occasional notes contain traces of his skepticism at the response of foreign countries to his poetic work; again and again we are reminded of the disappointed resignation which he once, in the thirty-fifth Venetian Epigram, had expressed quite frankly: that Europe had done little to oblige him, France not excepted, even if she was willing to read him and contribute her share to the more frightening than gratifying success of *Werther*. It was a settled matter for him that France on the basis of her intellectual and literary development could not find a genuine access to his poetry, and that the reaction to his endeavors in the country beyond the Rhine would always prove this river to be more than just a geographical and national dividing line. What at best might happen if the *génie* of France merged with his own, was, so he said,[3] a "strange competition" with highly curious results, but no actual understanding, no fertilization that could produce something living and pregnant with future. Whenever he en-

---

1. *Gespräche mit Eckermann*, January 3, 1830.
2. Not satisfied with this Goethean praise for Nerval's activities as a translator, his French friends Janin, Gautier and Audebrand later invented a letter which Goethe is supposed to have written to Nerval, and in which he assured him that he had understood his own work for the first time in the French translation. In his article, "Goethe und Gérard de Nerval," (*Goethe Jahrbuch* XVIII, 200 f.) Louis P. Betz proved conclusively that no such letter was ever written, that, in fact, Goethe never entered into a correspondence with Gérard.
3. In a note to his publisher Cotta (December 8, 1808), announcing Lemarquand's intention to prepare a *Faust* translation.

countered in these middle years uncomplimentary verdicts about his translated works, his response was never dictated by the hurt vanity of a self-assertive author, but by the melancholy realization that the gulf between the political, intellectual and temperamental attitudes of the two nations was unbridgeable. This suspicion was confirmed when he saw in *La Décade Philosophique* a negative review of the French translation of *Hermann und Dorothea*, and he could not help concluding that the French, curiously enough, had no feeling for the "basically Republican spirit" of his epic, because they were, now as before the Revolution, "died-in-the-wool aristocrats."[4] The French seemed to him constitutionally incapable of deriving pleasure from his works; and it is almost shocking to note the brusque frankness with which he expressed this conviction in a letter to the French diplomat Le Lorgne d'Ideville when sending him a copy of the *Wahlverwandtschaften* which had just come off the press: "Je ne puis espérer ni même désirer que ce petit ouvrage plaise à un Français, en tant que Français."[5]

One might expect that the year 1814, the publication date of the German translation of Mme. de Staël's *De L'Allemagne*, should have brought about a change. Goethe could not fail to realize — and he most assuredly did — that Mme. de Staël had made it her task to establish a beachhead for German literature abroad, and that her book indeed succeeded in proselytizing some of the best European minds to the cause of German letters. Goethe surely did not underrate the epochal significance of Mme. de Staël's work; he often and gladly attested to his profound satisfaction with a literary enterprise whose mediating function proved so effective and beneficial.[6] Yet he could not quite bring himself to believe that Mme. de Staël had really understood him, and that her interpretation would promote a genuine understanding of his works in France. It was during

---

4. Letter to Knebel, November 3, 1800; Goethe used the same phrase in his letter of November 19, 1800 to Bitaubé, the translator of *Hermann und Dorothea*.
5. To Le Lorgne d'Ideville, October 6, 1809.
6. To mention only some samples: to Heinrich Meyer, March 7, 1814, and to Knebel, May 18, 1814.—The literature about Goethe's relations with Mme. de Staël is so numerous that only a few references can be given here: Fernand Baldensperger, *Goethe en France* (Paris, 1920), pp. 60-64, et al; Comte d'Haussonville, *Mme. de Staël et l'Allemagne* (Paris, n.d.) 57 ff.; Jan Allan Henning, *L'Allemagne de Mme. de Staël et la polémique Romantique* (Paris, 1929) 240 ff.; Pauline de Pange, *Mme. de Staël et la découverte de l'Allemagne* (Paris, 1929).

these very years that he was engaged in reconstructing his past through the narration of his autobiography, and that, strengthened by this retrospective glance, he recognized more and more the insoluble unity between his life and his work, the power of "the law which was forever preordained to me." He could, therefore, not help being exasperated by Mme. de Staël's method of looking at all his "products piece-meal and isolated, without a notion of their inner cohesion, their genesis".[7] As late as 1823, when Mme. de Staël's work had already born rich fruit and awakened the interest of France and England in the golden age of German literature, Goethe still acted stand-offish, and confessed in a letter: "Dass meine früheren Arbeiten nun endlich auch in das Strudelgewebe der französischen Literatur aufgenommen werden, macht mir wenig Freude. Es bleibt allen diesen Dingen kaum etwas mehr als mein Name."[8]

But about the middle of the twenties the turning point had come. A number of factors contributed to having Goethe revise his attitude toward the efforts of his French admirers on behalf of his work. There was first the fact that in 1821 Albert Stapfer undertook to translate his entire dramatic work, thus offering his countrymen an opportunity to view Goethe's productions no longer "piecemeal and isolated." But still more decisive became the founding of a literary group which, using Stapfer's translation as a firm base, was willing to serve the beloved poet not only by sporadic, albeit fervent, enthusiasm, but by a serious concern with the organic wholeness of his work, with the creative energies from which it had grown. It was the group of Romanticists gathering around the literary magazine *Le Globe*; it was above all their spokesman in matters pertaining to Goethe: Jean-Jacques Ampère. Goethe considered the utterances of these young Frenchmen so important that he rendered large excerpts from Ampère's review of the Stapfer translation into German, and published them in his own periodical *Kunst und Altertum*.[9]

Surely he must have noticed that in many points, in stressing his Protean "multifariousness," the "originality" of every individual creation, the hypochondriac Werther-*Weltschmerz*, Am-

---
7. To Müller and Riemer, cf. W. Biedermann, *Goethes Gespräche* (Leipzig, n.d.) III, 129.
8. To Boisserée, December 12, 1823.
9. *Kunst und Altertum* V, iii, 131-145 and VI, i, 94-111; in *Goethes Werke* (Weimar Edition) XLI (2), 177ff. In the following this edition is referred to as *WA*.

père still followed quite obediently Mme. de Staël's cues. But what endeared Ampère's effort to him was the young critic's attempt to establish an intimate connection between his personal experiences and their objectivations in his works, a connection by which the total Goethe grew together into an insoluble organism that encompassed all his faculties, sensibilities and responses. Beyond that, however, Ampère had recognized and recorded a development within the wholeness of Goethe's life and work, a development of form, a development toward form whose demonstration was most welcome to the old Goethe. It is easy to imagine the high degree of satisfaction with which Goethe translated the following sentence from Ampère's review: "Genau besehen ist die Form im *Goetz* noch nicht entwickelt, sie herrscht schon in *Iphigenie*, und in der *Natürlichen Tochter* ist sie alles".[10] Seeing himself recognized was reason for rejoicing; but it was more than that: by being so recognized, he could recognize himself; by acting as a subject upon others, he could meet and face himself as an object. In his late years it seemed to him the fulfillment of his *entelecheia* to become an objectively historical phenomenon to himself, to conceive, as the title of his autobiography, *Dichtung und Wahrheit*, suggests, of his own life as a self-contained and self-sufficient work of art. In this endeavor his French admirers were helping him now, and he expressed his gratitude in his remarks à propos the "Notice sur la vie et les ouvrages de Goethe par Albert Stapfer" by saying that the efforts of his translator "have become so highly important to me, coming at a time when I consider it my duty to reflect upon myself and to ponder my achievements and accomplishments along with my failures and missed opportunities".[11]

But apart from and beyond this interest in self-awareness and self-realization there still existed something else that made Goethe listen so eagerly and curiously to the echo that reached him from the other side of the Rhine river. It was the idea and the ideal of *Weltliteratur*. Even if he did not use this term (which he himself coined) before 1827,[12] his thoughts had circled around this conception ever since the middle of the twenties. He understood by it a far-flung commerce and traffic of literary goods which, he hoped, would bring about in the

---
10. *Ibid.*, 197.
11. *Ibid.*, 203.
12. The word appears for the first time in Goethe's Diary of January 15, 1827.

future a pacified and humanized European community, supported and enriched by the permanent process of a mutual intellectual fertilization, of competing with each other, of clarifying one's own genius and inheritance through a never-ending act of measuring oneself against and comparing oneself with the foreign.[13] Seen from this vantage point, the interest which his poetry evoked in France became much more than a personal concern; it served as a station and a signpost on the road to world literature. The work that had sprung from his creative forces now turned before his eyes into a creative force again, capable of begetting, awakening, and fostering new life. The name of Goethe, which filled the air of France and came back to him from beyond the Rhine, now designated more for him than just his own name. It meant the invocation of and recourse to a power which created new forms according to its own laws. Of this he was very conscious, and when he rendered into German a selection of critical reviews of Alexandre Duval's play *Tasso* that had been inspired by his own, he could state, modestly and proudly at the same time, that he presented these excerpts to the readers of *Kunst und Altertum* "not only with the purpose of drawing attention to myself and my productions," but rather for the sake and good of world literature.[14]

Pronouncements like these have a very positive ring and might lead us to the conclusion that he was at peace with the world which so willingly seemed to absorb his work. Yet this view is deceptive. Behind this gentle and peaceful harmony there lurk historical irony and personal tragedy. The force which now conquered France under the name of Goethe was highly suspect to him. He became the idol of the young Romanticists, the powerful ally in their battle against the classic-rationalistic poetics and poetry of the *ancien régime*. What now proved so irresistible to the new generation of French writers was the emotional exaltation and exaltedness, the inner and outer abandon, the liberated and liberating naturalness of young Goethe. He realized only too well that he was, as he put it

---

13. The best treatment of Goethe's conception of world literature is to be found in Fritz Strich, "Goethe und die Weltliteratur," *Jahrbuch der Goethe Gesellschaft* XVIII, and in the same author's definitive and masterful monograph *Goethe und die Weltliteratur* (Bern, 1946). The present brief summary of Goethe's reaction to the reception of his works in France was written shortly before the publication of Strich's book. What Strich has to say, especially on pp. 225-241, covers much of the same ground and materials.
14. *WA* XLI (2), 265.

in his "Studien zur Weltliteratur", "grist to their mill,"[15] and the clatter of this mill was far from pleasing him. So he found himself again and again in the embarrassing position of warning against the force whose name was Goethe. It is not without a touch of sad irony that his very first report about the *Globe* is shot through with an element of argumentativeness, with a gentle and amusingly paradoxical polemic in which he, the author of *Faust,* explains to the young Frenchmen, who have just come away from defending the Faustian properties of deviltry and witchcraft against the attacks of the old-fashioned classicists, "that Greek mythology, highly and lucidly contoured as the embodiment of the purest and most vigorous form of humanity, deserves much more to be recommended than the ugly element of deviltry and witchcraft which could develop only in lightless, anxiety-ridden ages, emanating from an unenlightened and undisciplined imagination and feeding upon the dregs of human nature."[16]

He was bound to be frightened by the fact that the dark and unruly condition of his soul which he had outgrown with so much pain and self-abnegation, was now sweeping France triumphantly as a new revelation; and it was therefore quite fitting that he had his misgivings about the magnificent *Faust*-illustrations of Delacroix—not because he felt that Delacroix had not understood and captured the "unenlightened and undisciplined" mood and spirit of his *Faust,* but because he had understood and captured them too well and had brought them too powerfully to new life in his pictures.[17] It was not bad taste but a profound inner compulsion that made him prefer the mawkishly sweet illustrations of a Peter Cornelius to Delacroix's much more masterly drawings. He himself put the finger

---

15. *Ibid.,* 491.
16. "Aus dem Französischen des Globe," *WA* XLI (2), 233. In the original draft Goethe formulated his objection still more sharply and negatively. The last relative clause reads: "das nur . . . in der tiefsten Hefe menschlich-niederträchtiger Einbildungskraft zum scheinbaren Dasein kommen und eine unflätige Nahrung finden konnte" (*ibid.,* 538).
17. *Ibid.,* 233, and in the piece "Faust, Tragédie de Monsieur de Goethe," *ibid.,* 340ff.—A remark of Goethe, made on the occasion of his reading Nicolovius' study about him, clearly shows how much he was afraid of the reviving of a state of mind which he had overcome: "Ist es mehr oder weniger bedenklich, an dasjenige, was man getan und geleistet, in späteren Jahren erinnert zu werden, so ist es wohl noch viel apprehensiver, wie man auf andere gewirkt und wie man von ihnen durch Rückwirkung gefördert, gestört und gehindert worden, gewissermassen protokolliert zu sehen" (*ibid.,* 356).

on the crucial point when he remarked in a conversation with Foerster that a comparison between Cornelius and Delacroix led to the surprising conclusion that "the Frenchman may well be taken for a German, and the German contrariwise for a Frenchman,"[18]—a remark which can easily be extended to cover the entire relationship between Goethe and his *Globe*-disciples, in which the German reacted like a Frenchman, and the Frenchmen like Germans.

So it was much rather a human, a fatherly, concern than a strictly literary one which determined the old Goethe's attitude toward his admirers from beyond the frontiers. In this respect, as in any other aspect of his life, his old age had taught him the melancholy wisdom that fulfillment (and what higher fulfillment could he yearn for than the devoted love of the young generation?) was but another word for self-denial and self-abnegation. Having succeeded, by one painful act of renunciation after the other, in easing the explosive tensions of his overpowering inner drives and demands, he was loathe to see the youth of France losing themselves—in his name—in the same dangerous abyss.[19] Therefore, he was profoundly grateful for the fact that the French language itself acted as a bastion against all emotional excesses and exuberance, that what he had "conceived in the dark and gloomy element" presented itself in French "more serene, more lucid and purposeful".[20] Serene, fresh, full of

---
18. Biedermann, *op. cit.*, VII, 160.
19. It is surely significant that, when reproducing Ampère's critique (cf. fn.9), he did not translate the passages which refer to *Werther*, f. i. Ampère's observation: "Werther: c'est la tête de mort à la fin du banquet." He summarized Ampère's thoughts and presented them in a few brief and innocuous words. And it is still more significant, and highly amusing at that, that he claimed in a conversation with Eckermann (May 3, 1827), that Ampère had characterized *Tasso* as a "gesteigerter Werther," although Ampère had not done anything of the sort. The passage in question reads in Goethe's own translation of Ampère's text: "Er selbst (the poet) spricht aus dem Munde des Tasso und . . . man hört den Werther durch." No word about a "gesteigerter Werther;" but Goethe insisted on this "Steigerung," in order to create a distance between Werther and the later Goethe, and he insinuates this interpretation to Ampère, who had never thought of suggesting such a distance.—For well over a hundred years Goethe scholars have, with very few exceptions, fallen for Goethe's "trick" of putting into Ampère's mouth words which the French critic never uttered, among them the champion of "socialist realism," Georg Lukács, in his *Goethe und seine Zeit* (Bern, 1947), 28. It is to be hoped that the excellent study of Elizabeth M. Wilkinson, "Tasso—ein gesteigerter Werther in the Light of Goethe's Principle of 'Steigerung'," (*Modern Language Review* XLIV, 305ff.), published three years after the present article, will finally lay this ghost.
20. "Faust, Tragédie de M. de Goethe," *WA* XLI (2), 340.

*esprit*—these are the laudatory adjectives which he applied to the French translations of *Faust,* and, taking the statement with the necessary grain of salt, one might go as far as to claim that he was so inordinately fond of the Lemarquands, Stapfers and Nervals because they had, through the medium of the French language, de-demonized his *daimon,* and de-fausted his *Faust.*

The more eagerly and anxiously he observed the traces which his work left upon the French mind, the more they were bound to remind him again and again that he was out of tune with his times, that the roads which he had traveled in the maturity of his old age were not those now trod by the young generation which had written his name upon their flag. Yet such misgivings vanished and were replaced by profound satisfaction, because the echo from France proved to him that his life's work had become a creatively active force in the intellectual organism and metabolism of Europe. A little worried, to be sure, but happily resigned and expectingly hopeful, he could write to the French diplomat, Count Karl Friedrich Reinhard: "So wirkt unser alter Sauerteig immer auf neues Backwerk, das wir uns denn wohl gefallen lassen mögen, und da einmal das Eindringen der deutschen Literatur in Frankreich kein Hindernis findet, so mögen sie denn auch die guten und schlimmen Wirkungen unserer Produktionen, die wir selbst durchgenossen und durchgelitten haben, hinterdrein nachgeniessen und erdulden."[21] Looking toward France, being looked at from France, he now experienced the "anticipation of the highest moment," the premonition of the aeons in which, beneficial to all humanity, the traces of his earthly days would never vanish. He became timeless while still in time, and he enjoyed to the fullest degree the wise benediction of the French aphorism: "L'étranger, cette postérité contemporaine".

---

21. To Reinhard, March 12, 1827.

# SCHILLER: POET OF POLITICS*

A quarter of a century ago, when darkness descended upon Schiller's native country, a darkness that was to engulf all of mankind in the shortest possible time, a theater in Hamburg produced one of Schiller's great dramatic works, *Don Carlos*. It is the play which culminates in the stirring climax of its third act, the confrontation scene between King Philip of Spain and the Marquis Posa, the powerful verbal and intellectual battle between the rigid and autocratic monarch, contemptuous of mankind and gloomily convinced that only harsh and tyrannical suppression can preserve peace and order in his vast empire, and the young, enthusiastic advocate of revolutionary principles, who demands for his fellow citizens the untrammeled right to happiness, the possibility of unhampered self-development and self-realization of every individual. The scene rises to its pitch with Marquis Posa's brave challenge flung into the king's face: "Sire, give us all freedom of thought!" When this line, one of the most famous of all German dramatic literature, resounded from the Hamburg stage in the early years of Hitler's terror, the audience under the friendly protection of darkness burst out, night after night, into tumultuous applause. So dangerous and embarrassing to the new rulers proved a single verse of the greatest German playwright, who by then had been dead for fully a hundred and thirty years, that the management of the theater was forced to cut out the scandalous line. But the audience, knowing their classic well enough even if it were fed to them in an emasculated version, reacted quick-wittedly: from that evening on they interrupted the performance by thunderous applause at the moment when Marquis Posa should have uttered his famous plea on the stage—and did not. After these incidents the play was withdrawn from the repertoire altogether.

This is a touching and heart-warming story: people turning at a period of national calamity and shame to one of their great writers to find strength and direction in his words, protesting with him and through him against a vicious political system, which debased the noble thoughts that he, through his work, had bequeathed to his nation as a precious heritage. A touching, a heart-warming spectacle, and yet at the same time one that

---

*An address in commemoration of Schiller's two-hundredth anniversary (1959), delivered at the University of Cincinnati, the University of Texas, and the Ohio State University.

makes us feel somewhat ill at ease. Is he really a poet, we must ask, whose creation can so easily release a stark political demonstration, even if we happen to be in complete agreement with this demonstration? Is he really a great dramatist who speaks so directly to our political emotions, who turns the stage into a pulpit from which we are preached at, admonished and exhorted, nobly and loftily to be sure, but preached at nonetheless? Certainly we will not underrate or malign the need and importance of an appeal to our highest ideals, the inspiration and edification which we derive from the teachings of a great and venerable mentor; but very much aware of the borderline that has to be drawn between the word of wisdom and the word of poetry, we cannot help asking the anxious question: uplifting as all of that may be, is it really and primarily art?

The question becomes more pressing when our minds shift back from this scene in the Hamburg theater to the year 1859, to the celebrations on the occasion of Schiller's hundredth anniversary. It is perhaps no exaggeration to state that never before —and never since—in the history of Western civilization has a writer been so passionately and fervently honored in his own country—and by the German population of this country, too— as was Schiller in 1859. Again, a touching, a heart-warming spectacle: a man of letters, who, during a short life of barely forty-six years, though beset by incessant illness and poverty, had produced a body of uncompromisingly serious plays, of sophisticated aesthetic and philosophical essays, of high-flown poems and ambitious historical writings, assumes fifty-four years after his premature death the status of a popular hero, and is accorded the accolades of veneration which a nation generally reserves to the powerful and mighty, to its founding fathers and those who in moments of great historical decisions have established and saved its identity. Recalling the festivities of the year 1859, the torch-light parades of students and intellectuals in innumerable cities, the mass meetings of whole populations, the unveiling of dozens of monuments, the endless oratory reverberating through modest citizens' clubs no less than through huge assembly halls, we ask: was ever a poet so honored? But upon looking over the list of famous speakers, upon reading their words of praise and adulation, we realize that it was hardly the poet Friedrich Schiller who was thus honored. As in the Hamburg theater, it was one stormy political demonstration which in 1859 swept over Germany under the disguise of the centenary celebration of a great writer. A little more than ten years earlier, in 1848, the burning hopes of the German population for a fatherland united in the spirit of enlightened liberalism and constitutional government had died under the fusillades and deceitful machinations of the old regime. So dreadful was the shock, so thorough the blood-letting, that Germany lay numb for a whole decade. But then, in 1859, the muted voice of the German people arose again, and when it shouted the name of Friedrich Schiller, it actually bewailed the shattered dreams of a whole generation; it protested against a superannuated political and social order, and pledged itself to offer resistance and give new battle.

Was this the way, is this a way to honor a poet? Was it honorable of Robert Blum, the fiery tribune of radical republicanism, to ransack Schiller's works in search of stirring political slogans and to weave three such passages lifted from three different plays—the famous line of Marquis Posa was surely not missing —into one sentence, and by doing so make Schiller the crown witness of revolutionary convictions which impregnated the air a century ago? Becoming so very popular, being transferred so enthusiastically from the pantheon to the market place is a mixed blessing for a poet. As with no other man of letters before him, the nineteenth century transfigured and transformed Schiller into a political poet, political in the widest sense, meaning that he spoke on and for matters of the *polis*, the public life, warning and advising, chiding and guiding, judging and condemning—an orator and pamphleteer more than a poet. How easy it was to quote him, for he had an eminently quotable maxim for every noble purpose; how usable he was for every schoolmaster and dignitary who, facing serious crowds, needed something edifying, lofty and inspiring. The reaction became inevitable, inevitable the questions whether Schiller was a poet at all, whether his place was in the *agora* rather than on Mount Parnassus, on a glorified soap-box rather than in the theater. And Friedrich Nietzsche, disrespectful iconoclast that he was, denigrated Schiller neatly and devastatingly by calling the poet simply "that tedious and brassy trumpet player of moralism"

This is brutal, and it is utterly wrong; wrong because it confuses with his true image the crudely glossy lacquer which posterity has generously spread over Friedrich Schiller's features. The nineteenth century—and in this respect the nineteenth century is by no means over—was mistaken in forcing Schiller into a posture which was that of a tribune of the people rather than of a poet. Yet underneath the spurious overlay there exists a genuine and fundamental level upon which Schiller and politics meet. Though he was not a political poet, he was perhaps the greatest poet of politics. With a fervor unequalled, a passion unabated, his plays ask decisive and basic questions: what and where is man's place in this vital and fateful game called politics; how does he master it and how does it master him; in which sort of relationship does the private human being, his moral, emotional and divine essence, stand to the *zoon politikon*, the political animal, which man, equally essentially, is? Someone as obsessed with these questions as was Schiller is not a political poet who furnishes us with slogans, with marching orders and banners to be waved on the shifting battleground of ideologies, but one who, through memorable figures and configurations, elucidates for us our human existence, our existence as humans, its complexities and paradoxes, its defeats and triumphs, its condition and possible consequences. And this, indeed, is the poet's task.

After he outgrew the fervor and furor of his youthful subjectivism, starting with *Don Carlos*, Schiller used decisive moments of Western European history as the subject matter of his plays: the breaking away of the Netherlands from Spain in *Don Carlos*, the Thirty Years' War in the *Wallenstein* trilogy, the rise of Britain to a world power in *Mary Stuart*, the liberation of France from England's yoke in *The Maid of Orleans*, and the foundation of Swiss democracy in *Wilhelm Tell*. Yet he did not write dramatic chronicles in the manner of Shakespeare, nor give us a gallery of historical individuals, brave or cowardly, heroic or mean. Instead, he traced again and again man's fateful involvement in history, in that process which we determine while being determined by it, which uses us as its pawns by mobilizing in us our freedom to act.

This dialectic interplay of determining power and freedom of action, the friction and tension between our moral obligations and the dictates of the necessities which the historical moment imposes upon us, in short, the problems of political man, have been Schiller's most persistent themes. We may as readily and enthusiastically as did that audience in the Hamburg theater applaud Marquis Posa's plea for political freedom, for the right of every individual to full expression; but if we do nothing but this, we have missed the human condition and the human tragedy which Schiller's *Don Carlos* probes. For Marquis Posa's ringing line: "Sire, give us all freedom of thought" is only a station in a series of arguments in which not this or that political ideology, not this or that form of government, is being discussed and presented, but politics as such, its field and orbit, its function and aim. In the long speech that follows, Marquis Posa demands of the king: "Restore to man his lost nobility!" Now this, we must admit, is strange. Nobility, we would think, is a value of the inner man, a private, a personal value, something untouchable, whose loss or preservation does not lie within the public domain, cannot be jeopardized or secured by the head of state, be he ever so enlightened, tolerant and liberal. Since the dawn of Christianity political theories have again and again started from Christ's saying: "Render therefore unto Caesar the things which be Caesar's, and unto God the things which be God's", a clear separation between the powers that govern the public and the private existence of man, his outer and inner obligations, duties and rights. The most effective revolutionary attacks on various forms of tyranny were derived from the very conviction that Caesar had encroached upon a field that was God's, had demanded loyalties that were the prerogatives of the Highest. Yet Posa argues in the opposite direction: Caesar is to restore the lost nobility of mankind, the world is to be remade into paradise, the breach between this world and the other healed forever, and politics proclaimed as the field in which man in his totality, his truth and eternal essence, will rule supreme. Politics, as Posa sees it, is no longer carefully calculated to determine the distribution and balance of obligations and rights, the amount of freedom or freedoms which the citizen should enjoy, but is the very medium on which his total existence depends, not only his position and status within the machinery of the state, but the value, the inner verity, of his being man. No less than his nobility, the visible activation of his moral essence is here proclaimed as the starting point and ultimate aim of politics.

Marquis Posa's famous plea, then, so heavily taxed and overtaxed by every freedom-loving speech-maker as a program point of an enlightened liberal political platform, is not only that. Within its context it serves to define politics as the very climate in which man as man, as a moral and spiritual being, can and must fulfill himself. But at this point, after the basic foundation has been laid, Schiller, the great dialectician of politics, begins his probings. So far Marquis Posa has been a private citizen, unwilling to assume any political responsibilities at King Philip's court, traveling about the empire as a mentor and friend to those who share his advanced political philosophy, a living link between men who dream of and prepare a better future, and, above all, the source of inspiration of Don Carlos, the crown-prince, who one day, guided by Posa and Posa's principles, will usher in a new and brighter world. But now, more or less against his will, he becomes involved on the plane of action. The king, shivering in the cold isolation of his loneliness, surrounded by the sterile servility of his selfish courtiers, is struck and overwhelmed by meeting a free man, who speaks his bold mind freely, asking no favors, despising the shrewd game of the manipulation of power. Suddenly the idealistic dreamer of a better world, the theoretician not only of a new politics but of politics as the medium which can restore mankind's lost nobility,—he has become from one moment to the next the king's most powerful seal-bearer, the unchallenged master over the fate and future of his country. Schiller's question and ours is: what will he do with this unparalleled power?

Let us look at the outcome, at the fifth act. Marquis Posa, champion of a new, happy life growing from what he called the lethal stillness of a churchyard that was Philip's Spain, is shot to death; Don Carlos, the successor to the throne, in whom Posa implanted the high ideals of progressive, freedom-loving government, is arrested and turned over to the executioner at the very moment when he sets out to flee to the Netherlanders to lead their rebellion and topple the Spanish system of suppression; the Duke of Alba, the most sinister and blood-thirsty of the king's hangmen, marches North with his troops, his baggage filled with death sentences which are to break the Hollanders' spirit and will to resistance; King Philip himself, who, in spite or because of his rigidity and misanthropic distrust, had been longing for a gentle human voice to help and guide him, now delivers himself and his power unreservedly to the merciless grip of the Inquisition, and when he asks the Grand Inquisitor the pathetic question: "For whom have I planted and collected?", receives and **meekly accepts the brutal answer**: "For the graves and the worms rather than for liberty." What an ending after such high hopes, what a harvest of ruin and devastation growing from seeds that were meant to transform a barren field into a paradisiac garden!

What Schiller here presents is not only an accidental historical disaster, the pessimistically gloomy tableau of noble dreams destroyed and great expectations foiled. The dreadful outcome is, after all, the direct consequence of Marquis Posa's involvement in the political game, of his active participation in the battle of power and passions raging at the Spanish court. We are witness to a truly vital process of politics, to the tragic dilemma that arises when an ideal, be it ever so benevolent and noble, enters upon the plane of reality, is drawn into the orbit of pressures and counter-pressures, distorted and ruined by the very forces which it mobilizes in the course of its attempted realization. When telling the hapless story of the defeated idealist Marquis Posa, has not Schiller indeed touched upon a basic problem of politics *per se*, a problem which the twentieth century has only too brutally experienced; the disastrous and destructive effects of a political principle which, good in itself—meant as a panacea of all the social ills of mankind—is twisted by the currents which it unleashes into its very opposite, into a harbinger of darkness blacker than the one which it was to dispel? The true tragedy of politics, of man in the political arena is here revealed: the noble ideal, man's highest hope, is being ground to shreds by the inexorable maelstrom of uncontrollable forces; good itself has turned into an instrument of evil and destruction.

Yet Schiller's *Don Carlos* is more than a probing into the dialectic ambiguity of political ideologies. The play presents not only the havoc which the ideal can work when transferred from the realm of pure thought to the realm of concrete realities. More decisive, more tragic still, is the moral *impasse*, the dubious road onto which the idealist is forced in pursuit of his ideal. Nothing could be purer than the flame that burns in Marquis Posa, nothing nobler than his intentions. And yet, how questionable the means, how frightening the detours, that the realization of this ideal prescribes to him! The one who had proclaimed the securing of man's totality as the very justification of politics, and as its purpose the free display of man's nobility, has donned, since he entered the plane of politics, an impenetrable mask, has become so divided within himself that every action he commits is calculated to conceal his true objectives. His friendship with the king, who had turned to him because he saw in him the only genuine human being in his whole entourage, free, unselfish, unpurposeful, and therefore worthy of complete trust, is nothing but a subterfuge, a betrayal, that is to promote his revolutionary aims. And his betrayal of Don Carlos—at least what seems to everybody, including the prince himself, a betrayal—is nothing but a subterfuge which is to save the beloved friend from grave impending danger. Treason under the cloak of friendship, friendship under the cloak of treason—what a disturbing twilight in the champion of a new world who was fighting for everybody's freedom of thought, which is in the last analysis nothing else but the individual's right to be himself, to accept as the guiding light of his life nothing but his own inner truth, the authenticity of his being. But, when Marquis Posa laid down his life for his ideal, where was his authenticity?

Don Carlos, mourning at the bier of his friend and mentor, is convinced that he died for him, and taunts the king, who had tried in vain to gain Posa's heart and support:

> Mine was he, mine,
> While you were boasting loud of his esteem,
> While he, his nimble tricky eloquence
> Was playing with your proud, majestic mind . . .
> You showered him with tokens of your favor;
> He died for me. Your friendship and your heart
> You urged upon him. And yet your crown
> Was but a plaything in his hands.
> He threw it down—and died for me.

But did he really? Or is not perhaps King Philip closer to the truth when he arrives at a very different answer:

> For whom then did he sacrifice himself?
> For Karl, that boy and son of mine? Oh never!
> I don't believe it. A Posa does not die
> For a mere youth. The meagre flame of friendship
> Does not fill a Posa's heart. That beat
> For all mankind. His passion was
> The world at large, with all its future generations.

If this is the right answer, then Posa did not love the prince because he was Don Carlos; he loved Don Carlos because he was the prince, the future ruler who, under his tutelage, would usher in the new millenium. But what about man's nobility, if the human being, the closest friend is degraded to a tool, a tool, to be sure, that is to serve the loftiest purpose, but a tool nevertheless? Is the political idealist—and this is Schiller's most penetrating question in *Don Carlos*—who fights so bravely and passionately for humanity, not himself a human failure? Obsessed by the legitimate demands of mankind as a whole, he becomes blind to the legitimate demands of individual man. Infatuated by an abstract idea, a noble, a grand idea, he plays havoc with man's dignity, which consists of one fact and one fact alone: that every human being is, and must be treated as, an end in himself and not a means for a purpose, no matter how lofty— this is the very dignity for which Marquis Posa had spoken up so movingly and eloquently in his first encounter with the king.

How silly it was to call a poet who offered such trenchant insights into the complexities and perplexities of political man, into the ironies and paradoxes of political action, a "brassy trumpet player of moralism"! The duplicity of man—duplicity in the twofold meaning of the word—his position at the intersection of moral law and the inexorable force of circumstances, the tragic dilemma which results from the unavoidable intertwining of his emotional life with the demands of practical and responsible action in the world—this, and not an easy and starry-eyed proclamation of ethical conduct, was Schiller's vital concern. The intertwining, the crossings and counter-crossings of our personal drives and desires with the principles and ideas which guide our actions:—again it is *Don Carlos,* Schiller's first fully mature play, that develops this existential problem. From its publication, and for more than a century afterwards, the play has been pronounced, with all due respect of course, debatable from a dramatic point of view because, its critics argued, it contained two entirely different actions that were only artificially and forcibly joined together: on the one hand the perfectly private court intrigue arising from Don Carlos' illicit love of his step-mother, the present queen, and the necessarily ensuing conflict between father and son, and, on the other, the political action, which is completely dominated by the figure of Marquis Posa eclipsing in the course of the play the protagonist, who in spite of the title is at best a secondary hero. Even if it were true that these two strands do not properly merge—and I do not think that it is true—such an argument would only point to a problem without explaining it. We have to understand this division within the drama as the palpable presentation of that tenuous interplay, by no means smooth, by no means harmonious, between the private sphere of man, his impulses and emotional realities, and those principles and conceptions which stimulate and guide his actions on the stage of politics.

But were Schiller preoccupied only with the banal truth that man's subjective drives and motivations color his ideological aims and objectives, promote or obstruct them, deflect or pervert them, we might dismiss the poet as inconsequential. But here again, his eye probes much more deeply. He realizes that these objectives are essentially and fundamentally intertwined with the individual's personal and private life, that they can be translated into actions only when they enter the living tissue of man's total existence and form with the energies of his emotional being an amalgam in which alone they can become effective. Ideas and ideals which have not penetrated into the subsoil where passions rest are sterile and dead. If we want to make them realities, we can do so only by feeding them with our life-blood, by what in modern terms would be called a total commitment. And yet here arises another paradox in the existence of political man which Schiller has elucidated in his drama. If the political ideal, which as an ideal is an absolute and objective postulate, must necessarily enter into the tangle of man's impulses and drives in order to become effective, then its purity is automatically lost. The deed which he commits for the sake and in the service of the ideal becomes indistinguishable from the deed which his own often petty interest forces upon him. This insoluble dilemma—and it is truly insoluble—Schiller has made transparent in his most powerful evocations of political man, in those historical figures who are called upon to act as the servants of a great historical mission and yet are surrounded by the dubious light of selfishness and hypocrisy. Only by asserting themselves, their own personal needs and desires, can they hope to assert the ideal which they pursue: Wallenstein in the great trilogy, and Queen Elizabeth of England in *Mary Stuart.*

Seeing in Wallenstein and in Elizabeth nothing but hypocrites, evil schemers for the sake of their own power, means again to miss Schiller's essential point. It is idle to ask which of the many faces that Wallenstein presents to the viewer is the true one. We have to realize that for him, as a political man, all of them are true and depend on each other even if at first glance they may seem exclusive. The great general of the imperial army, the idol of his soldiers, wants to reassure himself by a written declaration of the unreserved loyalty of his officers so that they will follow him blindly wherever he leads them, even against the emperor, even into the camp of the enemy, the Swedes. Schiller presents a clear case of treason, a preparation of mutiny against the supreme overlord, motivated by the boundless ambition of a man who wants to be not only his ruler's mightiest sword but, if need be, the ruler himself. And yet, is it really only Wallenstein's thirst for unlimited power that leads him onto the road of clandestine conspiracy and, finally, to open rebellion? It is, and it is not. He does not simply feign when he casts himself—again not quite without ulterior motives—in the rôle of a harbinger of peace, who after sixteen years of the bloodiest holocaust wants to put an end to the immeasurable misery of war. But he knows that this ideal—and it is a noble ideal, after all—can be realized only by cutting through the religious intolerance and the entangled dynastic interests which dominate the emperor and his house, the house of Hapsburg, by uprooting old hatreds and old loyalties which, the longer they last, drive the course of history ever more deeply into a hopeless stalemate. If this be treason, and it surely is, then treason there must be.

From this summary of Wallenstein's deeds and motivations one might conclude that Schiller raises mainly the question of the legitimacy of certain means to achieve certain ends, a question which is, indeed, one of Schiller's vital concerns. It is a vital question for a poet who, as hardly any other, has been the merciless anatomist and dissector of political man. But Schiller goes one decisive step further, or rather he goes one step back, by asking the even more disturbing question: how do we, how can we, when on the stage of politics, decide at all upon the means we are to employ, be they good or foul? In order to arrive at any decision that is to inspire and guide an act, we must be free agents, independent of alien authority, not subject to the pressures which pure hazard or the necessity of the moment may exert upon us. Now Wallenstein's craving for power appears in a somewhat different light. It is not simply a selfish desire for self-aggrandizement, but the inevitable corollary of the make-up of a man who is basically political. If he acts, responsibly and fruitfully, he must be in complete command, must be able to exclude interference that could hamper his plans and deeds, to eliminate the unforeseen that could thwart the action in the very process of its realization. In short, political man, and the greater and truer he is, the more so, must of necessity strive for omnipotence and omniscience, a striving as monstrous as it is pathetically futile.

It is for this reason that Schiller's Wallenstein, the great man of action, appears so strangely inactive during much of the play, so hesitant and evasive, so resistant to those who want him to commit himself to a definite course. Just this Wallenstein is unwilling to do. Because committing himself means to relinquish some part of his freedom, to start a chain of events which may not be controllable and calculable at every point, to be, perhaps, drawn against his will into a constellation and a development in which he becomes the slave of a situation instead of its master. It is in the *Wallenstein* trilogy that Schiller pushes the problem of political man to its extreme consequence, to the point where the man of action can no longer act, because in order to act freely—and only if he acts freely can he make history instead of being made by it—he must be able to choose freely, to keep all avenues open, so that at no time will the direction of his course be dictated to him. Seen in this light, the freedom to act, which is the premise upon which the existence of political man rests, is transmuted into a freedom from action. Therefore Wallenstein waits until the constellation and his calculations become unbeatable.

And yet, what Schiller presents in *Wallenstein* is the fateful irony which is likely to beset all politics. In order to act decisively and infallibly—and this is the aim of all purposeful action—Wallenstein has again and again postponed his decision. But he has postponed it just a minute too long. One who has hesitated for many precious months in order to be able to act as a free agent is now forced by the weight of circumstances to decide upon a course which he wanted to keep open only as a last and ultimate possibility. Was he really determined to commit treason, to lead his troops over to the Swedes, the enemy he had been fighting so brilliantly for years? Just by trying to be uncommitted, to stand above the situation so that he could be its complete master, he has fastened the noose around his neck, and has no other choice but to battle for his very life under the most unfavorable of circumstances. In the great monologue at the beginning of the last part of the trilogy, one of the most powerful poetic passages that Schiller ever wrote, Wallenstein asks himself the question:

> Must I commit the deed because
> Just in my thoughts I toyed with it?

Yes, he must. Because even thoughts have a momentum of their own and create a reality which, from one moment to the next, changes the stage upon which political man acts. While taking the first step he is still free, but the second is already prescribed. And who can tell which is the first step? Such is the irony of politics that, when Wallenstein finally takes his first step, he has actually taken his last. Every plan, every bit of strategy, has created conditions which now prove overwhelming, which force him from a strong position to a precarious one, from a precarious position to a shattered one, from a shattered position to a lost one, until finally his doom is sealed.

It may seem like a hopelessly gloomy picture that Schiller in his *Wallenstein* trilogy draws of man acting on the political plane. But at this point Schiller the great dialectician takes over again. Indeed, the ironic and tragic fate of Wallenstein, the master tactitian and politician, is merciless and unrelieved. He who tried to insure for himself such complete freedom of action that he could move in any direction which would seem advantageous at a given moment is now fighting with his back to the wall, losing one support after the other, yielding inch by inch, until his last stronghold, the fortress of Eger, becomes a doorless trap where he finds an ignoble end at the hands of hired assassins. But it is this very downfall that Schiller surrounds with the halo of human greatness. The reckless scheme has now turned into a wild, pathetic gamble. The powerful schemer who acknowledged no other authority than his own unbridled will has become a plaything of forces he cannot control. The dream of scepter and crown has faded into the illusory hope of sheer survival. And yet, the moment has come when Wallenstein can act—because he must. Now he reaches the status of true greatness and, a man alone, relying only on his inner strength, he goes down in defeat with an austere uprightness which lends him the majesty that he never possessed in the days of his power and exaltation. The man of political action who is fully committed, committed with his entire existence and personality, achieves in the face of radical insecurity and extreme exposure an amount of freedom which no strategic shrewdness and calculation could give him; and while utterly failing in his objectives and ambitions, he demonstrates a nobility which no success could have granted him.

Indeed, success will not grant it. In *Mary Stuart*, his next tragedy, Schiller has given an almost complementary image of political man. At the end of the play, Elizabeth has vanquished her deadly rival, the hapless queen of the Scots. Her rule is now, and will in all the future be, secure and unchallenged, and England saved from the threat of civil war. Yet, what might seem the moment of her complete victory is in truth the moment of her utter defeat. The picture over which the curtain falls tells the whole story: Elizabeth, deserted by those who were close to her heart, holds herself painfully and forcibly upright, a human wreck whose hollowness is more exposed than concealed by the strained regal posture. No other poet has, I think, made us witness so closely the bitter and inexorable tragedy of political man, his defeated triumphs and triumphant defeats as Schiller did in the fate of Queen Elizabeth of England. Hers is the richest and most complex portrait of the human being as a political being, of his hopeless involvements, of the rôle which he is called upon to enact on the stage of history, and of the usurious price he has to pay for his actions.

Again, the task Elizabeth has to fulfill is not only an inevitable necessity, but a truly noble mission. She feels destined to bring peace to her country which, after the death of her reckless father, has been shaken by religious strife and unrest, by the undermining of governmental authority and civil security, by the permanent threat from powers abroad, from France and Spain, whose might and ruthless exploitation of England's internal tensions conspire to bring the heretic island to its knees. All these dangers have one name, the name of Mary Stuart, "the scourge of my life," as Elizabeth calls her. Mary, without any active guilt and against her will, has become the very center of all destructive forces: as a Catholic, the idol of the religious opposition; as a former queen of France and Scotland, a permanent invitation to the foreign enemy to meddle in England's affairs; as the direct descendant of Henry VII, the first Tudor, a living reminder of Elizabeth's disreputable birth and disputable claim to the throne. This woman, the innocent source of all disturbances, is now a prisoner in an English citadel, her life completely at Elizabeth's mercy.

Still, with all this, Elizabeth's hands are tied; because of the divergent drives and counterdrives she has to consider, because of the moral and legal problems which Mary's execution, a plain act of violence, would raise. How simple it would be if a clear demarcation line could be drawn between what is ethically right and justifiable and those impure motives that are the consequence of petty personal interests or of the cold demands of statecraft, between actions morally obnoxious but politically necessary, and motives personally pure perhaps but politically ineffectual. It is the impenetrable twilight shrouding the feelings and dealings of political man, the inseparable compound of values, energies, and impulses, that fascinate Schiller and make the character of Elizabeth as baffling as it is symptomatic. The vast field of ambiguities upon which political man moves is here outlined, the pitfalls of political action laid bare. If Elizabeth sends Mary to the block, does she do so because the welfare of her country demands of her this extreme and cruel decision? She does and she does not; because when signing the death warrant, she will at the same time give vent to her personal idiosyncracies, her jealousy of a rival whose beauty and youthful charm show up her own unloveliness. But apart from this interference of the petty and all-too-human, is there any way at all to distinguish between the postulates of morality and of political action? Killing Mary is, and Elizabeth knows it, an act of gross injustice that the public good, the unity of the country, seems to require unequivocally at this historical moment. But what if this dismissal and overriding of the dictates of morality for the sake of politics turn out to be the very means which jeopardize the desired end? Elizabeth's power rests on the approval and consent of her people, who are now clamoring for Mary's death. But will not the bloody verdict, once pronounced and executed, cause a shudder of disgust to run through these same people and open up a schism between queen and nation, the very schism Elizabeth wanted to prevent by sacrificing the voice of her conscience to the harsh interests of state? What if the question of morality which had to abdicate before the demands of politics becomes itself a political question creating a new political situation?

Of these perplexities Elizabeth herself is eminently aware. In the great monologue spoken before she finally signs the fateful death warrant, she penetrates to the very bottom of the political dilemma:

> Why have I practiced justice all my life
> And shunned tyrannic arbitrariness, so that
> For this, my first and inescapable
> Despotic act, I weakened my own hands?
> The pattern which I set now damns me . . .
> Yet was it, after all, my own free choice
> To practice justice? Necessity,
> All powerful and governing the will
> Even of kings, has forced this virtue upon me.

How insoluble the dilemma that confronts political man! Justice, which Elizabeth, a free moral agent and a responsible ruler, had chosen as the foundation stone upon which the edifice of her government was to rest, has turned into a strait-jacket which paralyzes her at the very moment when the existence of her state is at stake. Her own past—and a noble past it is—blocks the way into the future; and even this past, the rule of justice which she thought to have created by a free decision of her moral being, is now revealed as nothing but a response to a combination of circumstances that left her no other choice but to be just. Is there a way through the labyrinth, through the hopeless maze of duplicities, imperious necessities, high objectives, and unscrupulous means, in which Elizabeth, in which political man, is lost?

Schiller's answer to this question seems to be given in the character of Mary Stuart, as in his *Wallenstein* trilogy it was given in the youthfully idealistic figure of Max Piccolomini. Though in physical bondage, a helpless object whose fate is determined by forces and constellations she cannot control, Mary represents man in his freedom, in the veracity of his being, not innocent—Schiller takes great pains not to absolve her from the criminal complicities with which history charged Scotland's queen—but truthful, showing her genuine face and refusing to hide behind the screen of deviousness, opportunism, and disingenuous representation, in which Elizabeth is a master. It is from this vantage point that, in her dispute with Lord Burleigh, Elizabeth's prime minister, she challenges her regal rival:

> And what she really is
> She ought to dare appear,

a demand not for specific human qualities and virtues, not for this or that principle of action, but a demand for human authenticity, for the courage of one's own convictions and deeds, for the acceptance and frank display of one's own distinct and distinguishable individuality.

This, we may be inclined to argue, is a shirking of the issue. For is it not Schiller himself, the poet of politics, who has made us so acutely aware of the complexities of political man, the paradoxes of political action, the dissimulations that are part and parcel of the great game, and the dubious stratagems which even a noble intention needs on its road to realization? But all this, the very matrix of politics, which Schiller has so lucidly expounded in his dramatic works, is challenged by Mary Stuart's uncompromising insistence on human authenticity, an insistence which does not solve the perplexing problem that politics raises, but simply ignores and overrides it. Mary Stuart's voice, her very existence, represents, we might say, the attitude of a-political, even of anti-political man. She can easily display this attitude, since she has withdrawn from the stage of politics and is no longer faced with the harsh needs and decisions which the operation and preservation of the body politic exact. To put it quite cynically: she can well afford to insist on man's inner freedom, on his authenticity, on his exemplary submission to the highest and eternal moral values, because all that is left to her is to die, and to die nobly. But is dying nobly, the extreme sacrifice by which we liberate ourselves from the burden of our earthly existence, an answer to the burning question of how to live in and with the world, how to act responsibly, so that this world will bear the imprint of our existence as humans?

Surely it is not an answer, and Schiller did not offer it as an answer, since, being a poet and not a soap-box orator, he was concerned with the essence and condition of this creature called man, and not with solutions that might easily be applied. And being a poet of politics and not a political poet, he had to show, and insist on, the limits and limitations of politics, lest man, all of man, be transformed into a nefarious political automaton. Just because Schiller saw, and presented more sharply and unflinchingly than any other poet, man's fateful and inescapable involvement in politics, the unrelievable pressures to which we are subject, the vulnerability of even our highest ideals when they enter the web of overpowering historical forces, as they must—for this very reason he insisted sharply and unflinchingly on the preservation of a realm of freedom, the only realm in which man as a self-determining being, subject only to immutable moral law, can fathom his own dignity. Not sharing the shallow smugness of the optimist, he knew only too well that no political formula and no political form could ever open up this field of freedom, that it was and would remain a postulate that forever has to be raised, even if, or perhaps just because, it can never be fulfilled. Should our age, which is at the point of succumbing to the all-domineering demands of total politics, should a humanity, threatened by the fate of being paralyzed by suprapersonal powers and the inexorable pressures of state interests, should we not remember, commemorate and listen to a poet who, profoundly aware of the commitments we cannot escape, of the entanglements and ambiguities we cannot avoid, proclaimed again and again the fight for man's inner freedom, a fight, always on the brink of defeat and death, but never to be abandoned? Schiller's whole work is permeated by the spirit of the great scene in *Don Carlos*: man, proud and jealous of his independence and uniqueness, challenging forever the political power with the words: "Restore to man his lost nobility!" Defending this nobility, insisting upon it in the face of inevitable encroachments and threats, was Schiller's mission as a poet of politics, just as he himself pronounced this guardianship the supreme mission of any artist. In one of his philosophical poems, which he entitled "The Artists," he addressed his fellows:

> Man's dignity is laid into your hands.
> Do guard it well!
> It falls with you! With you it will rise high!

With him, with Friedrich Schiller, it rose to heights of which we must never lose sight.

# SCHILLER'S "TREACHEROUS SIGNS": THE FUNCTION OF THE LETTERS IN HIS EARLY PLAYS

We have become accustomed to regard the abundance of letters—which in Schiller's early plays engender, propel and, often enough, obfuscate the action—as clumsy technical devices and props, chargeable to the inexperience of a youthful beginner, and, therefore, to be dismissed and excused with a mixture of condescension and embarrassment. By doing so, we have relegated one of young Schiller's most persistent motifs to the level of mere dramatic machinery, and quite a maladroit one at that, uncognizant of the fact that we are thus committing one of the deadly sins of criticism: namely, considering formal and technical devices as merely extraneous matter, and abdicating before the imperative task to reveal, within all the elements of a work of art, the basic oneness without which a literary product is no more than an arbitrary agglomeration of unshaped materials. The plot of a drama, so Aristotle knew, is inseparable from its meaning; and the devices setting off the action are not an artificial mechanism, invented at will to serve an extrinsic purpose, but they are of the essence, the *energeia* of the play, in and through which the over-all design manifests itself. Seen as such, they are motifs in the very proper sense of the word; and they act, within the literary work of art, as metaphors, figures of speech in a speech universe.

If we cease to regard the letters in Schiller's early plays merely as crutches for the development of dramatic action, as mechanically manipulated gadgets, which produce and accelerate intrigue and counterintrigue, conflicts and *dénouements*, we may be able to recognize them as poetic symbols, which reveal, together with all other elements, the full meaning of the drama.[1]

---

1. The special perspective of this investigation precludes any heavy reliance on the large body of Schiller scholarship. Still, a few recent studies should be mentioned which are, though only remotely, related to this discussion. A similar functional or metaphorical interpretation of certain materials within Schiller's plays is offered by Ilse Appelbaum-Graham in "Reflection As a Function of Form in Schiller's Tragic Poetry," *Publications of the English Goethe Society*, XXIV (1955), 1 ff. Some points of contact are to be found in the much broader investigations of Kurt May, *Friedrich Schiller, Idee und Wirklichkeit* (Göttingen, 1948), and in Paul Böckmann, "Die innere Form in Schillers Jugenddramen," *Dichtung und Volkstum*, XXXIV (1934), 439 ff. Especially enlightening among more specialized studies were Fritz Martini's "Schillers *Kabale und Liebe*," *Der Deutschunterricht*, v (1952), 18 ff., and Walter Müller-Seidel's "Das

What, so we might ask first, is a letter? We may define it as a communicative sign; a sign, because it transmits a message which is not directly and spontaneously accessible; communicative, because it derives its very existence from the realization of distance, physical distance, and from the desire to bridge this distance, and to establish a connection between two separate and separated individuals. It has, as has all genuine human speech, the function to reveal a verity; but not being audible human speech, it can reveal its verity only indirectly.

This indirectness of the letter, its merely signatory character, leaves the field open for corruption to creep in; being but a sign and not the "thing *per se*" (quite consciously we are already using the Kantian term), it is prone to unwittingly distorted interpretation or, worse, to consciously treacherous manipulation. It is, of course, in this sense that Franz Moor (*Die Räuber*) uses it so masterfully and destructively.

If we want to assess the full range and symbolic richness of the motif, we have to realize how consistently and thoroughly the letter episodes reflect the very problems which Franz Moor's existence and ambitions raise. The hideous deceit which he perpetrates against his brother is exactly mirrored by the vicious game which he plays with the letters. By a trick of counterfeit he injects himself into a genuine correspondence, correspondence meaning here something much more vital than an exchange of letters. Hiding behind a screen, the decoy of "our correspondent in Leipzig," he substitutes his voice for the voice of the brother, who, through his letter of repentance, wanted to communicate

---

stumme Drama der Luise Millerin," *Goethe* (Neue Folge des Jahrbuchs der Goethe Gesellschaft), XVII (1955), 91 ff. Since, in the early works of Schiller, a letter appears again and again as the decisive instrument of plot and intrigue, some of those works should be mentioned here which deal extensively with the phenomenon of cabal and "false appearance" and demonstrate its constitutive importance in Schiller's dramatic practice as a whole: e.g., the two books of Benno von Wiese, *Die deutsche Tragödie von Lessing bis Hebbel* (Hamburg, 1949), I, 209 f., and *Friedrich Schiller* (Stuttgart, 1959), 145 ff., 207, 213; Paul Böckmann's *Formgeschichte der deutschen Dichtung* (Hamburg, 1949) I, 680 ff.; Gerhard Storz's *Der Dichter Friedrich Schiller* (Stuttgart, 1959), where we find the excellent formulation that with Schiller the intrigue can actually be taken as "one of the symbols for the human condition" (181); and finally Max Kommerell's observations about "Das Handeln und der Schein" in his essay "Schiller als Psychologe" in *Geist und Buchstabe der Dichtung* (Frankfurt/Main, 1944), 208 ff. In the Wallenstein-chapter of his book, *Schiller and the Changing Past* (London, 1957), 32-56, William F. Mainland deals quite specifically with a letter as the instrument of the intrigue. His attempt, however, to unmask Wallenstein's letter to the Imperial court concerning Buttler as a forgery of Octavio seems to me so unconvincing that no benefit could be derived from this publication.

to the father the genuine verity of his life; and finally succeeds in wresting from old Moor the right and power to answer, which are the prerogative of the father. The letter intrigue thus illuminates symbolically Franz's wanton destruction of a genuine "correspondence," his meddling and meddlesome interference between a father and his first-born, prodigal son. If we are responsive to the biological, social and religious implications which the constellation: father—first-born, prodigal son conjures up, then Franz's initial letter intrigue reveals the full measure of the grand, evil scheme: his self-interpolation into the natural, social and divine design of the universe, his displacement of the chosen brother and his arrogation of the authority of the father. As he rebels against and attempts to pervert the natural order of things, the law of primogeniture, the rule of the father, the holy autonomy and self-determination of love, so he rebels against and perverts the meaning and function of a letter; what is destined to establish communication, to bridge the distance which blurs the recognition of truth, is misused by him for the purpose of cutting off communication altogether, and of creating a void, in which he intends to rule supreme.

This stratagem is achieved by making vicious use of the indirectness which is inherent in the phenomenon of the letter. He fills the distance between addressor and addressee, which a genuine letter strives to overcome, with a host of intermediaries and middlemen: the correspondent from Leipzig, himself writing for the father, Hermann disguised as a military comrade of Karl, so that the message delivered, completely deprived of its immediacy, becomes a dead "letter," an empty sign whose meaning has been torn away, and was thus perverted into a communicator of outrageous falsehood. What Franz has to prevent at all cost is the possibility of sign and genuine meaning finding each other again, of eliminating the middleman through whose interference alone the hideous scheme can be put to work. Twice in short succession Schiller has his old Moor say: "Ich will ihm schreiben," and it is Franz's ultimate triumph that he can avert the impending danger of direct communication which would, indeed, heal the breach caused by misunderstanding and deception. It may not be quite insignificant that old Moor, when stating his intention a second time, stresses the immediacy by adding to his "Ich will ihm schreiben" an "auf der Stelle." To be sure, no more than speed and urgency is expressed here; but the spatial metaphor enhances the impression of directness, emphasizes the exclusion of all interfering and mediating elements.

Once the vulnerability of the letter as a communicative sign is established, we can tell from the different messages that are being delivered in the course of the play Franz's gradual progress in the art of deviltry. The three notes read aloud in the drama are, of course, all authored by Franz; what, in the universe of the play, purports to be communication, human intercourse, is actually always the same, self-imposing voice, drowning out everything else. In the first instance, in the faked letter of the Leipzig correspondent, he arrogates the voice of public opinion, of the world at large; in the third instance, in Karl's faked last message to Amalia, he arrogates the most intimate voice of the heart. Here is—and again it is Schiller's ingeniously invented letter design that brings it out fully—the portrait of a megalomaniac egotist, of a man who assumes all the signatures of the world to write the one character: I. Yet in the middle between the trumped-up voice of the world and the trumped-up whisper of the heart—almost exactly in the middle, by the way, so the dramatic balance of the play wills it—stands the masquerader unmasked, delivering the one message which is signed by his full and real name: Franz von Moor. However, in this letter, which functions as an axis between two extreme poles, the deviousness is doubly confounded. In the other two cases Franz invented mouthpieces through which his intentions could become articulate; here, in the one letter to which he signs his name, he presents himself as a mouthpiece only, as the speaker for the father, into whose mouth, however, he places his own, Franz's words. All transparency is gone, human speech has become so thoroughly refracted that understanding is no longer possible. If we try to unravel it: the one who speaks (Franz) is but a mouthpiece of someone who—supposedly—speaks (the father); but this supposed speaker is only the mouthpiece of his mouthpiece.

This only "genuine" letter of Franz's with its mischievous game of refractions and juggled identities is, indeed, the middle point of the route over which the letter traffic travels. With its intricate iridescence between speaker and mouthpiece it serves as a cue to the bewildering distortion of directness and indirectness which Franz's letter-schemes consistently exhibit. Let us look at the initial step. Here is a direct message: Karl's letter to his father; but this direct communication has been spirited away and supplanted by something entirely false, the letter of the correspondent from Leipzig: the immediate report *of* Karl has been transformed into a mediated report *about* Karl; the voice of a second person has been interpolated behind whom the direct speaker disappears. In the last message of the triad of communications this proportion is completely reversed. Karl's last will, inscribed with blood on his sword, is, as we know, a pure fabrication. Here Franz's juggling skills have succeeded in feigning the unmediated communication of a person whom death has removed from any immediate contact. A direct voice is heard behind which the mediating reporter Hermann disappears.

Seen from this aspect, even the repulsive way in which this last message is being delivered becomes meaningful. To be sure, this injunction smeared in blood on the blade of a sword, is intolerably gory and melodrama at its most melodramatic; but symbolically it is "right": it heightens the directness which Franz here feigns to the nth degree. What could be more direct than a communication which speaks through the very blood of a man, a message, in which "das warme Blut des Herzens," the very organon of life, becomes the organ through which a man's last will becomes articulate. To strengthen this shocklike impact of directness even further, Amalia, when seeing the sword, bursts out in the exclamation, "Heiliger Gott, es ist seine Hand." Surely, it is sheer nonsense that anyone should be able to recognize in these bloody smudges a specific handwriting, not to mention the fact that Amalia is dead wrong in her attribution. But what seems absurd and ludicrous on the level of action, is logical and consistent in the evolution of the motif. (It should be noted that Amalia in her exclamation uses the expression "hand" for "handwriting," thus preferring of two possibilities the synonym which conveys, as does the blood-ink, a literally bodily directness and presence.)

The letter, then, in its precarious correlation of sign and meaning, its ambiguous indirectness, is the proper symbolic medium through which the great interferer can work his destruction. What Franz does to, with, and through the letters is an exact reflection of his devilish philosophy of life: the blasphemous denial that there is an inviolate and holy correspondence between the sign and its meaning, between the characters of material nature, biological, social and emotional, and the supreme writer-creator of these characters, God. Out of this denial grows his sinful attempt to make such vicious use of the indirectness in the relationship between sign and signer that every communication turns into "a tale told by an idiot . . . signifying nothing."

The symbolic function of the letters within the structure of Schiller's first play may be thrown into bolder relief by looking briefly at the obverse position, i.e., Karl's. If the letter, thanks to its indirectness which can be shrewdly exploited, is Franz's very element, it is to Karl for the same reason the alien and hostile element which has to be negated. His very first words, his curse at the "tintenklecksende Säkulum," his outbursts against a mode of life which substitutes carpingly critical and petty judgments for the spontaneity and vitality of heroically strong acting and living, sound like a refutation of the emasculating and "debunking" *Tintengekleckse* with which Franz, at the beginning of the play, made his entrance. Karl is utterly unaware of and vehemently denounces the indirectness which is inherent in the letter as a communicative sign. The distance which the letter hopes to bridge is simply denied and wiped out by Karl. Of course, the father will hear, through the written words of his letter, the genuineness of his repentance—the sign can and will unequivocally carry and convey the meaning; of course, the father will unconditionally forgive him—the immediacy of complete communication is taken for granted.

When talking about the letter he dispatched to his father, he narrows the distance between addressor and addressee down to a minimum, stresses the violent directness of his appeal: "So eine rührende Bitte, so eine lebendige Schilderung des Elends und der zerfließenden Reue—die wilde Bestie wär' in Mitleid zerschmolzen! Steine hätten Tränen vergossen!" (I, 2). This is, of course, *Sturm und Drang* overorchestration. But it is, at the same time, the belief in and the glorification of the overwhelming impact of directness, the tearing down of the barriers which make for distance, and the transformation of even the most distant, "Bestie" and "Stein," into something like oneself. Before receiving the "father's" fateful answer, while still convinced that all will work out well, he jubilantly announces to Spiegelberg: "Die Verzeihung meines Vaters ist schon innerhalb dieser Stadtmauern." This is not only linguistic hyperbole, but has to be taken in its literal impact: not a letter containing the father's pardon has arrived, but pardon itself, in all its directness and immediacy, is within the city walls.

The letter qua letter, the refraction of the "thing *per se*" through the medium of a sign, is rejected by Karl as violently as it is exploited by Franz. Quite consistently there is and must be for Karl a very different means of communication: it is the picture, the portrait. When, after a long absence, he returns to Amalia in disguise, the communication is established not by words, not by signs, but by his portrait on the wall. For the portrait stands at the opposite pole of the letter; it represents the person directly, it is what it represents; it proclaims: here I am. This is the reason why the portrait, here in the *Räuber* and later in *Maria Stuart*, appears as the seal and voucher of genuineness.

As it was in the case of Franz, Karl's attitude toward the letter symbolically reveals his existential position and his crime. As Franz blasphemously severed and denied the ordained holy correlation of the message, the phenomenal world, and the giver of the message, God, so Karl denies blasphemously the holy and ordained disparity between the created world and its creator. He rebels against the immutable law that *this* world, *this* justice is no more than a mediated sign in which the essence is not directly and unrefractedly present. He feels himself to be and acts as the avenging angel, announcing and preparing for the Last Judgment, for that final moment when our world, whose order is indeed only a mediated and refracted sign of the eternal essence, will forever and directly coincide with the divine order. By his hubris, by his delusion that he has been chosen to fuse sign and meaning into immediate and self-evident communication he, no less than Franz, although working in the diametrically opposite direction, denies the correlation, frail as it surely is, between creation and creator, phenomenon and thing *per se*, and pushes the world to the brink of chaos. When he realizes what he has done, when he repents and accepts the distance between the visible sign and the One from Whom this sign emanates, he has renounced his heroically sinful insistence on directness. And Schiller, by a poetic symbol of the highest rank, makes him submit to the power of earthly justice through a "middleman," the poor laborer, who will earn the prize placed on Karl's head. It is Karl's understanding and acceptance of the communicative sign—and the letter metaphor opens the way to its interpretation—which marks his downfall as a victory.

As if he had exhausted in his first play the symbolic possibilities of the letter metaphor, Schiller makes scant use of it in *Die Verschwörung des Fiesco zu Genua*. Yet even the modest place which he assigns to the motif is of interest to our interpretative argument. Again, a bit of writing serves as an instrument of treachery; again it carries a "wrong" message; even more radically than with Franz's *Tintenkleckse* it is a dead letter from which all genuine meaning has been torn away. In fact, the note which the Moor hands to Fiesco in the ninth scene of the first act is utterly devoid of meaning. It does not communicate anything; for all we know, and as far as the action of the play is concerned, it might as well be a blank sheet of paper. Its only function is to allow the Moor easy access to his prospective victim, to deflect Fiesco's attention for a moment and thus afford the Moor a favorable opportunity to murder him. The whole ruse of the Moor, his use of a written communication as a means of approach to Fiesco (Schiller leaves us in the dark as to what the slip of paper actually contains), seems quite far-fetched and unconvincing. Yet the dramatic situation again was such as to suggest to Schiller the letter metaphor that had proved so fruitful and revelatory in *Die Räuber*. Someone wants to insinuate himself into another person's good graces; someone, while pretending to act as a well-meaning and solicitous warner, gets ready to strike the deadly blow; someone ruthlessly exploits tension and strife for the satisfaction of his own greedy purposes: this is a portrait of both Franz and of the Moor when they enter the universe of the respective plays. In both cases a letter, a written communication of spurious content, is their passport into a life full of deception, crime and nihilistic denial of any higher order.

It would be an inadmissible shifting of weights and a distortion of the essence of Schiller's first two plays if one overstressed the parallelism between Franz and the Moor, who is, after all, no more than an easily available tool in the hands of the powerful active schemers. Yet the Moor is the channel through which every bit of duplicity, every devious subterfuge flows: the attack upon Fiesco's life, the plan to poison Leonore, Gianettino's conscription list which decrees death to Genoa's twelve leading citizens, Fiesco's secret military preparations for his *coup d'état*. Though not, as is Franz Moor, the master of every hidden design, he is all corruption's agent, the sinister go-between, the man of *indirection*. That he is a creature of darkness has, of course, not only ethnic, social and religious significance. He moves in a shadowy no man's land where there is no direction and no directness, crossing all lines, from Gianettino to Fiesco, from

Fiesco to Andreas Doria, and ends, quite properly, with his feet high up in the air, strung up at the church gate: the model of a double-crosser in the word's most literal meaning. His business is going back and forth, covering distances, "communicating," but what he communicates are deceptive attitudes, "signs" whose meanings are ambiguous and undecipherable. The letter, the written communication, which in Schiller's storehouse of poetic metaphors is the symbol of treacherous indirectness and dubious mediation, is logically the instrument associated with the black double-crosser. Every single instance of written communication in *Die Verschwörung* is linked up with the Moor: the note he hands to Fiesco (I, 9), the letters from Fiesco's supporters in Rome, Piacenza and France (II, 15), Gianettino's conscription list (III, 4), Fiesco's invitation to the enemies of the Dorias (III, 4), and finally Andreas Doria's letter which unmasks the last betrayal of the Moor (IV, 9). And with these scene references we have enumerated almost all the instances in which the black man appears on the stage. Letters and the Moor—they belong together.

The pattern of the letter as the instrument of trickery and treachery is firmly established in Schiller's first two dramatic works. It plays, so we have pointed out, a minor part in *Die Verschwörung*; however, in Schiller's next play, *Kabale und Liebe*, the motif again assumes a dominant position. Yet the letter which Luise writes at Wurm's dictation represents a new variation whose metaphorical value we shall have to assess. All the letters considered up to this point, no matter how treacherous their contents, no matter how deceitful and falsified their signatures, were "genuine" in so far as they obeyed the will of their writers. They were true documents of their authors from which—though not an objective truth—the truth of the person could be gleaned who, whatever his disguise, was speaking through them. Luise's letter presents an entirely new situation. It is the first one that we actually see being written. In no other scene of any of Schiller's plays, in hardly any scene of all dramatic literature, does the brutal disparity between verity and phenomenal sign become as stark and shattering a reality as in the composition of Luise's letter. Here someone is writing before our very eyes, yet every word is a piece of monumental falsehood. Again a letter, and the circumstances under which a letter is being written serve—a symbolic abbreviation—as a metaphorical *summa* of the existential problem of man, presented by the play as a whole.

Luise's letter leads into depths of human misunderstandings, into fields of treachery much more devastating and tragic than Franz's comparatively simple mischievous concoctions. The truly frightening aspect of the letter episode in *Kabale und Liebe* lies in the fact that the very victim of the devilish intrigue becomes its instrument, that the destruction wrought is aimed at the writer's own heart and happiness. Thus, one of the decisive problems of Schiller's plays, the problematic interrelationship of human freedom and the tyrannic power of necessity, is reflected in the letter episode. It is man's real tragedy that in this world, on the plane of communications, the very sign of communication is poisoned at its inception, dictated by the "enemy": the world with its ruthless demands. Man's most genuine and natural loyalties, his very love of family and devotion to God, will, on the plane of communications, be perverted into instruments of destruction and self-destruction. This tragic irony which besets man, and of which Schiller's *Trauerspiele*—from *Kabale und Liebe* on—are a magnificent record, is the very essence of Luise's letter, and for this reason again a cue to the entire play.

There is hardly a scene anywhere which so powerfully and consistently in all its elements—atmosphere, situation, speech—symbolizes the existential condition of man: haunted, pursued and trapped by a hostile world which forcibly guides his hand to give a treacherous sign, which uses communication for the purpose of establishing an impenetrable silence. Every word dictated, every word spoken during the dictation scene is permeated by the corrosive spirit of ambiguity, the frightful equivocation which arises when letter and meaning are torn asunder. The scene lives on paradox and irony, those elements of the grand design which press the most natural, intimate and holy—love of parents, devotion to God—into the service of the unnatural, public and devilish. We have to follow the intentions and the dialogue of the scene almost line by line.

The letter is addressed ostensibly to the Hofmarschall, yet it is actually written for the "benefit" of Ferdinand, who will be its real recipient. Its content is the arrangement for an amorous rendezvous, yet in reality it successfully blocks forever the joining of the true lovers. It presents itself as a confession, yet the oath that Luise will have to swear will seal her mouth forever.

The ironic and paradoxical run through the entire dialogue of the dictation scene. Luise, the victim of extortion, the one who has become a powerless puppet, starts the scene by asking, "Kann ich ihn zwingen . . . ?" and she ends with the movingly ironic question: "Darf die Taube nun fliegen?" To her question to whom she is writing she receives three times the answer, "An den Henker Ihres Vaters," but it is the very purpose of her writing to change her father's hangman into his liberator. However, most revealing in this respect is the text of the dictated letter. Certain phrases are being repeated by Wurm in order to coordinate dictation and writing. Here are these phrases: "sind vorüber"—"an den Major"—"den ganzen Tag wie ein Argus hütet"—"zu einer Ohnmacht"—"unerträglich." And these interjections seem, within this document of brutal deception, like snatches of truth, like a genuine disclosure of Luise's real situation and predicament. This cruel and ironic interplay finds its apex when Luise—and she does that in one instance only—repeats a phrase which she is forced to write down, thus making this part of the dictation her very own utterance. These words are: "loskommen könnte." What do we hear in this stammered repetition? Is it the painful sigh of a tortured soul; is it just a little bit of backplay of the vicious document that is being drawn up? It is Luise who speaks from the bottom of her heart; but what she utters is an echo of Wurm's words, which will appear before the world as Luise's own. It is this frightening duplicity, this horrible perversion which is, so it seems, summarized in Luise's question with which the scene ends: "Gott! Gott! und du selbst musst das Siegel geben, die Werke der Hölle zu verwahren?"

In this duplicity, so we believe, lies the real tragedy that *Kabale und Liebe* represents; here much more than in the social and political conflict which too readily and often has been considered the very root of the play. How simple—and simplistic —would everything be if *Kabale und Liebe* presented two neatly separated and clear-cut camps: here "Kabale"—there "Liebe"; here the vicious realm of tyrannical wordly power—there the realm of man's genuine emotions, of his inalienable human rights; here the field of brutal necessity—there the field of glorious freedom! This is the light in which Präsident Walter sees the conflict, and his attempt to solve it by a head-on collision of the two opponents is bound to fail miserably. The true tragedy reaches into much deeper layers: it arises when man is so trapped that his very heart is compelled to act as a bond servant to the designs of the world, when, and this is Schiller's tragically ironic view, God himself must furnish the seal to safeguard the works of hell.[2] It is not by chance that the name of the real enemy is Wurm, the one who carries the rot into the inside, and not Walter, the one who rules and administers to the outside world.

Of this metaphysical *condition humaine*, of man's tragic fate in which everything—outer pressure, love, religious devotion—conspires to extort from him a sign brutally at variance with the genuine voice of his heart, to draw him into an act of communication which is predicated on the premise and promise of deepest silence—of all this Luise's letter is the most revealing symbol. The metaphoric meaning of the letter becomes even more revelatory when we turn to the letter's recipient. The way Ferdinand reacts to Luise's letter shows up not only the tragic blindness of the "idealist," which from now on will be one of Schiller's very persistent and personal themes. Ferdinands naïveté, quite incredible if viewed from the aspect of psychological verisimilitude (altogether a rather unfruitful aspect of Schiller interpretation), has been amply, more than amply, established otherwise. Ferdinand's undoing results from the fact that he cannot distinguish between the phenomenon and the "thing *per se*," between appearance and being, between the sign and the meaning. For him truth and expression coincide, there is no distance that has to be overcome, and which leaves room for ambiguity and distortion. He falls for the utterly incredible wiles of his father, for the noble confession of Lady Milford, for the "letter" of Luise's letter. But here, too, the letter is not only a metaphor of the tragedy of blindness and misunderstanding. It is, even more, a metaphor of fate's cruel irony.

It is the letter that reveals to him the disparity between reality and appearance. From the very moment the letter has fallen into his hands, he asks, almost monotonously, the question: how is it possible that a viper is hiding behind an angelic face, that the visible, the sign, is so brutally at variance with the essence. Every word, every expression of feeling can be, has been, so the letter teaches him, a vicious sample of dissimulation. And yet,

---

2. It is, for the sake of dramatic balance and completeness, only logical that the obverse condition is equally represented in the play: Lady Milford hoping to use the political intrigue, the machinations of the world, to implement the genuine desires of her heart.

the letter, the precarious communicative sign which has come to him in the most devious and circuitous way, is accepted by him on its face value. This is the tragic irony of Ferdinand's predicament: that the very instrument that could show him the true relationship of things destroys relationship altogether. What, in a less sinister world than ours, might be salvation, i.e., clarity, becomes the tool of destruction, i.e., complete darkness.

In a masterful figure of speech which occurs in the violent altercation between Ferdinand and the Hofmarschall, Schiller has inscribed man's blindness in the very face of truth, the insoluble ironic ambiguity of communication.

> HOFMARSCHALL: Es ist nichts—ist ja alles nichts. Haben Sie nur eine Minute Geduld. Sie sind ja betrogen.
>
> FERDINAND: Und daran mahnst du mich, Bösewicht?—Wie weit kamst du mit ihr? Du bist des Todes, oder bekenne!
>
> HOFMARSCHALL: Mon Dieu! Mein Gott! Ich spreche ja—So hören Sie doch nur—Ihr Vater—Ihr eigener leiblicher Vater—
>
> FERDINAND: Hat seine Tochter an dich verkuppelt? (IV, 3)

All human understanding has become impossible. Even the word of truth cannot break through the magic circle of deceit which the letter has drawn. We shall see in our discussion of the letters in *Don Carlos* how man's failure to hear the truth in a truthful communication becomes the decisively new concern of Schiller's thoughts.

But before we reach this point, there are still to be mentioned two additional letters from *Kabale und Liebe* which throw the problem of communication, as we have developed it from the letter metaphor, into bolder relief. The first is Lady Milford's "Karte" to the Duke (IV, 9); the second, Luise's letter to Ferdinand (V, 1). Here are two letters—and this is unique in the traffic of major communications we have analyzed so far—whose messages reveal truths which were hidden under the cloak of dissimulation and vicious fraud. In content, these two letters stand at opposite poles: the Lady revokes what is presented as a merely contractual association. Luise tries to cancel a dissociation weighted down by the heavy burden of the holy sacrament. Yet, and this is the decisive feature, both these communications are last statements, testaments so to speak. To be sure, they reveal genuine verities; sign and essence here, for once, coincide. But they can coincide only because the sign is given

## The Function of the Letters in Schiller

at the moment when the signer is already on his way to the "beyond." Truth is communicated and communicable only as a last, a final farewell: the sign that truly communicates can be given only from "über der Grenze," the phrase with which Lady Milford's letter characteristically closes.

It is for this reason that the "delivery" of these letters becomes a serious problem. Not being deliverable in this world, they hover, so to speak, in mid-air. Their contents are being made known to us by an outsider, rather than by their writers or their prospective recipients. Their words reach us through a reciter, the Hofmarschall and old Miller respectively, most unwilling reciters at that, who would like to suppress the very content which they communicate to us. Access to the addressee is even more problematic. Luise's letter will never arrive at its destination; it is being destroyed before it can be dispatched. And the Lady finds it very difficult to get a carrier for her message, so much so that she suggests: "Mein Rat wäre, man backte den Zettel in eine Wildpretpastete, so fänden ihn Serenissimus auf dem Teller." Will the Hofmarschall ever deliver it, knowing what the reward may be? But even if he does—the message of truth will sound from beyond the frontier; the truthful communication is, again, all communication's end.

In our previous discussion we have quite often used the terms "phenomenon" and "thing *per se*," terms which have found their final definitions in Kant's epistemology. In our context, however, this pair of concepts was used—and is to be taken—in an heuristic sense only, as an analogon which could, perhaps, illuminate the problem of the communicative sign, its duplicity and treachery which, so we believe, is one of the decisive strands of Schiller's tragic view. At the most, and only implicitly, the use of these terms might point at a certain *a priori* affinity to Kant which existed in Schiller long before he was exposed to the systematic thinking of the great philosopher. It is in the same spirit of heuristic analogy that we now, turning to *Don Carlos*, discover through the letter metaphor a shift to the critical attitude in the Kantian sense, i.e., the introduction of the subjective consciousness as a key to the understanding of reality, and, for the tragic playwright, a key to the human tragedy. The letters with which we have dealt so far, have—metaphorically—illustrated the opaqueness of the object given (the content of communication), the willful distortion of truth, its refraction through the sign, the indirectness inherent in the letter and, with it, its "illegibility," its proneness to misunderstanding and misinterpretation. To summarize our whole argument briefly, but loosely: the truth of things has been tampered with, the lie is rampant in the world, man, deceived by the sign, is sped to his perdition. One thing was clear in all our letters: the sign was at fault, its message deceptive, the reality presented was bound to mislead the recipient. Man became the victim of objectively faulty signs.

Now, however, with *Don Carlos* this situation changes, and again it is the letter metaphor which illuminates this change. The emphasis now shifts from the objective *datum* to the subjective apperception of the *datum*. Two of the letters or correspondences, which figure prominently in *Don Carlos*, show an entirely new pattern. The letters are genuine, their messages truthful; they lead, however, to catastrophic results because the recipient does not know how to read them. We are dealing in both cases with *bona fide* signs, the confusion that ensues is the fault of the letter reader, who imputes meanings to them which they do not have.

The letter which the page hands to Don Carlos (II, 4) is a cautiously worded but straightforward invitation of Princess Eboli to visit her in her chambers. It is Carlos' jumping at conclusions which makes him believe that he has in his hands a message of the queen, a mistake which is to have disastrous consequences. The same conditions prevail with regard to Carlos' love letters to the queen, which the king finds in the rifled strongbox of his wife. They are genuine. Wrong only is Philipp's conclusion that they prove the queen's unfaithfulness. In both cases it is not the sign which is at fault. The dilemma arises from the fact that every sign needs a reader, and that the reader cannot perceive the truth transmitted.

The decisive new turn which the *Don Carlos* letters exemplify lies in the fact that the message is being refracted and distorted by certain given conditions *within* the recipient.[3] Both Carlos and Philipp cannot receive the meaning "straight" because they

---

3. Without wanting to overstress the Kant analogy we cannot help pointing out the curious coincidence that Carlos' and Philipp's wrong judgments rest on a disorientation of what Kant calls the three "categories" which determine all apperception of the real world surrounding us: space, time and causality. In Carlos' case the sense of space has been disturbed (he finds himself in a wrong room); in Philipp's case, the sense of time has been disturbed (he attributes the love letters, written in the past, to the present); in both cases a false causal link has been established between the letters and their origins.

are human, i.e., involved in their own emotional lives: Carlos in his love of the queen, Philipp in his suspicious jealousy of his wife. The basic situation which the letter metaphor illuminates could be summarized as follows: the message, the "idea" (and, we may go one step further, the ideal) must, in order to become "real" and active, enter into the living tissue of man's emotional, moral and ideational existence; but by doing so, it loses its pristine purity, its unambiguous meaning. This tenuous interplay (we can and need not elaborate on it here) lies at the bottom of all Schiller's philosophical thinking, in the realm of ethics no less than in the field of aesthetics. Yet even if we cannot demonstrate the full range of this basic conception, it must be pointed out in how far it underlies the whole tragedy of *Don Carlos.*

In his *Briefe über Don Carlos* Schiller has given a very comprehensive and ingenious commentary to his own play. The whole burden of this lucid self-defense against unintelligent criticism is the demonstration that the political theme, the message which the dramatic poem wants to convey, can become activated—dramatically and existentially—only by anchoring it firmly in the sub-soil of subjective human emotions. Love (Don Carlos), friendship (Marquis Posa), frustration (Philipp) are the necessary vehicles to carry the ideas forward. But these very emotions are responsible for the ultimate failure of the realization of the message. Of this ironic paradox the figure of Marquis Posa is the most impressive and pure manifestation, and it is surely not accidental that in the *Briefe* Schiller considers him the genuine protagonist of the play. From this paradox emanates the twilight enveloping Posa's character. Here we have, as always with Schiller, not a psychological, characterological problem, but an existential one raised to the rank of a general rule. Schiller expresses it as follows:

> Und hier, deucht mir, treffe ich mit einer nicht unmerkwürdigen Erfahrung aus der moralischen Welt zusammen . . . Es ist diese: dass die moralischen Motive, welche von *einem zu erreichenden Ideale von Vortrefflichkeit* [Schiller's emphasis] hergenommen sind, nicht natürlich im Menschenherzen liegen, und eben darum, weil sie erst durch Kunst in dasselbe hineingebracht worden, nicht immer wohltätig wirken, gar oft aber durch einen sehr menschlichen Übergang einem schädlichen Missbrauch ausgesetzt sind . . . Schon allein dieses, dass jedes solche moralische Ideal . . . doch nie mehr ist als eine Idee, die, gleich allen andern Ideen, an dem eingeschränkten Gesichtspunkt des Individuums teilnimmt . . . , schon dieses allein, sage ich, müsste sie zu einem äusserst gefährlichen Instrument in seinen Händen machen: aber noch weit gefährlicher

wird sie durch die Verbindung, in die sie nur allzu schnell mit
gewissen Leidenschaften tritt, die sich mehr oder weniger in allen
Menschenherzen finden. (Eleventh Letter)

Many of Schiller's later "Kantian" positions are here already prefigured. Here are foreshadowed the problems which arise from the amalgam, both indispensable and fateful, of absolute verity and subjective consciousness, from the refraction of the message in the receiver. It is, so we believe, the handling of the letters in *Don Carlos* that illuminates, both dramatically and existentially, this central problem.

Seen in this light, even the circumstances surrounding the delivery of the first letter in *Don Carlos* are deeply meaningful. The prince exhorts the page, who brings him the letter, to be closemouthed about this message and any future one. This is his advice:

> Sei wie das tote Sprachrohr, das den Schall
> Empfängt und weitergibt und selbst nicht höret. (II, 4)

And a little later:

> Den allgemeinen Fahrweg der Gedanken
> Betrete deine Zeitung nicht! Du sprichst
> Mit deinen Wimpern, deinem Zeigefinger;
> Ich höre dir mit Blicken zu. (II, 4)

This may, on the surface, be no more than the warning: be very discreet. Yet it is, of course, more. It is the realization (and ironically it is Carlos who realizes it) that disaster is impending as soon as the message to be delivered is reflected (in the double meaning of the word), as soon as the verity travels through a subjective consciousness which is more than a "totes Sprachrohr."[4] The whole fallacy of the hope that the message might be transmissible directly, outside of the "Fahrweg der Gedanken," unaffected by human consciousness, is unsurpassingly expressed, as only great poetry can do it, in the self-invalidation of language as a medium of meaningful communication; for speaking with one's eyelids and fingers is not speaking at all, as listening with one's glances is not listening. What is here aimed at is the starkly impossible: a sign that does not have to communicate a meaning because it *is* this very meaning, the annulment of the phenomenon of the letter as we have identified it at the very beginning of our investigation: a communicative sign.

That this cannot be, that the message has to be translated (in the literal sense of the word) through man, is all misery's beginning. It is at the heart of Johanna's desperate plaint:

# The Function of the Letters in Schiller

> Willst du deine Macht verkünden,
> Wähle sie, die frei von Sünden
> Stehn in deinem ew'gen Haus,
> Deine Geister sende aus,
> Die Unsterblichen, die Reinen,
> Die nicht fühlen, die nicht weinen!
> Nicht die zarte Jungfrau wähle,
> Nicht der Hirtin weiche Seele! (*Jungfrau*, IV, 1)

It is certainly not accidental that Schiller in three different personal letters, written over a period of ten years, has inserted a discarded *Don Carlos* passage, which bewails the distortion of the pure "message" through the medium of communication:

> Schlimm, dass der *Gedanke*
> erst in der *Worte* tote Elemente
> zersplittern muss, die Seele sich im Schalle
> verkörpern muss, der Seele zu erscheinen.
> Den treuen Spiegel halte mir vor Augen,
> der meine Seele *ganz* empfängt und *ganz*
> sie wiedergibt . . . [5]

With the discussion of the Eboli letter and the correspondence from the ransacked strongbox we have by no means exhausted

---

4. From here, an explanation may be found for the astonishing and crude mistake Schiller made in connection with the Eboli letter. The fateful confusion, from which so much of the further development of the action issues, is possible only under the assumption that the prince does not know the queen's handwriting. And so he assures the page explicitly: "Noch hab' ich nichts von ihrer Hand gesehen." How could Schiller commit such a blatant error? After all, we know that Carlos and Elisabeth have exchanged letters during their engagement; moreover, Carlos continuously carries a letter of the queen in his wallet as his most precious possession. One might charge this inconsistency to the overlapping of the two original intentions and plots which did not merge completely and smoothly in the dramatic poem: the Eboli letter would then belong to the "Familiengemälde," while the one in Carlos' wallet were to be linked to the political tragedy centering around the character of Marquis Posa. Yet a speculation of a different sort may prove more fruitful. I suggest that the motif "letter" seems to release in Schiller a compulsive mechanism. "Letter" always points, as I am trying to show, to a break of immediacy, to something impenetrable, to an existential situation in which man is prone to deception, and becomes uncertain concerning the true *données* and concatenations. Seen from this aspect, the mistake which crept into Schiller's dramatic motivation surely does not rectify itself, but it may reveal a profound inner meaning: the written communication appears as a deceptive sign even at places where, by the logic of the dramatic action, it actually cannot be such. The letter is, to speak with Storz, so thoroughly "a symbol of the human condition" (cf. fn.1) that it imposes its symbolism "by mistake" even against the reasonable course of the plot.
5. Letter to Charlotte von Lengefeld, July 24, 1789. The emphases are Schiller's. The same quotation with slight variations was transmitted to Körner, April 15, 1786, and to Humboldt, February 1, 1796.

the richness of the letter motif in *Don Carlos*. There are three additional communications which require our attention. The first is the king's note to Princess Eboli which falls into Carlos' hands and reveals to him Philipp's illicit relationship to the princess. The second is the queen's letter to Carlos, resting as a precious keepsake in his wallet, until, so he mistakenly believes, it was turned over to the king by Posa. The third is Posa's letter, ostensibly written to William of Orange, but meant to fall into the king's hands, and "confessing" his treacherous behavior and plans. They all have in common that they fall into wrong hands (although Posa's letter does so by design), and this connects them with the letters in the strongbox of the queen. Yet the first two belong with the group we have discussed in detail, because they are genuine communications, embodying unfalsified messages. They both bespeak hidden truths: the king's affair with Eboli, the queen's attachment to the prince. Yet, what makes them, at least potentially, devastating is the "compound into which they enter all too quickly with certain passions," the meaning and function which a human consciousness bestows upon them. Dramatically, they might become active (might, because actually they are never used for the intended purpose) by the fact that they amalgamate with the subjective, even the egotistical, desires of those into whose hands they have fallen: in the case of Carlos, his love of the queen which may find justification and fulfillment by unmasking the king's adultery; in the case of Posa, his ambitiousness which may use the compromising letter as an easy road to the king's most intimate confidence and favor. To be sure, the two letters are never used; but their dramatic possibilities show the same pattern: a genuine, truthful communication is about to be perverted by foisting upon it a devious "meaning" inspired by human, all too human interests and entanglements.

The characteristic feature of all the *Don Carlos* letters discussed so far is the fact that they are *bona fide*, in contrast to all those in *Die Räuber* and Luise's in *Kabale und Liebe*. The only exception to this rule is Posa's letter to William of Orange—actually, of course, to the king—which seems like a throwback to the pattern, familiar from *Die Räuber* and *Kabale und Liebe*. It is, as are Franz's letters, an untrue statement; it is, as is Luise's letter, addressed to a decoy with the obvious purpose of having it fall into the "wrong" hands. With all this, it seems to belong to the old deception scheme, and to miss those properties which distinguish the other letters in *Don Carlos* and make them revealing symbols of Schiller's new existential and philosophical attitude.

The Posa letter, with its faked text, its purpose of deception, is like a relic from former days within the chain of *Don Carlos* letters. Yet the way Schiller handles it dramatically brings it closer to the new variant of the letter motif. Before we learn anything about the content of the Posa letter (actually quite long before it: the intermission between the fourth and fifth acts intervenes), we witness its impact upon the recipient, the king. We do not know for sure who is the author of the letter (Taxis' statement is no more than a tantalizing hint), we do not know at all what it is about, yet in a climax of almost unbearable suspense we realize its shattering effect: the noise in the king's cabinet, the deadly silence, and finally, after much coaxing from the bystanders, Lerma's breathtaking pronouncement: "Der König hat geweint." This is not only one of the most magnificently dramatic scenes Schiller has ever written; it is at the same time highly relevant to our investigation into the treatment of the letter motif. The message which the letter carries has not yet become a part of the action on-stage, the "object" is kept in the background; what emerges, and most powerfully at that, is the havoc that it works in a human being, the "compound" which the message, still unknown to us, forms by joining the emotional nuclei of a soul.

When finally, not before the third scene of the fifth act, the content of this truly devastating letter is being disclosed, the objective side, the message itself, is played down considerably. Before he tells us what he actually incorporated in his letter, Posa has this to say:

> Wenn ich den König irrte? Wenn es mir
> Gelänge, selbst der Schuldige zu scheinen?
> Wahrscheinlich oder nicht!—Für ihn genug,
> Scheinbar genug für König Philipp, weil
> Es übel ist. (V, 3)

It is noteworthy how casually the content that the letter will eventually embody is being treated. "Wahrscheinlich oder nicht": the objective message is of small importance as long as it has those properties to which the given disposition of its recipient, the king, will respond. As it befits great poetry, the language itself tells the story. Within three lines the root "schein-" appears no less than three times: "scheinen—wahrscheinlich—scheinbar." What matters is the "appearance;" not the objective reality, but that which enters the subjective consciouness, be it ever so illusionary. Here again, disaster is not caused so much by the communication *per se*, but by the human involvements of the receiver, who will find in the message what he is conditioned and inclined to find anywhere. It is man's taint which taints the communicative sign.

To break off our discussion at this point, is justified by more than the merely arbitrary reason of convenience. The "treacherous sign" will indeed continue to play its fateful part in the dramatic productions of the fully mature Schiller. Yet hardly ever will it again appear in the guise of the letter. Its function will be taken over by suprahuman "messages": the stars in the *Wallenstein* trilogy, the thunderclaps in *Die Jungfrau von Orleans*, the oracles in *Die Braut von Messina*. To assess their relevance we must await a later investigation. The burden of the present discussion was to restore to the letters in Schiller's early plays, so often maligned as clumsy and contrived theatrical gadgets, their value as metaphors of the highest order. The justification for our attempt at giving a purely mechanical device its rightful poetic dignity is to be found, if such justification were needed, in Schiller's Preface to *Die Braut von Messina*. "Alles Äussere bei einer dramatischen Vorstellung... ist nur ein Symbol des Wirklichen. Der Tag selbst auf dem Theater ist nur ein künstlicher, die Architektur ist nur eine symbolische, die metrische Sprache selbst ist ideal." And "ideal" in this sense is the technical instrument which appears in Schiller's early plays so consistently as the lever of plot and action: the letter.

# GLORY AND DECLINE OF THE *BOURGEOIS:*
# SCHILLER AND DUMAS *FILS*

Whole generations have shed bitter tears over her fate, crowned heads in their regal *boudoirs* no less than cooks and chambermaids in their servant quarters. Strait-laced and unrelentingly proper matrons of the most respectable families had just as good a cry as the slightly worn girls of easy virtue; and storms of applause shook backdrops and stage sets, when Marguerite Gautier whispered herself to death in a score of languages or, as La Traviata, poured her last breath into breathtaking runs of coloratura in all the opera houses from San Francisco to Moscow. Yet we know that "Marguerite Gautier" is only a stage name, a pseudonym for Marie Duplessis, who, as one of the brightest stars in the sky of the Parisian demimonde, inspired the author of *La Dame aux Camélias* no less than she was to inspire, a little later, Théophile Gautier and Franz Liszt, and a host of other young artists—more or less gifted, but always qualifying well financially. For her contemporaries Marguerite Gautier and Marie Duplessis became so indistinguishable that, in a niche of the tombstone of the real Parisian grisette, a wreath of artificial camellias was sealed in order to identify her forever with her glamorous sister on the stage. In 1848—the year of the publication of Dumas' novel from which the play was to be drawn—everyone in Paris knew that Marguerite Gautier and Marie Duplessis were one and the same. And yet it may be that Marguerite has quite a different ancestry as well, that she borrowed traits from a literary model no less than from a living one, and that her real sister is not buried under a wreath of camellias in the Montmartre cemetery but lives on in one of the great plays of German literature, Schiller's *Kabale und Liebe.*

At first thought this hypothesis may seem absurd, and there is indeed no direct evidence to support it. Only this can be stated with certainty: the rise and fall of Marie Duplessis does not account entirely for the lachrymose story of Marguerite Gautier; to be sure, Marguerite's physical appearance, her seductive charm, her consumptive cough are Marie's; but neither her character nor the plot of the play corresponds to the historical facts. In his "A propos de la Dame aux Camélias," Dumas admits: "Marie Duplessis n'a pas eu toutes les aventures pathétiques que je prête à Marguerite Gautier. Elle n'a pu jouer, à son grand regret, que le premier et le deuxième acte de la pièce." There is no indication that the remaining three acts owe anything to a play so different in tone, intention, and literary value as Schiller's *Kabale und Liebe*.

The only reference in Dumas' play to anything German is Gustave's remark: "Nous avons l'air d'un roman allemand ou d'une idylle de Goethe, avec de la musique de Schubert" (III, 3), from which it would be hard to infer any serious familiarity with German literature on the part of the playwright. Yet, granted the author's ignorance, there is still a possibility that he became acquainted with the action of Schiller's play in French form, and at a time so propitious as to suggest strongly an influence upon *La Dame aux Camélias*.

Early in 1847 Dumas *père* and *fils* returned from an extended journey through Spain. Shortly after their arrival in Marseilles, the younger Dumas learned of the premature death of Marie Duplessis, his former mistress. He decided that a fictionalized story of Marie Duplessis would provide a good way to break into print and to pay homage, at the same time, to a not yet forgotten stormy love affair. He must have started work almost immediately, for in 1848 the novel, *La Dame aux Camélias*, was published.

On June 11, 1847 the Théâtre-Historique, owned and managed by Dumas *père*, opened its new season with a performance of the elder Dumas' *Intrigue et Amour*, a translation of Schiller's *Kabale und Liebe*, executed with the highhandedness and dash characteristic of the author of *Le Comte de Monte-Cristo*. Père and *fils*, always on good terms, were particularly close during this period. It is probable that the father was working on the translation of Schiller's play while traveling in Spain, and it is equally probable that the son became familiar with its plot.

In setting out on his own first literary venture, the younger Dumas may have found his father's translation of *Kabale und Liebe* quite fruitful. The basic situation, commonplace as it may be, could be taken with little change from Schiller's play: the passionate love of two young people, doomed to shipwreck on the rock of social conventions uncompromisingly upheld by the young man's father. To be sure, Luise Miller and Marguerite Gautier belong to two different moral and historical worlds; yet it is easily conceivable that Luise's offer of renunciation gave young Dumas the idea for Marguerite's noble gesture. In the corresponding passage of his father's overdrawn translation, twice the length of the original text, young Dumas could read the following:

> Laisse-moi tout entier le mérite de mon dévouement, garde à ma douleur cette consolation de mon héroïsme; permets à ma conscience de se dire que j'ai rendu un fils à son père! C'est moi la véritable coupable . . . Ferdinand, résignons-nous, mon bien-aimé! Fuis-moi! Oh! comprends donc! je ne suis qu'un accident au milieu de ta vie, une pauvre fille que tu as rencontrée, par hasard, en te détournant de ton chemin. Reprends ce chemin que Dieu t'avait tracé et que tu eusses dû suivre toujours. Au bout de ce chemin tu trouveras un cœur noble, aimant, digne de toi. Beauté, richesse, naissance . . . qui te feront oublier la pauvre pâquerette perdue sous la mousse près de laquelle tu ne comprendras pas un jour que tu aies pu t'arrêter un seul instant (III, 4).

The entire plot, those three acts which Marie Duplessis had failed to live through, are here preshaped. There is only a small step from Luise's maudlin vision of the future to Marguerite's sentimental farewell to the world in which she bequeathes Armand to a future "belle jeune fille que tu épouses" (V, 8). In addition to the overall plot which *Kabale und Liebe* may have furnished, the tricks by which the intrigue is set in motion are strikingly similar. A letter written under pressure causes the lover to believe in the unworthiness of the loving and beloved girl. What Luise does under the threat of Wurm (III, 6), Marguerite does under the impulsion of her aroused conscience (III, 6). In both cases the purpose is the same—to tear the lover away from an undesirable attachment. In both cases the hero is made susceptible to the fabricated accusations by his jealousy, which, however, fails to account satisfactorily for his extraordinary credulousness both in Schiller and in Dumas. There is a family resemblance between the two young men so cruelly and easily cheated of their happiness. Is this brotherhood in misfortune and defeat not etched like an anagram into their very names? It certainly cannot be quite accidental that Ar*mand* D*u*val sounds like a clearly recognizable echo of Ferdi*nand* de *Wal*ter.

The deceit leads to the same results in both plays. The duped lover vents his rage on the woman who has so cruelly hurt him (*KL*, V, 2 and 7; *DC*, IV, 7), and subjects her to a brutal inquisition in order to force from her the admission that the shattering letter did not convey her real feelings. Marguerite's desperate affirmation, "pars, oublie-moi, il le faut, je l'ai juré," echoes Luise's self-condemnation: "Par l'inexorable vérité, Ferdinand, j'ai écrit cette lettre . . . Vous avez mon aveu, je me suis condamnée moi-même. Oh partez maintenant, partez." In both plays the rivals who have been used as decoys in the destructive scheme, Maréchal de Kalb and M. de Varvilles, respectively, will meet the heartbroken heroes at pistol point (*KL*, IV, 3; *DC*, IV 7). The duels, of course, fail to resolve the tragic misunderstanding. The heroine must perish, and only with her last breath will she be allowed to assure the hero once more of her undying love. In each case, her death amounts to a half-conscious suicide —Marguerite returning to her exhausting way of life, Luise snatching from Ferdinand the poisoned drink with which he wants to end his own misery in the version of Dumas *père*, which here takes the utmost liberty with Schiller's text.

More important than the elements of plot and action which *Kabale und Liebe* could supply, the very character of the heroine is already in the German play. The courtesan with the heart of gold is hardly a faithful portrait of Marie Duplessis, who always had considered the bank-account a more suitable place for gold deposits than the heart. To be sure, the *fille de joie* capable of true love and noble feelings is a familiar enough figure in French literature from *Manon Lescaut* to *Marion Delorme*; yet none of these courtesans are closer relatives of Marguerite Gautier than Lady Milford in *Kabale und Liebe*. There is little of Lady Milford's grandiloquent majesty and intellectual superiority in Marguerite Gautier. But the human pattern is the same—the woman who, facing hardship and the prospect of a dire future, permits herself to be supported by the wealthy or powerful men whom she despises, yet is never quite able to drown out the whisper of her conscience; and who, after meeting the man she can really love, is willing to sacrifice wealth and power in order to attain happiness and to regain some human decency. Apart from the references to prince and principality, could not Marguerite speak in exactly the same terms in which Lady Milford confides to her chambermaid?

> N'as-tu pas deviné que toutes ces fantaisies capricieuses, que cette soif incessante de plaisirs, n'étaient rien autre chose que des moyens d'étouffer dans mon cœur le seul désir que je n'avoue jamais, parce qu'il le remplit sans cesse? . . . je jetterai aux pieds du prince son cœur et sa principauté, et je fuirai, avec Walter, jusqu'au fond des déserts les plus reculés, jusqu'aux dernières limites de ce monde (II, 1).

This flight from a degrading world, the Rousseauan idyl "aux dernières limites de ce monde" which the princely mistress of

Schiller's play envisages as her supreme bliss and the means for her purification, become reality, a very precarious and transitory reality, in the withdrawal of Armand and Marguerite from Paris. Scattered throughout Dumas' play (II, 13; III, 3; III, 4) are echoes of Lady Milford's desperate pleadings with Ferdinand not to permit her to "se rejeter plus avant qu'elle n'avait fait encore dans les profondeurs du vice" (II, 4). Of course, these are more or less stock-in-trade responses of the fallen woman who, in the midst of dissipation, yearns for a dignified and untainted happiness. The same may be said of the extraordinary generosity in material matters, the goodheartedness and compassion, evident in both Marguerite and Lady Milford. Still, Schiller's courtesan certainly sharpened the image which Dumas was to project in his work. Although Marguerite is lacking in Lady Milford's resourcefulness, in her virile determination to impose her will upon the beloved and her entire surroundings, there is in both women, at least in the beginning of their planning for the future, a certain amount of unscrupulousness and recklessness. Lady Milford is willing to exploit the political intrigue and the prince's infatuation to further her own plans, and to feign at least consent to the plot that is being hatched by Minister von Walter. By the same token, Marguerite sees nothing objectionable in obtaining from a former admirer the considerable sum of money which will enable her to live comfortably with Armand.

## II

The demonstration of this generic dependence and relationship between the two plays would be idle and pedantic, were it not for the fact that it can illustrate the change of the mental climate which occurred in Europe in the decades between the composition of Schiller's *Kabale und Liebe* and Dumas' *Dame aux Camélias*. Precisely because the two plays are so similar, the shift that has come about in the underlying social and moral philosophies becomes conspicuous and significant. Needless to say that a view concentrating only on the sociological implications does not do full justice to Schiller's play and the depth of his tragic vision.

Schiller's play is worthy of the man on whom the French bourgeoisie, victorious in the great Revolution, was to bestow the patent of an honorary citizen. It is the battle cry and marching order of a class determined to challenge and to fight the *ancien régime*, which brutally destroys the happiness of two innocent people destined for each other. The lines are drawn as sharply as possible—here the rotten court which taints all who traffic with it, there the honest world of the upright, industrious bourgeois. The private human tragedy of the two lovers transcends itself at every point; it serves as an inexorable accusation of a political system which feeds upon the heartblood of its citizens. One of the most impressive features of the play's structure is that the violent, open accusation of the guilty rises, so to speak, from the corpses of the victims.

Seventy years pass. The bourgeoisie has won and secured its victory. There is no external enemy left to be fought. The aristocrats in Dumas' play are harmless playboys whose charm fights a losing battle with their insipid foolishness. The only function they can still fulfill is that of the exploited substitute; they have become substitute fathers, substitute lovers. The little power that is left to them they owe to money, which is actually the instrument and yardstick of power of the bourgeoisie. The financial transaction—loan and sale, mortgage and liquidation—has become the objective correlative of man's deeds and emotions. In *Kabale und Liebe* money and valuables point toward a distorted order of values; they are tainted and demoniacal, the fruit and tool of man's dehumanization. Lady Milford's jewels are the transformed lifeblood of the Duke's subjects, and the purse filled with ducats which Ferdinand offers old Miller represents the shabby indemnity for the death of Luise. Wherever money and money's worth hold sway, human dignity and human rights have been viciously violated. In *La Dame aux Camélias*, on the other hand, man has settled comfortably into a money-oriented society, he buys and sells, he borrows and lends, from the first act to the last. As the focus of power, there stands behind *Kabale und Liebe* the morally degenerate castle, behind *La Dame aux Camélias* the morally neutral stock exchange.

In the world of Dumas, the very respectability which the bourgeois has attained represents the wall which will crush the love of two young people. In Schiller's view the moral rectitude of the bourgeois was his main weapon. Just because he was pure and on the side of the angels, he was capable of love, man's loftiest gift and resource against the degrading power of intrigue, the weapon of the mighty. Love was his supreme and inalienable right, which a social order unwilling to grant him his inalienable rights had to fight with utter ruthlessness. His love itself was revolutionary. Seventy years later, it is the bourgeois who demands the abdication of man's most legitimate and vital urge—for the sake of the good reputation without which he would lose face and his highest values. Love must fall a victim to respectability. It is for this reason that the father who steps between the two lovers has changed his features so completely. Schiller's Minister von Walter is the unadulterated villain; his demand that the son renounce his happiness and the bent of his heart is clearly inhuman and indefensible, except from a perverted political point of view. But old M. Duval is in his full rights when he persuades Marguerite to give up her lover. He can afford to be the perfectly understanding, fair-minded gentleman that he is, because his argument is irresistible; the desire of the heart has to be stifled so that a righteous and unquestioned social system may be upheld. Who could possibly revolt against so sensible a demand, except one who is blinded by a misguided passion? Love's freedom has turned into "free love" which, just because it is so irresponsibly free, must give way to the austere responsibilities to which the bourgeoisie fell heir in its conquest of power. All that is left to us is tears that the heartbreaking separation is necessary; but necessary it certainly is.

Characteristically, the protagonists of Schiller's play must be swept from the stage by violence; murder and suicide are marshalled to bring about the solution. These "unnatural" deaths are a clear indication that the natural order of things has been crassly mutilated. In *La Dame aux Camélias*, nature obligingly cooperates with the established social system. No unnatural death is needed here; nature, with the help of an overgrowth of tuberculosis bacilli, sees to it that the disturbing element is eliminated. Love, as here presented, is a wayward upsetting experience that has to be outgrown. Schiller defiantly proclaimed the rights of love, because it was so genuine and beautiful that it must be victorious. Dumas bewails the helplessness of a love which has no possible claim to victory and exhausts itself in being merely beautiful.

A double standard has been evolved which to Schiller would have been unthinkable. The private and public spheres of man's life have fallen apart. Just because love is unacceptable, it gains the bitter-sweetness of a beautiful thing which is doomed, rightly doomed, to failure. It is, almost by definition, only temporary;

but its very frailty, its secretness, give it an irresistible appeal. Beauty is lavished upon the forbidden outcast (Marguerite with her charm and her cough is but a symbol of this fascinating and sickly world), as a compensation, so to speak, for social unacceptability.

The soundness and health of bourgeois existence have to be strictly maintained, but there is a great deal of bad conscience underneath this strictness. Beauty, lightness of heart, joy, and spontaneity have fled from this respectable world and have found refuge in a "half-world" which, no matter how despised and slandered, offers an outlet for the unfulfilled desires of the heart. The social morality of the bourgeoisie and human morality in general, for Schiller identical and inseparable, have parted company. The human heart goes begging in the clean but cold air of the accepted social world. A heavy price is extracted for the flawless impressiveness of the social structure—happiness and love have gone underground. Safe in his position, but impoverished in his heart, the bourgeois has become a melancholy skeptic.

There is in this world no longer room for a full existence, and for this reason substance and appearance fall apart. The bad girls and some of the bad boys are not so bad, after all; in fact, Marguerite outshines in her noble resignation all the decency and propriety with which the bourgeois has decked himself out. However, Marguerite's nobility consists precisely in the fact that she is willing to sacrifice herself to the concepts and ideas of the very class which has marked her as an outcast. By her readiness to become a victim she tacitly testifies to the superiority of those values which victimize her. Indeed, the great gesture of renunciation is not alien to Luise either. She can enact it because there stands behind this world and this life another realm, in which all distinctions of class and status become non-existent, in which truth eternal will triumph over the breach that runs through everything temporal. This way out is closed to Marguerite: she knows only *this* world with its tangled play of essence and appearance, and therefore this dizzying play becomes the all-pervading game and last law of her life.

But the same is true of the opposite camp. M. Duval, the champion of respectability and decency, is easily persuaded that the fallen woman is the truly noble one whom he can fully respect as a "human being," although he cannot possibly permit her to be even remotely connected with his family. There is a strikingly similar situation in *Kabale und Liebe*. In the course of Ferdinand's pathetic story a moment comes, when the father declares himself convinced and won over by the goodness and human decency of Luise. Actually, this admission is, of course, itself a gross deception and part of the hideous cabal, designed to sharpen and precipitate the disaster that is being prepared for the two lovers. But Minister von Walter's attitude is quite consistent at this moment: as soon as he announces this (feigned) change of mind, he withdraws his objections against the union between Luise and his son. Since he now finds Luise worthy of Ferdinand, all the obstacles are removed. How differently works the same constellation in *La Dame aux Camélias*! Old M. Duval is genuinely convinced of Marguerite's goodness and human decency. But this cannot sway him for a moment in his attempt to prevent the marriage of the two lovers. A somewhat tenuous compromise has been concluded between the two camps that actually exclude each other. The bourgeois admits that the noble heart beats on the opposite side, but the noble heart realizes full well that it has no place in the world of society.

Since one can no longer take onself and one's moral and social foundations quite seriously, since the mental reservation about one's own existence is always present, it can happen that the feigned and pretended take moral precedence over the true and real. It is characteristic that in Dumas' play the gesture by which the heroine achieves her greatest human stature is a lie, a concealment of the true emotions of her heart. Her greatness consists in the very fact that she is capable of playing a role which is utterly at variance with her innermost being.

The great moment of Schiller's *cocotte* comes when, after a long life of pretense and untruthfulness, she finally throws off her mask and frees herself from her sham existence. With Schiller, the revolutionary idealist, the awe-inspiring deed is a deed of liberation, of transcending in a heroic effort one's own petty existence, and making one's essential goodness and truth manifest in and against a hostile world. With Dumas, the tolerant and melancholy skeptic, the great deed is a deed of noble deceit, of accepting the onus of a sinful life, of playing, brave and resigned, the game of the world, with no other satisfaction than one's own consciousness of having done something good, which is good for the very reason that it will remain secret and utterly private.

With Dumas' *Dame aux Camélias* the proud genre of *bürger-*

*liches Trauerspiel* has run its course. What started as a clarion call against an inhuman social order which had to be overthrown now ends on the melancholy note of a resigned "such is life"—sad indeed, but "realistically" to be endured with a smile on one's lips while the heart is breaking. The tears which in Schiller were intended to wash away social ignominy and shame are now allowed to flow away freely, private and inconsequential tears dedicated to a sweet but private and inconsequential love affair.

# EICHENDORFF'S SYMBOLIC LANDSCAPE

It seems to me one of the most exciting and baffling characteristics of Eichendorff's art that, if I may use this paradox, his most profound insights are hidden on the surface. They travel, a strangely elusive contraband, in the full light of day, so that the last truths of his poetic vision, the whole web of his religious beliefs, his intellectual conceptions, his socio-ethical postulates transform themselves into the most deceptively simple folktunes, sung by his people with an ease and unconcern usually assigned in the secular psalter of a nation to that section which is headed "folk song, author unknown." Goethe's solemn warning with regard to the ultimate secret and mystery of life, his injunction "Tell it no one but the sages," was utterly lost on Eichendorff. He told it to every listening ear; and so it could happen that what in reality was an exploration and manifestation of truth, the poetic transmission of knowledge, was taken—or mistaken—as a bewitching play of lyrical mood and atmosphere.[1] A comprehensive and integrated view of life thus turned in the public's hand into a picture book, lovely and self-contained, easy to peruse; and for the reader it was easy to absorb its sensuous refulgence without comprehending the meaning of design, color, and composition.

Since this is the situation, it may not be amiss to focus, when searching for some of the hidden secrets of Eichendorff's art, on the smooth surface, to start with one of his most popular songs, a favorite with every youngster—and every *Männerchor*. Here is its third stanza:

> Da steht im Wald geschrieben
> Ein stilles, ernstes Wort
> Vom rechten Tun und Lieben,
> Und was des Menschen Hort.
> Ich habe treu gelesen
> Die Worte schlicht und wahr,
> Und durch mein ganzes Wesen
> Ward's unaussprechlich klar.[2]

---

1. Even so discerning and recent a critic as Otto F. Bollnow, *Unruhe und Geborgenheit* (Stuttgart, 1953), p. 146, labels Eichendorff's poetry as "im ausgeprägtesten Sinne Stimmungsdichtung." In his chapter on Eichendorff in *Geist der Goethezeit*, IV (Leipzig, 1953), 232-246, Hermann A. Korff shows a curious indecision whether to see in Eichendorff a creator of symbols or a weaver of bewitching moods. After some interesting initial attempts at interpretation, Korff loses himself in the shopworn generalities about music, spell, mood pictures.
2. *Eichendorffs Werke*, (Stuttgart: Cotta, 1953), I, 36. Throughout this

Here, as in a nutshell, we can grasp Eichendorff's conception of nature. It is for him the spatial medium upon which the word, the logos, is projected; not, to stress that right at the beginning, a second revelation by which the spirit manifests itself directly; not Scripture with a capital S, but the tablet on which the inscription appears; not the meaning but the hull in whose shape man's love and doing, his treasures and resort become visible; not the voice itself but the lips which actualize the speech. If we take Eichendorff's metaphor seriously, the word of which he speaks does not transmit itself spontaneously, is not absorbed by feeling, not unlocked by intuition or immersion, but it has to be read faithfully in order to yield its light inexpressible. All this is but another way of saying that for Eichendorff and in Eichendorff's work nature and landscape are a system of symbols; not, as has been so readily and generally assumed, an evocation of moods, a hypnotic stimulant of feeling, but a cryptogram which has to be deciphered, a pictorial sign language which (and this cannot surprise us now) is often referred to as a mass of hieroglyphs.[3] In his first great work, in *Ahnung und Gegenwart*, we read: "How true it is that each landscape has by nature an idea of its own which tries to become articulate, as if by stammering words, in its brooks, trees and mountains" (II, 96). And in his late short novel, *Eine Meerfahrt*, the hieroglyph is no longer used simply as a simile for nature, but actually becomes one and the same with her: "All around them the rising morning gilded over the initials of a wondrous, unknown writing" (II, 765)

Thus forewarned we ought not to yield unquestioningly to the sensuous magic of Eichendorff's landscapes, to the lure of their atmospheric spell; we shall have to "read" them faithfully, all the more faithfully the more plainly and truly they seem to speak. So it may be appropriate to begin with the plainest and truest of Eichendorff's works, with *Aus dem Leben eines Taugenichts*, and further with the plainest and truest scene of the whole book. By "plain and true" I mean that here more plainly than anywhere in the little story a locality is clearly identified

---

article I refer to this edition, vol. I: *Gedichte Epen Dramen;* vol. II: *Erzählende Dichtungen.*

3. See Liselotte Dieckmann's penetrating article, "The Metaphor of Hieroglyphics in German Romanticism," *CL*, VII (1955), 306-312. Alice Hirschfeld's dissertation, *Die Natur als Hieroglyphe* (Breslau, 1936), deals only, and quite unimaginatively at that, with Hamann, Herder, Lenz, and Novalis.

and geographically fixed: the immediate surroundings of Rome, and finally the city itself.[4] Yet what does our little hero see when he approaches the goal of his long and circuitous roamings? Still quite some distance away, at the mere mention of the name, there rises from his memory a fantastic landscape. As a boy, still in his childhood home, he saw mirrored on the sky among the moving clouds a city with strange mountains and precipices on the blue sea, with golden gates and shimmering towers upon which angels are singing in golden gowns—a fairy tale dream, we must say, hardly a description of the city of Rome. But then, after all, he is still some distance away, just imagining things in anticipation. Yet now he comes closer; the city, so he tells us, is actually spreading underneath his feet. But what does he see now? A long wisp of fog hovering above a sleeping lion, over whom mountains stand guard like dark giants. At that point we are thoroughly in doubt whether the landscape which Eichendorff conjures up before us has anything to do with Rome and its environs. Our doubts become certainty when, reading on, we hear that before finally reaching the city gates the little Good-for-nothing has to cross a big lonely heath, bleak and still as the grave, covered with ruins and withered, twisted shrubbery. But that isn't enough. Suddenly the underworld opens up before us: buried below the gloomy heath there is an old city from which the heathens often rise to the surface to lead the lonely wanderers astray. No less than three times does the word "grave" appear in this short description of the bleak plain, and three times as well the word "heath" plus its derivation "heathen"—a derivation which, we are convinced now, we must not take as an etymological pun, but as a metaphysical signpost. Those ghosts from the underworld have no power over our little hero; he strides on without looking to right or left. For now the city rises before him, and lo and behold! it *is* the city he had seen in his childhood dreams, with gates and towers shimmering in golden light as if angels were standing on every pinnacle. Do we still have to ask what this Roman landscape means? Is it not clear that we are treated here not to a scenic description but to a theological vision: the celestial city, beginning and end of man's roaming, primordial image and distant lure of salvation,

---

4. I have given a close reading of this passage in my article, "Der Taugenichts ante portas," *JEGP*, LII (1953), 509-524; now also reprinted in *Aurora, 1956* [Eichendorff Almanach] (Kulturwerk Schlesien, Neumarkt), pp. 70-81.

reachable only by crossing, undaunted, the heathenish heath, dry, lightless, and full of subterranean temptations? Only if we faithfully read the "word" which transmits the hope for redemption and terror of damnation as it is inscribed in this Roman landscape, only then shall we discover the little Good-for-nothing in his full stature. He is the brave Christian knight on the road: his childish naïveté is the seal of innocence, his stubborn love for the lady fair is the shield and weapon of faith, his wanderlust is the quest for man's true homestead, his moments of dejection are the fear and trembling which seize us at the realization that we do not belong, do not rest secure in God's hand, his merry singing and fiddling are a grateful paean in praise of the Creator.

Landscape as visible theology, serving as the key with which deeper perspectives of the unfolding story are opened up—this is a feature occurring again and again in Eichendorff's writings. Sometimes the scenic picture carries within itself its own commentary, or at least a clue to its meaning. In *Ahnung und Gegenwart* Friedrich, the protagonist, has a dream in which

> he saw an unlimited horizon, sea, rivers and countries, immense wrecked cities with broken gigantic columns, the old manor house of his childhood strangely in ruins. Some ships floated in the background toward the sea; upon one of them stood his deceased father as he had often seen him in portraits, looking unusually serious. Yet everything was as if wrested from the twilight, vague and unrecognizable as a huge blurred picture; for a dark storm swept over the whole view, as if the world were burnt, and the immense smoke settling down over the devastation. (II, 165 f.)

Here there is no doubt for a moment that we are observing the eschatological vision of the apocalypse and not simply an uncanny Romantic landscape. In the foreground of the picture is a child of "wonderful dignity and beauty" who points with a rosy finger at the wild scenery and, at the end of the description, emerges again, this time leaning against a huge cross, and talking to the sleeper: "If you love me truly, go down with me; as a sun you will rise again, and the world will be free." The whole Christian doctrine of salvation, including the passion, the day of judgment, and the resurrection has here become tangible in a land- and seascape.

It will not do to dismiss the almost allegorical character of this scene and scenery by pointing out that we are, after all, dealing with a dream vision. The very greatness of Eichendorff's work and world consists just in the fact that vision and description of so-called reality are inseparable, that for him vision is really that which can be seen. It can almost be stated as a rule that the more clearly a description is related to a specific locality, the more visionary it turns out to be. We noticed it in the Rome episode of *Aus dem Leben eines Taugenichts*; we find it anew in the opening scene of *Ahnung und Gegenwart*. Again, it is the only instance in the whole voluminous novel where a concrete locality is pictured.

> Whoever has traveled up river on the Danube from Regensburg knows the magnificent spot which is called "the whirl." Steep mountain gorges surround the strange place. In the middle of the stream rises a curiously shaped rock, from which a tall cross looks down, consoling and peaceable, into the chute and collision of the raging waves. No human being is to be seen here, no bird sings; there is only the continuous, century-old roaring of the woods on the slopes, and of the terrible vortex which draws all life into its unfathomable abyss. The mouth of the vortex opens from time to time, with a glimmer dark as the eye of death. (II, 9 f.)

For all we know that may be the description of a specific scene near Regensburg, but undeniably it is the vision of life's stream, rushing madly and in circular motion into the dark mouth of death but for the unshakable rock upon which the sign and voucher of salvation was erected. Clearly, then, Eichendorff's landscapes are not self-contained pictures, vehicles for the transmission of subjective emotions, but they express the ontology of man's fate and existence.

He certainly meant it seriously, and not merely as a noncommittal outburst of lyric enthusiasm when, in *Ahnung und Gegenwart*, he had Leontin exclaim: "How earnestly and mirthfully life, boundless and still unknown, looks at us out of woods and mountains, out of young girls' faces beckoning from bright castles, out of streams and old fortresses!" (II, 40). Indeed, woods and mountains, streams and fortresses serve again and again as a prefiguration of life still unknown; they are not picturesque surroundings, but the pictorial interior of action, situation, and character. The empty highways which the Good-for-nothing sees from the treetop, extending in the early morning light like bridges far over the mountains and valleys, are not simply a panorama, but the very reminder to go on with his quest; and the Danube is not just a river, but the promise and, finally, the actuality of finding one's way home. For this reason, in our story it can flow through a geographical location we know to be incorrect: very close to the Italian frontier, so close that the Good-for-nothing can see it as a shimmering ribbon from the mountain ridge that separates Italy and Austria. Should we call to Eichendorff's attention that there is actually a distance of a good three hundred kilometers between the northernmost point of Italy and the Danube? And what if he wanted to call to our attention that the Good-for-nothing is coming home, sailing into port, and that for this occasion the Danube must be on hand? Landscape, thus presented, is not ornamental but emblematic; its iconography will again and again reveal the existential condition of man, or at least the existential condition of the particular character who moves in this scenery. Indeed, it should be possible to read the whole action of the short story *Das Marmorbild*—search and temptation and final redemption of its hero, Florio—by just looking at the scenery through which he passes: initiation into life and into the community of the living—a lovely green meadow strewn with flowers, dotted with friendly tents in whose shadows a gay crowd is strolling; the threat of seduction and sin—a mysterious garden, full of exotic, burningly bright flowers; the breaking of the deadly languid spell of the enchantress—a bright peaceful plein-air scene with a sturdy gardener who, shovel over his shoulder, starts his day's work on his little plot of land; the final shaking off of the evil bewitchment and the opening up of the new good life—a horseback journey into the blossoming, fertile spring country, bathed in the light of the morning sun, in the company of the true friend, the true beloved and her father.

To realize the degree of complexity and completeness with which the emblematic landscape foreshadows the existential condition, it may be worth looking more closely at one of the scenic designs within the sequence just mentioned. When Florio for the first time strays into the orbit of the dangerous enchantress, her garden is described as follows:

> High galleries formed by arched beech trees received him there with their solemn shadows, among which golden birds fluttered like blown-off blossoms while tall, strange flowers, the like of which Florio had never seen, dreamily moved to and fro in the soft wind with their yellow and red chalices. In the great loneliness there splashed monotonously innumerable fountains, playing with gilded spheres ... Florio looked in surprise at the trees, fountains, and flowers, for it seemed to him as if all this had become submerged long ago, as if the stream of days were flowing above him with light, bright ripples, and the garden were lying down there enchanted and in bondage, dreaming of life gone by. (II, 321).

No doubt the park itself lives under a spell, but beyond that the things in the garden reveal the very nature of the spell which, soon enough, will envelop Florio himself. Let us try to decipher the hieroglyph which this strange garden represents.[5] It is a space sealed off by the vaulted tree branches against the sky, the heavenly light, filled with shadows, uncanny shadows indeed. For if, as we are told, the birds are fluttering among them, we cannot conceive of them as simply shadows on the ground thrown by the beech trees, but willy-nilly they assume a third dimension, and with that the lightless, shadowy world of the tree gallery changes imperceptibly into the ominous world of shadows. The birds which populate this world move like blown-off blossoms, not propelled by their own will, but drifting passively, helplessly gliding downwards, animals without anima. In this world vegetative life, telluric life, the flowers, grow tall, they are bound to the earth, caught within themselves—dreaming —glowing proudly in their fiery colors—red and yellow—burning with their own light since we know that the light from above, from the genuine source of all light, cannot filter through to them. And the fountains complete the picture of vacuity and futility: a monotonous *perpetuum mobile*, a motion continuously sinking back into itself, a senseless playing with shimmering toys, up and down, rising and falling, incessantly. Do we still need Florio's observation that this garden is submerged, cut off from the stream of days which, in bright ripples, passes over it? The shadowiness which the day cannot penetrate, the emasculated will, the captivity in one's own self, the burning color which needs no outside source of light, the automatic motion spending and replenishing itself by inane circling—this is the garden of sin, sin as a garden; and if we were called upon to give it a name, sloth, the deadliest of the seven deadly sins, might do better than any other. This garden, as scenery, evokes precisely the horror which a little later, when Florio enters the castle of the enchantress, will be produced in a scene. The spell which the garden prefigured will then become actuality, with all the familiar elements present: the shadows, the paralysis of the will, the deadly introversion and repetition, magnificently expressed by the fact that in all the female pictures on the tapestries Florio seems to recognize the sorceress' countenance, in all the male

---

5. A short allusion to the "meaning" of this garden is found in Josef Kunz, *Eichendorff: Höhepunkt und Krise der Spätromantik* (Oberursel, 1951), pp. 171 f.

likenesses his own features. Yet Florio will be saved. While the temptation is closing in on him, he hears from the outside an old pious song, and at the moment of highest danger he prays "from the deepest depth of his soul: God, my Lord, do not let me get lost in the world!" (II, 338). The break-through has come: grace, waiting and offered, has been accepted by man's prayer; sloth has been vanquished. The spell is broken. When Florio emerges, he finds another garden, tiny and modest, shimmering in the bright light of morning, with vines growing sturdily around a little farmhouse on whose roof there strut, merrily cooing, the turtle-doves, the birds of sweet and faithful love.

Since Eichendorff's landscape is not meant to be taken as rich and diversified ornament, nor as the expression of psychological moods with their innumerable possibilities of nuance, it becomes understandable that he can, yes, that he must, limit himself to a bare minimum of scenic features.[6] He has often been blamed for his narrow range, his almost monomaniac fixation on the same basic settings—garden, forest, meadow, river, mountain gorges, heath—and for the primitive simplicity of the colors which he has on his palette, and which are lacking in variety, shades, and transitions.[7] Yet if we realize that his landscapes actually enact the basic situations of religious existence, quest and home-coming, threat of temptation and hope for salvation, nearness to and distance from God, then it will not surprise us to see the same panorama over and over again. What mattered to him was to bring into sharp focus, through the hieroglyph of the landscape, the essential truth he had to convey, and for this reason the scenic view had to be revelatory, but not richly impressionistic or realistically individualized. The two gardens in *Eine Meerfahrt*, one barren and shadowed by rocks, the other neat, green, and nestling under a cross, picture not just real estate, but the real state of souls, some dried up, the others fertile because they

---

6. Rudolf Ibel, *Weltschau deutscher Dichter* (Hamburg, 1948), p. 106, states somewhat too sharply; "Die Elemente seiner Dichtung, der Spielraum der Bilder und Situationen sind sehr begrenzt. Wer *eine* Erzählung kennt, kennt sie fast alle."
7. René Wehrli offers a very thorough investigation into the materials of Eichendorff's scenic views in *Eichendorffs Erlebnis und Gestaltung der Sinnenwelt*, Wege zur Dichtung, XXXII (Frauenfeld/Leipzig, 1938). See also Bollnow, pp. 228-231. In his essay, "Die symbolische Formelhaftigkeit von Eichendorffs Prosastil" (in *Form und Innerlichkeit*, Bern, 1955, pp. 177-209) Werner Kohlschmidt discusses these stereotypic views as genuine poetic *topoi*, and not just picturesque props.

have been moistened by the waters of eternal life. Any attempt at being more explicit about the two gardens would have made their meaning less explicit. To be sure, it is undeniable that the same essential scenic feature, the garden for instance, appears with an almost monotonous frequency in Eichendorff's work. Yet the word that it transmits can be made highly variable by a slight rearrangement of its basic elements, just as the same letters in a different sequence result in very different meanings. Let us look at the scenic surroundings of Romana's castle in *Ahnung und Gegenwart*: "It stood like a mirage high above a vast indescribable chaos of gardens, vineyards, trees, and rivers; the very slope around the manor house was one big garden in which innumerable fountains jetted from the green . . . Strange exotic trees and plants stood there like half-uttered, bewitched thoughts, shimmering water rays crisscrossed in crystal arches high above them, foreign birds, brooding and dreaming, sat everywhere among the dark green shades" (II, 155). We surely recognize every single feature in this scenery as old acquaintances: the trees and fountains, the exotic birds and flowers. And yet this landscape does have a character and a meaning very much its own. What strikes us is the impression of formlessness, the intermingling of land, water, vegetative growth, which all seem to run into one. In fact, the different features of this scenery are quite indistinguishable to our eye—we cannot draw a clear line between them. The slope which the castle crowns is, so we are told, one big garden, but in the preceding line we read that the manor house rises over a blend of gardens, vineyards, trees, and rivers. It is more than mere carelessness when the author pronounces this kaleidoscopic confusion "indescribable"; what we are here dealing with is the unformed, the unarticulated, and it is certainly more than accidental that the trees and plants stand in this *tohu-bohu* like half-uttered thoughts. We may do well to take quite literally the word "chaos" in our passage, a state in which the elements, not yet separated, shapeless, not bent by the creative command into a clear order, rule supreme. With this we have arrived at the very essence of the mistress of the chaotic garden, of Romana. She is undefined and undefinable, a kaleidoscopic soul in revolt against the principle of the all-ordering spirit; matter, pure element, which refuses to acknowledge the creative, form-giving will of the Highest. From here stem her strange iridescence, her abrupt and bewildering appearances and disappearances, her indistinctness uncannily symbolized in the hunting scene where, madly galloping on her steed, she seems to materialize in different places at the same time. As in her garden, the elements, intermingling, not yielding to the hand which makes cosmos out of chaos, hold sway, and it will not surprise us that after her suicide the consuming element, the fire, breaks loose and destroys her world, her castle. Before the catastrophe occurs Friedrich talks to Romana in her house, and pointing to the scenery which becomes visible through the windows he exhorts her: "have a good look at the miraculous structure of the century-old trees down there, at the aged giant rocks and the eternal sky above, see how the elements, usually destroying each other as enemies, willingly bend their rough, ragged necks and their innate wildness before their Lord, carry and maintain the world in wise order and piety" (II, 223). This is Friedrich's rejection of Romana, but is not the scenery which he points to, the stress on structure, order, clear distinction of forms, a rejection and refutation of Romana's original garden with its blurred outlines, its intermingling of land, water, and vegetation, its inarticulateness and chaos?

I hope it has become clear from the foregoing examples that Eichendorff's landscapes are not decorative material introduced at will for the sake of background or atmosphere. Yet it is not even enough to state that they are illustrative of metaphysical positions, revealing that "life still unknown" which will become manifest as the story unfolds. They have beyond that a definitely structural function and serve as the joints and hinges on which the whole work moves and swings. The scenic views are like landmarks on a net of coordinates which, if properly connected, represent the curve, the rise, turning point, and fall of the outer and inner action. They are the form into which the concrete is being poured, the scaffold which helps determine shape, angle, and perspective of the edifice. To trace the whole complicated pattern of design is clearly impossible, yet the demonstration of some points of intersection may elucidate the structural function of Eichendorff's landscapes. On the simplest level the two gardens in *Eine Meerfahrt,* of which we have spoken, may serve as a case in point. Taken separately, they symbolize pagan and Christian life. Yet if we connect these two landmarks, we arrive at an axis around which the inner and outer action of the story revolves. Again and again, landscape is used as a leitmotif, not only in the sense that we associate previous situations, physical or emotional adventures, with recurring features, but in the very literal sense that they guide us through the layout and the curve of the story. If, for instance, we take the mill of Good-for-nothing's father as a landmark, we can plot the structure of the whole book. Three times the mill appears at the beginning of a chapter, and every time it proclaims readiness and exodus: I'm set to go; set for any place, at the beginning of the first chapter; set for Italy, at the beginning of the third; set for Rome, at the beginning of the seventh. But the same view, the mill in the green valley, also appears three times in the middle of chapters, and then it means: I'm lost, oh were I home!; in the middle of the first chapter when the close air of the midday heat oppresses our little hero; in the middle of the third when he is about to be caught in the dark forest by the two "robbers"; in the middle of the sixth when he whiles away his days, without aim and direction, in the strange Italian castle. Interestingly enough, after the Good-for-nothing has entered Rome, after the real Rome, the celestial city, has once appeared on the scene, the mill in the father's meadow can vanish from the pages of the book. The remainder, even if it still offers detours and confusion, is dénouement, home-coming; the scenic image which signalized the high points of departure to new horizons, the low points of forlornness in the world, is no longer used because it is no longer needed.

A glance at *Ahnung und Gegenwart* may even more convincingly reveal the structural function of Eichendorff's landscapes, their use in illuminating the pattern and design—all the more illuminating since here the pattern proves extremely complex. At the beginning of the twentieth chapter we read that Friedrich suddenly recognizes the landscape around him as the one where his journey had started at the beginning of the book. Quite literally the story has returned to its origin, Friedrich is again at his starting point. But starting point means home, and man's home is at the same time his destination. Advancing, if it is real advancing and not just running in circles, consists in tracing one's steps back to the origin. And this is exactly what the novel does from this point on: while it advances it traces its steps back, and it is through the reappearance of the landscapes that this movement is achieved and organized. The story moves ahead toward its end, the many loose threads of action are now being gathered up and woven into the final pattern and resolution, but the scenery, familiar to us from the beginning, proclaims at every point: we are back again, returning to the origin, approaching home. There is the mill in the dark glade where Friedrich had his first encounter with a hostile world, and now it has reappeared, cleansed of danger and threat; what at his start into the world was a deceptive and treacherous refuge, is now a true and friendly shelter. The landscape of his childhood years, which he conjured up at the beginning of the book in his confessions to Rosa, is present again, really spreading out before him: "Suddenly Friedrich remembered: 'This is my home,' he called out. 'What I see here and all around, everything reminds me like a magic mirror of the place where I grew up as a child. The same forests, the same paths, only the beautiful ancient castle I find no more on the mountain'" (II, 250). While the line of the story and action declines and falls toward its end, the scene and scenery rise higher and higher until Friedrich will finally reach the top of the mountain, and on it the cross, home and destination, point of origin and terminal in one. It is the landscape that makes the design apparent, design in its double meaning: purpose and aim as well as structure and composition of the narrative.

    Here again we have been made aware that the true function of Eichendorff's landscapes is the creation of perspectives, the opening up of vistas into the metaphysical depth of his stories, into the organism and pattern of his literary designs. And it is the very phenomenon of perspective which offers a most fascinating problem of Eichendorff's presentation of scenery. It has been often and duly noted that his favorite view of the land is from a point above, a total panorama seen from great height.[8] The same situation repeats itself in his works over and over: a horseback ride or a walk through the mountains and forests, a sudden clearing in the woods, and there, far below the observer, stretches the green valley with fields, gardens, and villages, and in the distance, but still quite distinct, the shimmering band of a river. Without exaggeration we might call it *the* Eichendorff perspective. But why is this specific view so persistent? It is clear that Eichendorff insists on distance; nature and landscape are experienced as objects, distinctly removed from the organ through which they are perceived. "Man is," so we read in Eichendorff's *Geschichte des Romans*, "so to speak the eye of nature"; while being part of it he sees it as the thing opposite him, he is at every moment actor and spectator in one. Yet this means

---

8. Also noted by Ibel, p. 106.

that his view is in perspective, that he rejects the blissful claim of identity of man and nature which has always been considered the hallmark of romanticism. A scene like the one in *Werther*— the hero lying in the field, feeling the little blades of grass, the tiny worms and insects pressing against his heart, overcome by the moment "when the world grows dim before my eyes, and earth and sky are absorbed into my soul"—such a scene of mystic exaltation is unthinkable in Eichendorff, and I suspect he would find it quite revolting.[9] He knew nothing of this ardent union with the universe and, through it, the universal spirit which is so overpoweringly expressed in young Goethe's Ganymede-cry "embracing while embraced," this ecstatic fusion of subject and object in a quasi-erotic act. Faust's attempt to burrow into the heart of nature is the very opposite of Eichendorff's attitude, of the distance-conscious view from mountain peak down into the valley which is so permanent a feature in his work. Against Faust's exclamation "Feeling is all," the superman's empathic dissolution into the great Oneness, Eichendorff would pit a "Seeing is all," watching a spectacle offered to our eyes. Indeed, "What a spectacle!;" yet Eichendorff would never continue with Faust's exasperated and morose complaint "but oh, naught but a spectacle!"

All this is, of course, nothing but a corollary to Eichendorff's more basic insistence upon the separation of nature, the created world, and God, the Creator. Ever since the days of the dawning Renaissance God had been drawn into the creation, until finally in the pantheistic creed of identity nature became the direct revelation of the absolute spirit. German romanticism was a high point in this development; here the complete fusion of the material and the spiritual was proclaimed—God had immersed himself totally into the world. In Novalis' and Schelling's magic idealism matter and spirit are only two different forms of the same substance; Schleiermacher could call nature poetry a manifestation of religion; the great painter Philipp Otto Runge, when making a first sketch for his "Ruhe auf der Flucht," transformed

---

9. A passage in *Ahnung und Gegenwart* seems almost a direct refutation of Werther's self-abandonment in nature, his loving embrace of "blades of grass and tiny worms": "He [Leontin] tried to fall asleep. But when the blades of grass, amidst the incessant and monotonous humming of the bees, moved to and fro over his head . . . his heart was oppressed by such an anxiety that he jumped up quickly. He climbed a high tree which stood upon the ridge and rocked himself in its wavering crown over the sultry valley just to rid himself of the terrible stillness in and around him" (II, 102).

the Biblical scene into pure landscape: Joseph represented by an old, gnarled tree, the Christ Child by a blooming shrub, Mary by a gentle slope to which the shrub is clinging. For Eichendorff, the devout Catholic, such a divinization of nature amounted to paganism; and I think it is for this reason that his work does not contain the infinite, all-enveloping landscape in which the romanticists reveled, the fusion of the real and the ideal, the temporal and the eternal.[10] This explains the great clarity of Eichendorff's scenic views no matter how wide the vista that is being offered. Even the river in the far distance is still distinct; it does not merge with the sky above.[11] It has been often noted that one of his favorite landscape features, the garden, has, its tendency to relapse into a wilderness notwithstanding, a definite eighteenth-century rococo tinge. But I would take exception to the common explanation that the form and pattern of his gardens were determined by the park of Lubowitz manor, the estate where he was born and grew up. He needed the rococo garden because its clear arrangement, its distinct form and design point to a gardener in the background, a creator, a supreme maker who has drawn, sketched, and shaped this plot of land. Eichendorff hardly ever allows the separating line between heaven and earth to become hazy and melting. To be sure, in his most beautiful poem, "Mondnacht" (I, 360), one of the—shall we say ten—perfect lyrical marvels in the German language, the heavens do kiss the earth. But it seems to me significant that this union of above and below is presented as an unreal condition

---

10. In his authoritative book *Die Philosophie der unendlichen Landschaft* (Halle, 1932), Helmut Rehder has dealt fully with the gradual rise and ultimate triumph of this fusion in romantic thinking and poetry. He does not overlook the fact that Eichendorff stands outside of this general tendency. Whether he is right in claiming this this "unromantic" attitude toward nature marks Eichendorff as a child of the Biedermeier (p. 194 f.), I am not prepared to argue. The fact as such is undeniable in spite of Bollnow's assertion of Eichendorff's "pantheism" (p. 213), a statement somewhat qualified later (p. 244), and Ibel's remark that Eichendorff "Gott immer wieder als das allumfassende und alldurchdringende Weltwesen, als die Weltseele, erlebt und erfasst" (p. 133). This "divinization" of the landscape, as revealed in romantic landscape painting, especially in the work of Philipp Otto Runge, is lucidly demonstrated—and rejected from a Catholic point of view—by Otto Georg von Simson in his article, "Philipp Otto Runge and the Mythology of Landscape," *Art Bull.*, XXIV (1942), 335-350. I am greatly indebted to Professor Simson's exposition. Runge's picture "Ruhe auf der Flucht," to which I referred, is reproduced in this article, both the first sketch and the final version.
11. I definitely contradict Ibel's contention that Eichendorff's landscape "meist in eine unermessliche Ferne mündet" (p. 107).

—"It was *as if* the heavens/Had softly kissed the earth"—and that the second stanza with its sharp line-contours, its almost uncannily neat sequence of landscape images, banishes the fluidity and intermingling which is so appropriate to the mystic experience. Eichendorff's favorite view from on high creates distance between the here and there, it rejects the pantheistic monism of the phenomenal and absolute realms, of being and essence, of life and that which gives life. His nature and landscapes do not embody the meaning but they point to the meaning, they have the function of a cipher through which the real, which is the absolute transcendency, can be divined. It may very well be that it was this mode of experiencing the world which induced Dorothea Schlegel to suggest to Eichendorff "Ahnung und Gegenwart" as a suitable title for his first book.

Eichendorff's landscape—we stressed this at the very outset—is not revelation, not the manifestation of the eternal spirit, but it is creature and as such finite and temporal, so much so that one of the most fascinating features of his art is the mysterious correspondence between and coincidence of landscape and time. This is a topic much too comprehensive to be discussed here.[12] Yet everyone even slightly familiar with Eichendorff will recall how consistently at the climactic point of his stories the image of home, the castle with its gardens and forests, appears, this almost stereotyped landscape which points to youth, origin, to the whole cluster of metaphysical concepts and associations which Eichendorff connects with "origin."[13] Landscape and nature envelop time, keep it dormant and enchanted, preserve the past for the future, ready to be reactivated, waiting to be called forth from its hiding place. The numerous ruins, covered with creepers and grass, are not scattered about as picturesque props, but they symbolize lived time which is being kept slumbering or imprisoned by nature. In *Ahnung und Gegenwart* we read: "When they [Friedrich and Leontin] emerged from the woods and stepped upon a projecting rock, they suddenly saw coming from the miraculous far away distance, from old fortresses and eternal forests the stream of ages past... the royal river Rhine" (II, 179). The river Rhine is here the "stream of ages past"; it not

---

12. A first but most rewarding investigation into the problem of time in Eichendorff's work is to be found in Wilhelm Emrich's "Eichendorff: Skizze einer Ästhetik der Geschichte," *Germanisch-Romanische Monatsschrift*, XXVII (1939), 192-207.
13. For the importance of "origin" in Eichendorff, see especially the chapter called "Ewige Heimat" in Ibel, pp. 99-125.

only conveys and alludes to, but actually is history. And the swim which the two friends take in the river clearly indicates that scenic view stands here for historic event; for the leap into the Rhine takes place in our novel just before the two friends enter upon their soldierly careers and exploits by which Eichendorff anticipated the war of liberation against Napoleon. This dive into the Rhine, the stream of ages past, is actually the hero's commitment to and leap into German history. What is presented here as a scenic view is in reality history, past, present and future. Through the medium of landscape Eichendorff articulates again and again the perspective of time, its pastness and future encompassed in the present—a time perspective which in our days has been given such striking expression in the first three lines of T. S. Eliot's *Four Quartets*:

> Time present and time past
> Are both perhaps present in time future,
> And time future contained in time past.

Yet this perspective of time which opens up in the landscape, this intermingling, crossing, and blending of past, present, and future as revealed in scenic images, point symptomatically to Eichendorff's basic conviction that nature herself stands within the process and under the dictate of history and time, of *that* history and time of which all actual history and time is only a preliminary reflection: namely, the history of salvation. Nature, being creature, lives the same cycle, the same possibilities of innocence, sin, resurrection, and redemption as does her fellow creature, man. The life of nature as Eichendorff sees and renders it is not primarily the biological rhythm of birth, growth, decay, and death, but the religious tension between distance from God and closeness to grace. In this connection it seems interesting to me that death of and in the scenic surroundings is not rendered by Eichendorff through the common metaphor of winter, which does represent the low point of *bios*, but through the sultry midday landscape,[14] cornfields and woods in their full biological growth, yet oppressed by the heavy, stifling air in which no breath, no anima stirs. It is more than a metaphor when Eichendorff speaks of the "innocent" garden, when the park in *Schloß Dürande* is called "petrified," when, at nightfall, "the world down there in the valley is locked in a wrestling grip with the huge

---

14. Strangely enough and against overwhelming evidence to the contrary, Bollnow states: "Eichendorffs Weltbild kennt den Tag nicht, oder gar in einem betonten Sinne den Mittag" (p. 146).

masses of color" (II, 251), when he clearly states in his *Literaturgeschichte*: "Nature is a veiled struggle toward the invisible above her." The same thought is repeated in his essay on the life of St. Hedwig, where we read that "Nature continuously strives from the dead chambers of the earth toward the light, reaching up and, touched by light, breaking out into blossom, fragrance, and song." This is nature working up toward God—but just as often Eichendorff presents us with the opposite view: landscape falling into the depth of the demonic, bound by a spell to the lower regions, elemental in the sense that, as vegetative life, it is pinned down to the earth and does not hear the call and challenge of salvation from above. There are the innumerable enchanted gardens—we met one of them in our discussion of the temptations in the *Marmorbild*, the green meadow which turns into a crystalline castle in the ballad "Der Gefangene" (I, 347) —the spellbound forests, the paralyzed fields smoldering in the heat of noon. This is nature unredeemed, caught in its earthbound origin, cut off from the light above—again and again the idea appears that these places are submerged, have sunk below the surface, motionless, lifeless. The concept of the enchanted landscape which appears in Eichendorff's work with such persistence is anything but the ubiquitous stock-in-trade used to titillate our nerves and to give us esthetically pleasant goose flesh. "Spellbound" is here to be taken as literally as possible: the state of hypnotic fixation on one's own self, the sinking back into the inside, the dreamy imprisonment in brooding and introspection, in short, a state of life arrested within its own magic circle, and incapable of breaking through its own shell. Its most profound pictorial representation seems to me Dürer's "Melencolia" with her sad, gazing eyes, a world under the sign of Saturn, the earthgod, touched by the dead hour, filled with the fearful stillness of oblivion.

What this landscape needs to return to life is a shock, a sudden act of awakening, a quick tearing away of the heavy shroud. And this is exactly what it gets again and again in Eichendorff's work. Here we may find the answer to the question why Eichendorff so persistently prefers one specific mode of daybreak. It is literally a break, stressing the suddenness, the almost explosive quality, the momentous act of awakening. There is no lingering in the twilight zone, no slow seeping through of the light; Eichendorff's morning comes not with a whimper but with a bang. It seems to me much more than an idiosyncratic formula when we read over and over in his works: the sun was *just* rising, *at this very moment* the sun rose, always the emphasis on the shock, on the active and activating moment of day's arrival. For Eichendorff it is the first ray that matters, the ray into which the lark throws herself, rising higher and higher, almost drunk with the feeling of being awake. This is more than just morning; this is the moment of resurrection when the first ray of grace suddenly touches the dark, sleeping landscape.[15]

Thus Eichendorff's landscapes are not simply props, not simply background against which a play is being enacted; they are, as much as man himself, dramatis personae, the drama being the miracle play of God and his creation. His stage is a genuine *gran teatro del mundo*—it is certainly not accidental that he dedicated himself so assiduously to the translation of Calderón —and rivers, gardens, mountains, and woods play their roles in the great action. That they are so much alive, not with borrowed but with their own life, gives Eichendorff's natural scenery a vitality and concreteness which is probably unmatched in German literature. Yet this very liveliness has given rise to the misconception that Eichendorff's landscape is thoroughly anthropomorphic, that he transfers human situations, emotions, and problems to the scenery which surrounds man. I do not think that this is the case, although I realize that a good deal of what I have presented earlier may have given credence to the anthropomorphism of Eichendorff's landscape. To be sure, we can read man's ultimate condition, and this is his relationship to God, the readiness or unreadiness of his soul, from the countenance of a garden and a heath, from a pond and a ravine in whose shadow a mill is hidden. But this close connection is not established by a simple reflection of the human in nature. The bond is not created by a projection or transference of one upon the other, but by the concept of analogy, the very principle which in the Scholastic philosophy of an Aquinas furnishes the link between the divine, the human, and the natural. It is not the relationship of a model to its reflection in a mirror, but it is a system of vast and subtle correspondences, a multiple design of perspectives all of which point to the ultimate question: What is the meaning and destiny of life as God created it?

---

15. What morning means to Eichendorff (especially in the *Taugenichts*) is clearly brought out by Kunz, pp. 75-77; also Ibel, p. 138. Starting from a typical morning scene, Richard Alewyn develops the very essence of Eichendorff's *Raumgefühl* in a superb interpretation of "Eine Landschaft Eichendorffs," *Euphorion*, LI (1957), 42-60.

Correspondences and perspectives: this seems the answer which, on different levels, our inquiry into the symbolism of Eichendorff's landscape has yielded. But if this answer is correct, then it is evident that landscape is not just a material ingredient inserted at will, and capable of being viewed, enjoyed and recognized per se, but that it is of a structural nature, not merely content but formal principle through which the materials used are organized into a work of art. It is not an element subjectively chosen by the author *for* his creation, but it objectively determines the meaningful design of the organism of which it is a part. By sharpening my argument to this point, I may make the polemic undertone of my interpretation too clearly audible. It is directed against a view, especially rampant in the Anglo-Saxon countries and authoritatively expounded by T. S. Eliot and his disciples, who reject the works of the romanticists—and Eichendorff is certainly one of them—as a mass of unorganized, subjective feelings, unverifiable because they are a matter of purely personal expression, a release of moods to which we may or may not respond with our nerves, but which do not guide us toward meaning and truth. The romanticists are, in the eyes of these denigrators, anathema because they exhaust themselves in the uncontrollable and irresponsible play of fancy, lead to a debasement of creative imagination and form, and, instead of sharpening our minds and eye for the universals, becloud them with the shapeless fog of the particulars. I hope I have been able to show, by one specific demonstration, how baseless and unjust such a view is. It stems, so it seems to me, from a vulgarized and cheapened form of romanticism as it spread after the real and creative impetus of the movement had spent itself. But these more or less tasteful arrangers of atmospheric details for their own sake, these users of empty props and meaningless effects are not the true heirs of the genuine German romanticists. Their true heirs live in a camp to which T. S. Eliot is, and knows himself to be, greatly indebted: the camp of the French symbolists.[16] Their concern, as passionate as Eichendorff's, was to illuminate the word, the cipher that appears on the face of the visible world, to

---

16. It is now exactly 20 years since this succession was irrefutably and impressively proven by Albert Béguin, *L'âme romantique et le rêve: Essai sur le romantisme allemand et la poésie française* (Paris, 1939), the first edition of which was published in 1937 (2 vols.). Yet this remarkable book does not seem to have had the impact which it deserves. Only occasionally one finds Béguin's insights and proofs accepted, as e.g. in Liselotte Dieckmann, p. 312.

let us divine the truth which is encoded in the hieroglyph. It may very well be that my whole presentation is nothing more than a clumsy elaboration on the two quatrains of Baudelaire's sonnet:

> La nature est un temple où de vivants piliers
> Laissent parfois sortir de confuses paroles;
> L'homme y passe à travers des forêts de symboles
> Qui l'observent avec des regards familiers.
>
> Comme de longs échos qui de loin se confondent
> Dans une ténébreuse et profonde unité,
> Vaste comme la nuit et comme la clarté,
> Les parfums, les couleurs et les sons se répondent.

Are we surprised at the discovery that the title of this poem reads: "Correspondances"?

# PICARESQUE ELEMENTS IN THOMAS MANN'S WORK

Whether little Lazarus of Tormes or any of his rascally breed should or should not be considered the direct ancestor of the protagonist of the German *Schelmenroman,* it is to the picaresque spirit that German literature owes one of its most lively and impressive fictional characters, Simplicius Simplicissimus.[1] Never before and hardly ever since did Germany move so close to the country beyond the Pyrenees as in the seventeenth century. Lessing's critical hammer-blows had severed the ties between German letters and those of the Romance countries, and the efforts of the Romanticists to mend the broken alliance with Spain bore fruit only on a secondary plane, in the field of translation to which Tieck contributed his unsurpassable German *Don Quijote* and his charming rendition of Vincente Espinel's *Vida y aventuras del escudero Marcos de Obregon.*[2] Only in the dramatic works of Franz Grillparzer and Hugo von Hofmannsthal have Spain and her literary heritage acted again as a leaven on the creative imagination, although the scene, now conjured up, is not the misery-ridden dwelling of the picaresque guttersnipe, but the resplendent *teatro del mundo* of the Catholic universe. That this revival took place in the Hapsburg Empire was not surprising, because it was here that, for political and religious reasons, the memory of the *siglo de oro* had lingered on, waiting for the opportune moment to rise again to the surface.

Yet it seems that even after more than three centuries Picaro is not dead. Again he has appeared on the scene of great literature, and although his features have changed, although the primitive little hoodlum of the sixteenth and seventeenth centuries has turned into a highly sophisticated and psychologically

---

1. For the impact of the picaresque novel on German literature and on Grimmelshausen in particular, cf. Albert Schultheiss, *Der Schelmenroman der Spanier und seine Nachbildungen* (Hamburg, 1893); Adam Schneider, *Spaniens Anteil an der deutschen Literatur des 16. und 17. Jahrhunderts* (Strassburg, 1898), 205-22; Julius Schwering, *Litterarische Beziehungen zwischen Spanien und Deutschland* (Münster, 1902), 65-71; Hubert Rausse, *Zur Geschichte des spanischen Schelmenromans in Deutschland* (Münster, 1908); J. J. A. Bertrand, "Ludwig Tieck et le roman picaresque," *Revue Germanique,* X (1914), 443 ff.
2. At about the same time, 1801 and 1802 respectively, two additional Spanish picaresque novels appeared in Germany. C. A. Fischer translated *Gran Tacaño* and published a new and literal version of Mateo Aleman's *Vida y hechos del picaro Guzman de Alfarache,* the first picaresque novel to be imported to Germany in Aegidius Albertus' "translation" of 1615.

complex character, it may still be possible to discern the long familiar, amusingly shocking type underneath the new clothes, in the midst of an entirely transformed spiritual and cultural setting. To find Thomas Mann among those who in their works have again brought the disrespectful rascal to life, may, at first glance, be startling and incredible. His acquaintance with Spanish literature is comparatively slight, and that he ever found suitable companions in such questionable characters as Lazarillo, Guzman, and their ilk is more than doubtful. Yet it is quite imaginable that a historical and cultural situation which prepared the soil on which Picaro could grow, was, in its basic elements, duplicated in another country and another era, so that a new Picaro was bound to emerge.

Undoubtedly, Thomas Mann, when recreating the old type, was originally quite unconscious of its literary ancestors. But, in due course, he became more and more aware of the fundamental affinity beween a specific age-old tradition and some of his own work. In recent years, the term *Schelmenroman* has become quite familiar to him, and it is not in the least surprising that he applies this term to two of his own works in which, indeed, a new Picaro has come to life, *Die Bekenntnisse des Hochstaplers Felix Krull*[3] and *Joseph und seine Brüder*.[4] To be sure, the word is used with a broad meaning—as it must be pointed out that the German term *Schelm* has a much wider range than the Spanish *picaro*—yet there is no doubt that Thomas Mann's extremely subtle feeling for Western heritage and tradition has gradually made him aware of subterranean communications between his own work and long-established types of the European novel.

The fragmentary novel, *Die Bekenntnisse des Hochstaplers Felix Krull*, was begun, and left unfinished, in 1911, and clearly belongs to the phase in which the *Künstler-Bürger* conflict, the problematic situation of the man of imagination in a soberly realistic and commonplace world, formed the center of Thomas Mann's thinking and writing. It may seem no more than a satyr-interlude between *Tonio Kröger* and *Tod in Venedig* with the outsider, the "artist," frankly transgressing the line of lawful ex-

---

3. *Die Entstehung des Dr. Faustus* (Amsterdam, 1949), 24. It may be more than a coincidence that in these late years Thomas Mann was seriously preoccupied with *Simplicissimus*. Cf. *ibid.*, pp. 71, 84.
4. Karl Kerenyi, *Romandichtung und Mythologie* (Zürich, 1945), 83. In a letter to Kerenyi Thomas Mann writes: "Joseph's actions and transactions are morally-aesthetically acceptable only from the vantage point of the divine *Schelmenroman.*"

istence and becoming overtly what Thomas Mann's artists, when viewed from the vantage point of bourgeois society, always have been latently: *Hochstapler,* mountebanks. Unquestionably the most humorous and light-hearted of all of Thomas Mann's productions, it carries so many undertones that a slight shift in emphasis will reveal Thomas Mann's "hero" as a member of a family much older than the clan of outcast artists who have populated the Continental novel since the beginning of the nineteenth century. If he is not Picaro himself, he is at least one of his first cousins.

Picaro was born when an empire, which could boast that the sun did not set on its confines, was gradually being undermined by slow yet steady decay; when values and institutions whose strength was still officially proclaimed had step by step fallen victims to doubt and corruption; when behind the noble façade of a world dreaming of fabulous expansion and unheard-of exploits, the reality of exhaustion, poverty, and disillusion made its wretched appearance. The scenery upon which Picaro moves is an empire on the eve of disintegration, its atmosphere the bitter and comic dichotomy between a hollow claim to greatness and the inexorable misery of everyday life. Since, at every turn, reality contradicts all high-flown pretensions, every act becomes an act of unmasking, and the little rascal who laughs at the ethical code of established society emerges as the victor in the battle for life. To be sure, he is a rogue, a cheat, a conniver— but what else can he be in a world from which every trace of true stability has gone, where the pillars of society are rotten to the core, false theatrical props which, in the merciless light of day, prove to be shallow, ludicrous, or, at best, pitiful? Life has become a cat-and-mouse game, and the only way to deal with it is to outwit it.

That was Spain in the sixteenth century. And now a glance at Thomas Mann's German family shortly before the outbreak of the First World War in which the great European structure received the death blow. There is the father, Mr. Engelbert Krull, the "backbone" of the family. Yet his entire existence is a most dubious, though amiable, fraud. He manufactures champagne,[5] wine with bubbles, a most spurious product by the way, whose

---

5. The German word *Schaumwein* renders the symbolic meaning of Mr. Krull's business much more aptly, because the word ("foaming wine") implies the degree of flimsiness which has been injected into a product of nature which once, in mythical days, was held sacred as a symbol of the nourishing solidity of the good earth (Bread and Wine).

only merit is the "coiffure" (11),[6] the attractive make-up, culminating in a highly decorative and misleading label. On a much more elegant level, he shortchanges his customers no less than Lazarillo's father who makes his little profit by tampering with the sacks of flour he has to deliver. In both cases the "coiffure," be it wine bottles or flour bags, is flawless, but the contents, the substance, show a deplorable deficiency. A higher and brutal justice, which seems unable to take a joke, catches up with both of them: Lazarillo's father ends in jail, Felix's "poor" father makes an end of it with the help of a revolver after the glamorous edifice of his bourgeois existence, erected on sham, fraudulent credits, and well-concealed insolvency, has come crashing down on him. He goes bankrupt, as thoroughly bankrupt as the father of Guzman de Alfarache whose economic position was about as sound as Engelbert Krull's.

Of course, it would be unfair to compare Mrs. Krull, a lady of worldly refinement, to Lazarillo's mother, who is evidently nothing but a cheap trollop. Yet we cannot forget that one of the main attractions which draws a crowd of devoted cronies into Mrs. Krull's lavish *salon* is of a somewhat questionable nature, too; for what she and her daughter Olympia gladly offer their male guests are "deep insights" (29)—into their shockingly low-cut décolletés when bending gracefully over the back of an elegant davenport. And after the disaster has descended upon the "backbone" of the families, the two ladies, Mrs. Krull and Lazarillo's mother, move to the big city to open boarding houses: homeless and deracinated people providing a pseudo-home for other homeless and deracinated people, a pied-à-terre for a night or a week or a month; and although we do not wish to cast any disparaging light upon Mrs. Krull's new profession, it must be mentioned that her lodgers enjoyed her liberality and tolerance, her gaiety and comfort no less than her cuisine (117).

This is the stock, a worm-eaten and shaky stock, from which the old and the new Picaro descend. Even their respective places of birth seem to have a symbolical meaning. Is it just an accident that Lazarillo first saw the light of day on the river Tormes, in the midst of the river actually, so that his very entrance into life is marked by an ominous lack of stability, of firm ground on which to stand? And it is the nearness to the unstable element,

---

6. References to *Bekenntnisse des Hochstaplers Felix Krull* are taken from the 1937 edition of the fragment (Amsterdam). This article was written five years before the publication of the "complete" *Krull* (1954), which is, of course, still a fragment.

the water, with which Felix Krull begins his autobiography, the charming description of the banks of the Rhine, the laughing and wine-studded countenance of the stream flowing past such famous spas as Wiesbaden, Homburg, Langenschwalbach, and Schlangenbad (10) whose very names evoke the association of casinos, vacation from life, and playful insincerity. It is not until *Tod in Venedig*, for the sake of which Thomas Mann interrupted the story of the mountebank and which represents the tragic continuation of what he had started, in his *Felix Krull*, as the comic autobiography of an "anti-hero,"[7] that the city on the water, the city in the water, becomes a symbol of the dissolution and disintegration of a structurally solid existence; but that both Lazarillo's and Felix's first glimpse of the world is the glimpse at the "bottomless" element may not be without meaning for the further course of their lives. Indeed, it should be pointed out that among Thomas Mann's fictional characters Felix Krull is the only one to grow up in Western Germany, in the Rhineland more specifically, that part of Germany which, through history and mentality, has preserved the most noticeable affinity to the Latin, the Mediterranean world. The spirited "cheat" is Thomas Mann's only Catholic hero,[8] and it may very well be that only the Catholic world could produce the figure of Picaro: a world enamoured of color and lightheartedness so that the imaginative performance of even a rascal can be relished; credulous enough to accept the miracle even if it is no more than the ingenious feat of a prestidigitator; so used to transubstantiation that the volteface of the actor who is a number of persons in one becomes acceptable; a world skeptical enough to take lightly the grim call "to prove oneself," which makes it perfectly legitimate to play a trick on reality; a world so conscious of the meaning and importance of the symbolic act that it must seem pedestrian and humorless to submit to the gray literalness of life.

To fight against the gray literalness of life—that is Felix Krull's mission, and with all its dubious and perverted slant, a mission indeed, not less edifying and entertaining than Picaro's mission to keep alive despite the stubborn resistance offered by

---

7. Frank W. Chandler in his *Literature of Roguery* (Boston, 1907), I, 5, calls the picaresque novel "the comic biography (or more often the autobiography) of an anti-hero."

8. I disregard here consciously the Catholic as a humanist as he appears in Thomas Mann's last great work, *Doktor Faustus*, because, characteristically enough, Serenus Zeitblom is only the prism in which the bitter Protestant fate of Adrian Leverkühn is reflected.

circumstances, to come out on top although everything and everybody conspire to keep him down. It is true, Picaro is no more than a little animal equipped with a shrewd and spontaneous instinct, while Thomas Mann's hero has worked out his program with such refinement and subtlety that he stands before us as the supreme artist of life. But both of them have one objective: *corriger la fortune*; and it makes little difference that, for Lazarillo, the highest satisfaction consists in getting his belly full, while Felix Krull aims at a complete victory of the creative ingenuity of mind over dead and sluggish matter. If, by a sheer act of will, he produces all the symptoms of a gastric disturbance (60 ff.), fever, fits of convulsion, and vomiting, he does so not only in order to stay away from the loathed classroom—which, to be sure, is the primary objective—but for the exalted purpose of proving that the unimaginative lethargy of the body can be forced under the control of a supreme mind:

> Now I had produced them, these symptoms, I had endowed them with as much effectiveness as they might ever have had, if they had come about without my help. I had corrected nature, I had realized a dream, and only he who out of nothing, out of the mere knowledge of things and the insight into them, in brief: out of imagination, is able to produce an effective reality, can appreciate the strange and dream-like satisfaction with which I rested after my act of creation. (66)

Every action of Krull manifests the victory of imagination over the silly seriousness of reality. You need not be a violinist to revel in the ovation reserved for a great artistic performance. Two little sticks of wood are enough, and if you manipulate them with the dexterous charm of a child prodigy in front of a music pavilion, the crowd will burst into applause as if there had been heavenly music where actually there was none (31 ff.). We could run through every instance of young Felix's life, through every incident from which he learns the great mastery of things; it will always be the triumph of wit, ingenuity, graceful shrewdness over the dullwittedness and clumsiness of matter and fact. The proud satisfaction that Felix consciously enjoys is the same satisfaction which the reader of the pranks of Lazarillo, Guzman, and their brethren unconsciously derives from the delightful fact that the weakling is not so weak after all; that, when he puts his scheming brain to work, he can snap his fingers at the powers that be; that he can lead by the nose the pompous, the mighty, the respectable.

What Krull enacts is a permanent and triumphant rejection

of reality, and this is basically the masterful game of the Picaro as well. But not to be subject to the dictates of a given situation, creating steadily one's own reality, means to be free. This is the boundless freedom of the Picaro who roams as he pleases, taking up an engagement today and leaving it tomorrow, not tied down by any responsibilities, open to every suggestion that may come along. There is no home, no family, no profession, no possession that can hold the roving rascal, and it seems only natural that the picaresque novel should so soon have been transformed into a novel of travel and adventure, with the wide world as a background. Lazarillo setting sail and being brought back as a sea-monster, Guzman in Rome, Guzman among the pirates, Alonso thrown in with a gypsy band—these are the stock situations of the picaresque novel, and at the very beginning of his autobiography Felix Krull drops modest hints at the world-wide trips he made in pursuit of his "profession." So powerful is the atmosphere of freedom that the world in which Picaro moves loses all cohesion, dissolves into a sequence of disconnected "tableaux," held together only by the accidental and haphazard journeys of the hero. This lack of integration explains the typical "flash-light" technique of the picaresque novel. Places and faces emerge as if conjured up out of the void, fulfill their functions as background, as partners in the Picaro's life-game, and disappear as quickly as they have come into existence. The hero is too weak, or too free, to hold fast to anything for any length of time. His world, so lacking in stability, offers the kind of spectacle we enjoy in a kaleidoscope, and casts upon the reader the same sort of magic, fairytale-like spell. It is quite characteristic that Thomas Mann notes: "In Krull the world could have been phantasmagoric."[9] In fact, it had to be phantasmagoric, a loose and uncoordinated jumble of time and space, in order to express the disintegration of a structural pattern in the midst of boundless freedom. It is not by chance that Felix Krull, when setting down the facts of his life, does not feel bound to any sequence of time, but freely jumps from experiences of his early youth to events of his adolescence.

The unwillingness or the incapacity of the Picaro to hold on, to steady himself, to renounce his utter freedom, transforms his life into an uncoordinated succession of "strokes of luck," good luck and bad luck, a whimsical wave of ups and downs, unexpected riches today, pitiful misery tomorrow. Life itself has become a

---

9. *Die Entstehung des Dr. Faustus*, 27.

roulette game, and we do not need the anticipatory hints in Krull's autobiography to predict that the casino will become the scene of some of his most remarkable exploits. Life, given over to extreme freedom, cannot help losing all clear destination, moving along without "destiny" and exhibiting at every point the arbitrariness of pure chance.

It is only logical that the unrooted hero finds himself drawn to groups which have "freed" themselves from the organic whole of society, irregulars and outcasts whose existence is through and through anarchic. Alcala Yavez y Rivera's Alonso falls in with the gypsies, Guzman concludes a mischievous pact with the pirates, Queveda Villegas' Buscon joins a group of strolling actors, Cervantes' Rinconete y Cortadillo become members of a highly ingenious gang of pickpockets, burglars, and pimps.[10] It is very much in the spirit of the picaresque novel, although anything but a literal rendering of the text when, around 1620, the first German "translator" of the second part of *Guzman* (he used the unauthentic second part by Sayavedra[11]) leads his hero through Germany as a member of a theatrical group. Needless to point out what magic threat the word "gypsy" wields in Thomas Mann's early work (*Tonio Kröger*); that Felix Krull is being initiated into the highest wisdom by an artist whose respectability is not exactly heightened by the fact that he has added, without any authorization, the title "Professor" to his name; that Felix's first overwhelming experience which shows him the irresistible power of dissimulation, takes place in a theater, with an operetta tenor officiating as the high priest of bewitchment (41 ff.). (Of course, it is an operetta, music with bubbles, about as cheap and unsubstantial as old Mr. Krull's merchandise.)

Picaro, the free hero, free from everything and everybody, is by this very token the lonely hero as well. He is always and basically an orphan, which is in his case not simply a matter of the premature disappearance of his parents, but the true and tragic

---

10. Cervantes' *novela* is so clearly a story of outright criminals that, strictly speaking, it does not belong to the genre of the picaresque novel. Yet the author himself states that it was conceived "in gusto picaresco." Its first German version, under the title *Isaak Winckelfelder und Jobst von der Schneid*, appeared in 1617, bound together with the first German translation of *Lazarillo de Tormes*. The translator, Nikolas Ulenhart, presented Cervantes' story as his own work. He could do that the much more easily since he had cleverly transplanted the locale to Germany, specifically Bohemia.
11. The actual author of this pseudo-*Guzman* was Juan Marti, a lawyer from Valencia.

signature of his existence. The authors of the picaresque novels take great pains to avoid in their stories any note of pathos and obvious compassion, yet the terrible loneliness of the roguish hero cannot fail to move us, even if such an emotion is not "in the book."[12] There is in all the picaresque novels the painful inability of the hero to establish human relationships, be it friendship or love, because the one who is so free that he belongs to nothing and nobody, has nothing and nobody that will ever belong to him. There is a remarkable similarity between Lazarillo's and Felix Krull's first experience with the other sex. Toward the end of Lazarillo's report the lonely Picaro seems to find marital happiness. Yet it turns out that the girl who becomes his wife actually "belongs" to a very affluent gentleman who marries this servant girl off to Lazarillo so that he can carry on with her all the more safely and inconspicuously. Felix is initiated into the secrets of sex by a buxom chambermaid, yet, delightful as this initiation turns out to be, he too is only a "substitute" for the dully respectable stationmaster to whom the girl has been engaged for many years and whom she cannot marry for financial reasons. In this episode (80 ff.) Felix Krull lives up to his role of a perfect cheat, and actually fulfills the picaresque pattern much better than his sixteenth-century counterpart who is, after all, only a pitiful cuckold; yet, although he gets the utmost pleasure out of his "love" affair, is he not actually the cheated one, a mere fill-in, condemned to be alone even in the rapture of the most intimate union? Is there in this case really any difference between being a poor little Lazarus and a "Felix"? Thomas Mann has clearly recognized that one of the mainsprings of his picaresque novel, if not *the* mainspring altogether, is the "motif of loneliness," no less noticeable for the fact that it is treated here "in a humorous and criminal fashion."[13] It is not surprising that in both the periods of his life when his mind was preoccupied with the charming cheat—in 1911 when he wrote the first chap-

---

12. It is certainly more than accidental that the name of the first and liveliest of all Picaros is a play on the name of poor Lazarus, prototype of all human wretchedness. Indeed, one should not miss the ironic undertone in this name-giving, as little as one should miss the ironic undertone in Krull's name, Felix. That the names of our heroes show this strong similarity—through contrast—must not go unnoticed. L. Gauchat in his article, "Lazarillo de Tormes und die Anfänge des Schelmenromans," *Archiv für das Studium der neueren Sprachen und Literaturen*, LXVI (1912), 430 ff., fails to note the ironic connotation of the name Lazarillo and sees in Picaro mainly "the image of a poor devil." This is definitely much too narrow and oversimplified an interpretation of the character of the immortal rascal.
13. *Die Entstehung des Dr. Faustus*, 26.

ters of *Felix Krull,* and in 1943 when he toyed with the idea of finishing the fragment—the problem of loneliness generated such a vehement driving power that it could no longer be handled in a "humorous and criminal fashion," but had to reveal itself in its stark and merciless cruelty, in the inexorable fates of Gustav Aschenbach and Adrian Leverkühn.

Is it too much to assume that the typical form of the picaresque novel, the autobiographic report, has something to do with this "motif of loneliness"? It is startling that almost every picaresque novel presents itself as a first-person narrative, and this may indeed be the proper form to communicate the lonely life in a world from which all cohesion has gone. If the validity of all norms, all authority, all reality, is rejected; if there is no center powerful enough to organize the dissolute fragments of life into an organic whole, what is there left but the lonely "I" which rules supreme and remains the only focus which can hold and release the fleeting phenomena of the world? For the human being who is not "involved" but a free outsider, life is no longer a fabric into which the thread of his own existence is woven, an objective reality valid and binding beyond his own personal experience, but loose and unshaped raw material for his subjective apperception. Such an existential situation becomes expressible only under the narrative form of "I." Of all Thomas Mann's major works it is only his picaresque novel that presents itself as an autobiography.[14]

In an autobiography the world has no autonomous weight, life does not present itself as something that "happens" before our eyes, but as something that has happened, something gone by, "finished," dead. It has no actuality, no presentness ("keine Zuhandenheit," as Heidegger would put it), it does not occur, but is "only" remembered—and the word "remembered" is to be taken here in its most literal meaning, as the re-membering of something which is basically dis-membered and disjointed. The van-

---

14. The only other narrative in the first person worth mentioning is his short story *Der Bajazzo* in which the problem of human loneliness and pernicious freedom is no less acute. The very title, clownishness as a principle of life, brings this *Novelle* into the neighborhood of the picaresque genre. *Doktor Faustus* is a pseudo-autobiographical novel with the narrator telling the life-story of the hero, his friend Adrian Leverkühn. Yet Thomas Mann points out (*Die Entstehung des Dr. Faustus,* 26) that his renewed preoccupation with the *Krull*-fragment may be responsible for the narrative form which his last great novel was to exhibit.

tage point of the narrator, of the "I," is always "after the event," never "in the midst of the event." Life becomes relatable only after it has passed, in the calm of deadness. It is for this reason that so many of the picaresque novels are told by a recluse, a hero who, after an exciting life, has completely withdrawn from the world, thoroughly and utterly alone with himself, living in a void which he now fills retrospectively with "things past," with images existing only in and through his own isolated consciousness. The world is nothing but a memory, indeed "phantasmagoric," and every picaresque novel, every autobiography could start with the opening words of *Felix Krull*: "While seizing the pen, in full leisure and withdrawal, healthy by the way, though tired, very tired . . ." (7). It is no accident that the greatest autobiography in world literature, St. Augustine's *Confessions*, was written after a conversion, after life, one way of life, had come to an end, after its hero, completely detached from his previous existence, had become dead to the world, or rather after this particular world had become nonexistent to him.[15]

It is the basic implication of a first-person narrative that the world has been swallowed up, that the "I" has become the center of all things. In this very form, the form of the autobiography, lies the intrinsic ironical connotation of the picaresque novel. The discrepancy between the wretched, lowly Picaro who does not amount to anything in this world, and the effrontery with which he dares to say "I," is in itself a piece of *blague*, of persiflage and roguery, probably felt much more keenly than today in the sixteenth and seventeenth centuries when the weight and dignity of a person depended heavily on his status in life, although the conviction that it is presumptuous to write one's autobiography is by no means dead today and unwittingly leads

---

15. Goethe's *Dichtung und Wahrheit* seems to me the only exception to this basic principle of great autobiographical writing. It is the only example where, in an autobiography, the full autonomy of reality is preserved, where the world is more than just a catalyst, an obstacle, digested or to-be-digested raw material for an ego. It is for this reason that Goethe's autobiography develops again and again into an objective narrative with situations, historical events, cultural movements actually "present" and not automatically and immediately related to the relating "I." At a certain point Goethe goes so far as to apologize for soliciting the reader's attention to his own person, a very strange remark indeed in an autobiography, but very indicative of the unique objective attitude of *Dichtung und Wahrheit*. In accordance with this "objectiveness" Goethe sometimes slips into a third person-narrative: "We have seen in the course of this autobiographical report how the child, the boy, the adolescent tried to approach the supra-sensual in various ways . . . When *he*, then, at certain intervals . . ." (part IV, book 20).

to the question: "Who is he, after all, to claim our attention for his 'I'?" In the case of Thomas Mann this persiflage, only tacitly implied in the picaresque novels by their very form, is quite conscious and one of the sources of most refined delight. That the unreformed scoundrel dares call the report on his mischievous tricks *Bekenntnisse,* thus evoking associations with two of the most profound and soul-searching literary documents of mankind, St. Augustine's and Jean Jacques Rousseau's *Confessions,* is in itself the height of impertinence, a slap in the face of anything honest, sincere, and serious. The frivolous masquerader, whose whole life is nothing but a sequence of frauds, deceits, and petty crimes, usurps words and forms that belong to an entirely different human level and thus ridicules and "unmasks" values and emotional patterns that once, when the world was still "whole," were respected, binding, and holy.[16] From this act of usurpation results the devastating humor of Thomas Mann's novelistic fragment. The profound hilarity of the book does not rest on the recital of the ingenious exploits of the hero, no matter how genuinely funny they are, but in the dichotomy between a dignified and noble style—style meaning here both human bearing and verbal expression—and the flimsy person who decks himself out with this ill-fitting robe. Instead of giving grandeur to the hero, it makes fun of the "heroic" attitude and reveals this form of life as a ludicrous hoax.

There is another form of implied or insinuated *blague* and parody which links the picaresque novel and *Felix Krull*: the didactic element. In the picaresque novel, with the noticeable exception of *Lazarillo de Tormes,* the moral preaching of the author takes up long and, for the modern reader, extremely tedious stretches. These insertions have always been explained as a *captatio benevolentiae,* a concession of the author to pacify the ire of the Inquisition and other institutions set up to prevent moral and religious infractions. Yet is must be pointed out that a *captatio benevolentiae* always contains an element of cynicism, of tongue-in-cheek irony. How is it possible for the author to take delight in the evidently immoral career of his hero, how can he possibly arouse in the reader delight at his hero's mischievous-

---

16. It should be pointed out here that the literary persiflage of Spain's greatest book, *Don Quijote,* rests on the same principle: the ridiculing of a once meaningful pattern of life by its reënactment, deadly serious and for this reason foolish, at the "wrong" historical moment and by a "wrong" person. Thomas Mann has paid tribute to one of mankind's greatest books in his beautiful essay "Meerfahrt mit Don Quijote," *Leiden und Größe der Meister* (Berlin, 1935), 212 ff.

ness, and then with a straight face go into long exhortations and edifying sermons? But what if the face is not quite straight, what if, unwittingly and unwillingly, there is a twinkle in the author's and the reader's eyes when switching from the roguish laughter to the grim pounding of the moralistic drums? There is an episode in *Don Quijote,* one of the most heart-rending episodes in the book, which rests on the same principle. It is the story of the expelled Moor who assures us in the most cruelly self-accusing words that he has been righty expelled, because he and his racial fellows are enemies of the country and had to be driven out in the interest of the state. And then he goes on to tell how he dreams day and night of his beloved Spain, how wretched his life has become since he had to leave the country of his forefathers. Here, as in the picaresque novels with their long declamations on the "official" moral code, a strangely ironic cancellation of the accepted and loudly professed standards—in Cervantes' case Philip's policy of mass expulsion—is at work. Evidently, the good Moor who loves his fatherland with all his heart cannot possibly be an enemy of his country, no matter how eloquently he accuses himself of high treason and renders lip service to the official political "line." This process of undermining the valid and accepted moral code just by professing it loudly is most likely entirely unconscious in the picaresque author, as it is most unlikely that Cervantes consciously wanted to attack Philip's policy of depopulation. Yet the effect of a devaluation of the very values so pompously upheld within earshot of a Picaro is undeniable.

Of course, in the case of Thomas Mann the ironic effect is quite conscious, and leads to a constant "twinkling of the eye." The irresponsible rascal is full of a most substantial philosophy of life, if we look closely enough, a strict and outspoken "idealism," permanently and most convincingly expounding the power of spirit over dull matter. He arrives at lofty philosophical conclusions, not by confessing things which are at variance with his own convictions, but by verbalizing the very philosophical foundations of his existence. Listen to him:

> Life, to be sure, is not at all the highest of all goods to which we have to cling because it is so enjoyable. On the contrary, it is to be taken as a hard and austere task, confronting us or, as it seems to me, chosen by us voluntarily, which it is our duty to sustain with steadfastness and faithfulness and from which to run away prematurely bespeaks unquestionably a most slovenly conduct. (104)

What a magnificent piece of double-talk, we are inclined to say.

Yet the amusing fact is that it is no double-talk, but the perfectly "honest" confession of the cheat, and, by being just that, the most murderous parody of the solemnity of idealism. This, indeed, is highest irony, the devilish workings of a process by which the shallowness of all high-sounding principles is revealed —not by attacking them, but by professing them in all sincerity.

The old and familiar feature of didacticism is preserved in Thomas Mann's novel not only in the philosophical pronunciamentos of the hero, but in the introduction of a character who fulfills the function of the "mentor" of old picaresque literature, and is specifically described by the hero as such. He appears as the wise old man with penetrating eyes who guides Felix at the decisive turns of his life. Yet his very name gives away the direction and the aspects of life which he opens up for his disciple. "Professor" Schimmelpreester is only too willing to disclose the etymological origin of his name (and the name is certainly more than "sound and smoke" in this case) : " 'Nature,' so he said, 'is nothing but putrefaction and mould, and I am ordained as its priest; therefore my name is Schimmelpreester' " (35). The priest as mentor, this is the old pattern of the didactic novel, yet what a strange and perverted priesthood which, in our special case, communicates the essence of life to the novice! But even the disdainful condemnation: "Nature is nothing but putrefaction and mould" makes this dubious "priest" still more akin to the zealous and ascetic hermit in the wilderness who plays the part of the mentor and spiritual guide in the picaresque novel, at least in its German version *Simplicius Simplicissimus.*

It is not difficult to distinguish in *Lazarillo* an analogous character, the figure of an ironically warped mentor. He is the beggar who, at the very beginning, promises the innocent and trusting little hero to initiate him into life. That he is blind, dead to the sight of the world, qualifies him about as well for his educational mission as the "putrefaction priesthood" qualifies the "Professor" for his lofty office. What he teaches his charge is about as wholesome to Lazarillo as Mr. Schimmelpreester's philosophy of life is to Felix. It is a school of thievery and petty crime through which the beggar puts Lazarillo, and when, at the end of the apprenticeship, Lazarillo leads his master into a trap and robs him of his last coppers, we cannot feel too sorry that the mentor is given a dose of his own medicine. Yet the archetype of mentorship is discernible in the wretched tramp no less than in Mr. Schimmelpreester's priesthood. The lack and the renunciation of earthly riches have been associated again and again with the highest wisdom, with a concentration on the "essentials." Yet in the "mouldy" priest and the thieving beggar the role of mentorship is ironically devaluated and travestied.

To play tricks on everything respectable, powerful institutions, noble traditions, established values, this is, as we have tried to show, the Picaro's chief "mission." The free hero, not being subject to the powers that be, can show them up in all their absurdity and rottenness. It is for this reason that the picaresque novel represents one of the highpoints of satirical literature, and this, indeed, quite consciously. Reality is laughed out of existence, and pompous and righteous representatives of the existing order stand revealed in their hypocrisy and corruption. As we follow the little rascal on his devious and twisted tours and detours, we cannot help reacting to his exploits in a most "immoral" way by saying "More power to him," more power over the miserly and heartless priests, the learned pedants, the inflated politicians, the corrupt sellers of indulgences. Indeed, these attacks upon the pillars of society are so strong that we understand the reluctance of many authors of picaresque novels to sign their names to their works. The bitter satire is by no means only a by-product of the picaresque novel, and it was not taken as such by contemporary readers. The little rogue was meant to be much more than merely a carrier and conveyor of jokes and pranks, and in his introductory epigram to Mateo Aleman's *Guzman de Alfarache* Vincente Espinel could flatly state: "You put your finger on festering sores."[17] A great deal of Alcala Yavez y Rivera's *Alonso* is a bitter take-off on the corruption of the various professions and social estates; the same is true for Queveda Villegas' *Vida del Buscon*.

With Thomas Mann, the satire is much subtler and much more veiled. Yet our perverse sympathy for the mountebank is based on the fact that his antagonists, the representatives of the respectable world, are revoltingly stupid—or worse. Why should one not cheat those gullible fools who almost ask to have the wool pulled over their eyes, falling into spasms of admiration at the performance of a child prodigy who uses two wooden sticks as a violin, or of an operetta tenor, a coarse and ugly individual,

---

17. The ambitious and serious aims of *Guzman de Alfarache* are equally indicated by its subtitle "Atalaya de la Vida Humana," although we should not fail to hear in this edifying flourish the same ironical undertone which we distinguished in the slightly mocking name of Lazarillo.

who bewitches the audience with the help of half a pound of make-up and an insipid make-believe of "high life?" As in the picaresque novel our reaction is: it serves them right. It surely serves Dr. Düsing right to be deceived by a perfect humbug (66 ff.), conceited fool that he is, basically indifferent to the health of his patients and only concerned with his own reputation and advancement.[18] However, Felix's master stroke—and, in my opinion, the funniest episode in all of modern German prose literature—is his gulling of the military commission to which he reports for induction, or rather for the prevention of his induction ( 152 ff.). Here is "authority" pilloried at its most merciless, in its pompously learned stupidity, its pedantic thoroughness, its stern righteousness, its tricky pseudo-benevolence, its lurking suspicion that everybody and everything is out to deceive it—and all this outwitted and outtricked by a splendid performance, not by resistance, but by meek submission, by homely "honesty," by eager readiness to serve—in short, by all the qualities that befit a good and desirable subject of the crown. On this occasion Felix Krull excels himself, he plays all his trumps, and he knows that he has to. For it is the most deadly danger that threatens him, the very negation of his "free" existence: the threat to be put into "the service," to be subjected to regimentation and "uniformation," to be molded into a useful member of an equalized society. What he wards off here is the frontal attack on his aristocratic aloofness, on the proud feeling of superiority and uniqueness which is the birthright of the free.

The cheat, the rejector of reality, as the aristocrat—this is a perfectly logical equation, and with Thomas Mann it is so prominent that it cannot be overlooked. Yet, strange as it may sound, even the ragged and tossed-about Picaro is basically an aristocratic figure, and his characterization as a "bastard of pride and pauperization"[19] thoroughly acceptable. He is too proud and too good for a humdrum existence, for earning his

---

18. Poking fun at ridiculously "learned" and corrupt health-practitioners and quacks seems to be particularly popular with the picaresque genre, e.g., Guzman's plotting with the two surgeons to gain access to the cardinal's castle in Rome. This feature is quite prominent in the overwhelmingly funny "medical" polemics of Laurence Sterne's *Tristram Shandy*, whose affinity to the "Spanish temper," the Quixotic in particular, is obvious enough. About the connection between Thomas Mann and Laurence Sterne, cf. the following essay, "Laurence Sterne's *Tristram Shandy* and Thomas Mann's *Joseph the Provider*."
19. Ludwig Pfandl, *Geschichte der spanischen Literatur in ihrer Blütezeit* (Freiburg, 1929), 267.

livelihood in the sweat of his brow. Even though we should not miss the latent satiric attack on the arrogant laziness of nobility, there is genuine dignity in the confession of Vincente Espinel's Picaro: "My name is Marcos de Obregon, and I am ignorant of any skill; for hidalgos do not acquire such things, and rather endure misery and servitude than work as craftsmen." Characteristically enough, the only likable partner whom Lazarillo finds in his rovings is the utterly pauperized and declassed hidalgo who, with an empty stomach and only one extra shirt, creates for himself a completely fictitious life of elegance, romance, and high distinction. To be sure, he is a fool, but it is the only instance where our laughter and the author's cease to be bitter and are mellowed by respect, compassion, even love.[20] This contempt of the vulgar business and utilitarianism of life is truly aristocratic, and only a pedant without any sense of humor can fail to detect the dignity in this refusal to be useful and practical, and call this attitude by the harsh name of laziness. The lazy little rascal knows perfectly well why the most beneficial activity, the only "activity" in which he indulges, is sleep. It shuts him off from the indecent hustle and bustle, and strengthens his inner forces so that he can resist the crude and vulgar onslaught of reality. It is the same aristocratic attitude which makes Felix Krull proudly confess his phlegmatic disposition and chronic sleepiness (15).

Both the picaresque novel and *Felix Krull* signalize, unconsciously or consciously, the decay of an established order, of a world which tenaciously clings to the appearance of greatness while its real substance, its real greatness, are gone. They are books of farewell, of a rather cruel farewell, convinced that what is destined to fall should be helped along with a strong, merciless push. In spite of the laughter they aim to arouse, they are basic-

---

20. Here is the germ from which, out of the same soil, just half a century later, the most lovable "fool" of all world literature was to emerge, the most magnificent image of human dignity growing out of an *idée fixe*. When F. M. Warren, in his *History of the Novel* (New York, 1908), writes that the picaresque genre "was a protest against the predominance in literature of the aristocratic type" (289), he states but a surface truth and fails to see the more complex and profound connotation of this type of literature. By the same token, *Don Quijote* is on the surface level nothing but a travesty of the Amadis novel, yet who could fail to see that the overtly ridiculous *idée fixe* of knighthood is, at the same time, the hidden source of the hero's true nobility? This thought has been most sensitively developed by Thomas Mann in his *Don Quijote* essay, *op. cit.*, 223.

ally melancholy, even pessimistic books,[21] and it was a profound inner necessity which led Thomas Mann, when immersed in the pranks of his mountebank, to his two most pessimistic creations, the stories of a frightening human breakdown, of the invasion of a precious and highly developed culture by the sinister forces of a barbaric and demonic underworld. The Picaro is the offspring of twilight, yet negative as his character may be, it contains enormous potentialities of rebirth. He is a creature of nihilism, but he is already the bridge which will lead beyond the abyss. The Spanish Picaro carries the hopeful message of the sheer force of survival, come what may, the cheerful promise that, even if an empire may reel and founder, the cheating, thieving, begging rascal will outlast every possible disaster. This stubborn animalistic endurance holds a guarantee, just as Felix's ability to create a "world" out of his imagination holds a guarantee, once the old and sluggish world is defeated by jokes and trickery. If Felix's existence is developed to the bitter end, Gustav Aschenbach and Adrian Leverkühn must appear on the scene. But if Felix's existence is developed beyond the end, if it is possible to turn the Picaro's "freedom from" into a "freedom to," if man's ingenuity joins in a covenant with the highest creativeness, with God and his universe, if *ad majorem gloriam hominis* becomes indistinguishable from *ad majorem gloriam Dei*, then a new day of mankind will break, then the *Schelmenroman* will transform itself into a divine *Schelmenroman*, and Felix's name will change to Joseph.

There can be no doubt that, in Thomas Mann's biblical Joseph, the Picaro has found his most elevated and most elevating revival. All the elements are here; yet what once was a bitter jest has now turned into "God's own jest." There is all the cheating, the double-crossing, the aloofness, the aristocratic arrogance, the "twinkling with the eye," the playacting, the *corriger la fortune,* the shrewd self-promotion, the "down" into the pit and the "up" to the highest heights, the travels into a "phantasmagoric" fairyland, the glib and golden tongue, the naïveté that is devilishly clever, the aloneness of the "orphan" who is torn from his father's breast and sold into servitude. Yet all of it is the fulfillment of a great plan, the plan God has for man and the world, and it is man who consciously helps God to carry out

---

21. Ludwig Pfandl, *op. cit.*, 278, states quite correctly: "Pessimism is the key-note of the true *novela picaresca*," although he arrives at this definition rather by intuition than by concrete demonstration.

His plan; because a covenant has been concluded to which man remains basically true, notwithstanding the little cheating, a highly beneficial cheating, which he has to do to promote God in the world. Felix Krull, justified, i.e., blessed by and in alliance with the highest authority—that is the story of *Joseph und seine Brüder*.

It begins with Abraham, the patriarch, who creates his God out of "arrogance," the very highest possible God, because so great is this man's "impertinence" that he is willing only to serve the very highest, the God of all Gods. From him issues a whole tribe of rascals, shrewd outwitters of reality, realizers of great dreams, yet their schemes and their dreams are signs of their being chosen, true children of the Spirit which through them plays a trick on heavy, stupid, and soulless matter. Jacob cheating his brother out of his birthright, becoming prosperous and "heavy" by cleverly manipulating nature and forcing her to give him an undue share of Laban's sheep herds—he is truly a divine rogue, and the word "rogue," so constantly applied to him by Pharaoh in his conversation with Joseph, assumes the dignity of a title of honor. He takes "liberties" with the established order of things, because he is free, yet free under the covenant, most sensitively aware of the great pattern which he has to fill, not being stupidly and passively lived by life, but taking it into his hands and, by a willful course of conduct, fulfilling the will of the Highest. To play one's role consciously within God's great scheme—that is man's highest destiny, to arrange and handle freely the dicta and data of the world and yet to listen obediently to what God wants with us and with Himself. To fulfill a covenant by "promoting" oneself—and the one can be achieved only through the other—that is the point where the highest human freedom and man's strictest submission coincide.

Joseph's whole career is the story of promotion and fulfillment. It is the most roguish mixture of mischievousness and innocence, and when he dreams his arrogant dreams, manipulated and true at the same time, Reuben cannot help thinking: "Mischievous in innocence, and innocent in mischief, so that the innocence becomes dangerous and the mischief holy, these are the unmistakable signs of the blessing, and there is nothing to be done against it, even if one wanted to, but one does not want to, really, because here is God."[22] It is not accidental that Hermes, the god of the "promoters," wayfarers, and thieves plays such a

---

22. *Der junge Joseph* (Berlin, 1934), 135.

prominent role in Thomas Mann's biblical story. He is, on a divine level, young Joseph's "Professor" Schimmelpreester, even if his name is Eliezer, the "oldest" servant, who, at the most decisive point of his career (which is not "his" career anyway, but the reënactment of an old and hallowed pattern), ran so fast that you would think he had little wings on his feet and his cap. The winged god appears again, half seducer, half saving guide, when Joseph travels to his brothers to meet his outrageous fate. It is on this ominous trip that Joseph himself takes on the features of Hermes, a frail little messenger with a hooded cape and a papyrus scroll, and it is not at all startling that Thomas Mann has nicknamed the career of his biblical hero the story of "an American Hermes."[23]

Blessed roguishness, roguishness under the blessing, a most beneficial, dream-born manipulation of reality—that is Joseph's mission, it is the mission of the "new man"—yet who could fail to discover the delightful resemblance to Felix Krull's *Hochstapelei*? Joseph's fabulous rise to the highest office in Egypt is a series of self-promoting covenants, with the major-domo Mont-kaw, with Potiphar, with Pharaoh himself. They all are only the conscious "filling-out" of the great covenant which Abraham concluded with God to help Him by helping himself. After the last battle, the conquest of Pharaoh, is won, the ruler's mother succinctly characterizes Joseph's scheming:

> "Fiddlesticks," she said impatiently, "you have plotted the whole thing and talked yourself under his skin from your very first word on. You needn't play the innocent child for me. . . . I do not have anything against politics. . . . I do not reproach you for having made good use of your hour."[24]

Surely, all this is "morally-aesthetically acceptable only from the vantage point of the divine *Schelmenroman*."[25] And from this vantage point only Joseph's proudest feat, his feeding of and providing for the starving world, is acceptable. Forewarned by a dream, he outwits nature, making the seven fat years relatively lean, in order to make the following seven lean years relatively fat. It is the most grandiose and triumphant stroke of *corriger la fortune* in the career of a Picaro. It is not by chance that the chapter which describes Joseph's agrarian policy and reform, his shrewd scheme of hoarding and distributing, is entitled "Of

---

23. Introduction to the new edition (in one volume) of *Joseph and His Brothers* (New York, 1947).
24. *Joseph der Ernährer* (Stockholm, 1943), 234.
25. Cf. footnote 4.

the Roguish Servant." Here is the counterpart of Krull's devastating "political" game with the stubborn and sheepish military commission. As in the case of Krull's greatest achievement, the joke is so delightful that the Egyptians and all the people of the world whom the great Provider feeds are almost split with laughter.

> Full of bewitching charm seemed to them the meeting of precaution and evil, that is: the way the Provider of Shadow played a trick on the evil, drew from it profit and gain, made it subservient to ends which would never have occurred to the honestly stupid and to the ogre only out for destruction—full of bewitching charm, incredibly funny and arousing immense laughter.[26]

Thus in Joseph the highest potentialities of the Picaro are fulfilled and exhausted. Picaro, ennobled to the point where he becomes the representative of the Third Humanism, has cast the bridge over the abyss from which he emerged. It is quite understandable that Thomas Mann, when playing for a while with the idea of finishing the "confessions" of his cheat, came to the conclusion that "the continuation of Krull . . . was superannuated and superseded by the Joseph-cycle."[27] Yet, in spite of this assertion, the disrespectful rascal did not cease to exert his fascination on his author. Beyond his resurrection as Joseph on the one hand and Gustav Aschenbach and Adrian Leverkühn on the other, he contained potentialities of life which did not let themselves be smothered, even if his master had officially declared him dead. So it happened that the writer to whom German literature owes its greatest realistic novel (*Buddenbrooks*), the most exciting revival of the *Bildungsroman* (*Der Zauberberg*), the most modern re-creation of the historio-mythological novel (*Joseph und seine Brüder*) has given us the great picaresque novel of our century as well. Through his own life's work he thus established creative activity as the variation of an old pattern, new beginnings as the continuation of an age-hallowed tradition. And he proved as the great writer's task what he considers man's highest task altogether: to activate and regenerate the eternal essence of our heritage.

---
26. *Joseph der Ernährer*, 568 ff.
27. *Die Entstehung des Dr. Faustus*, 24.

# LAURENCE STERNE'S *TRISTRAM SHANDY* AND THOMAS MANN'S *JOSEPH THE PROVIDER*

At first glance, it may seem no more than a whim to bring into neighborly relationship two authors and books,[1] separated from each other by time, language, intellectual scope, motive, and purpose—a whim utterly arbitrary at the worst, amusingly eccentric at the best. Where is the connecting link between the rambling and, more often than not, naughty chitchat of the eighteenth-century Englishman and the monumental reëvocation of the Biblical story by the twentieth-century German; between the "hobby-horsical" inanities of uncle Toby and the deep probing into a venerable myth, yes into the nature of myth itself; between the scholastic nonsense of father Shandy and the inspired brooding of the great father Jacob about God, man, and their holy covenant; between the provincial English household centering around Mrs. Shandy's accouchement, an ungreased door-hinge, and a pair of breeches, and the intricate sociopolitical machinery of the old Egyptian empire?

Indeed, when skimming over some of the most authoritative critical verdicts on Laurence Sterne, we happen upon statements that seem to make the gap between our two authors definitely unbridgeable, and any attempt to establish a kinship between the two both presumptuous and futile. Wilbur Cross, the Englishman's most exhaustive biographer, finds in Sterne "a humorist pure and simple, and nothing else";[2] and while it is easy to contend that Thomas Mann is one of the greatest humorists in German letters, it would obviously be foolish to claim that he is nothing else, and that his humor is ever "pure and simple." Laurence Sterne, says Walter Bagehot, "excels all other writers in mere simple description of common sensitive human action";[3] but very little, indeed, would such a gift alone benefit a writer who has taken upon himself to retell a story sacred to us by its origin, its remoteness in time and space, its joyful solemnity.

---

1. Quotations refer to the Modern Library edition of Laurence Sterne, *Tristram Shandy* (New York, 1941), quoted as *TS*, and to Thomas Mann, *Joseph the Provider* (New York, 1944) quoted as *JP*. Since in a number of instances the text of this translation does not convey the exact meaning of the original, some changes had to be made. When reference is made to the German edition, *Joseph der Ernährer* (Stockholm, 1944), the reference reads *JE*.
2. Wilbur Cross, *The Life and Times of Laurence Sterne* (New Haven, 1925), II, 226.
3. Walter Bagehot, *Literary Studies*, Everyman's Library, II, 104.

And what are we to say when we read in Traill's book on Sterne that the only purpose of his writing *Tristram Shandy* "was to amuse the lightminded and scandalize the demure"?[4] Is there any kinship conceivable between such an author and Thomas Mann, who has probably less "amused the lightminded and scandalized the demure" than any figure in contemporary world literature? No, we seem to be on the wrong track: if we trust the obvious evidence, the weighty testimony of qualified witnesses, Thomas Mann and Laurence Sterne seem to be separated by worlds, and any attempt to break down the barriers between the two is doomed to failure.

Yet we have overlooked one witness, and quite an important one at that: Thomas Mann himself. In his lecture, *The Theme of the Joseph Novels,* delivered in the Library of Congress in 1942, Thomas Mann tells us that during the last *Joseph* years two books have been his steady companions: Laurence Sterne's *Tristram Shandy* and Goethe's *Faust,*[5] a combination which he himself calls "perplexing." But however perplexing this choice of books may be, Thomas Mann defines quite clearly what specific function the reading of *Tristram Shandy* had to fulfill during the creative process of the great Biblical story. "It was the humorous side of Joseph which profited by this reading. Sterne's wealth of humorous expressions and inventions, his genuine comical technique attracted me; for to refresh my work, I needed something like this."[6] This statement, then, makes it plain that there *is* a tangible relationship between the tale of the eccentric Shandy family and the tale of the twelve brothers who were to become the founders of a God-chosen, because God-choosing, people. And again, it is Thomas Mann himself who indicates the particular kind of relationship:

> There is a symptom for the innate character of a work, for the category toward which it strives, the opinion it secretly has of itself: that is the reading matter which the author prefers and which he finds helpful while working on it. I am not thinking, in this connection, about factual sources and material research, but about great works of literature which in a broad sense seem related to his own effort, models whose contemplation keeps him in the right mood . . . All that can be of no use, does not fit, has no reference to the subject—is hygienically excluded; it is not conducive at the moment and therefore disallowed.[7]

---
4. H. D. Traill, *Laurence Sterne* (New York, 1882), 36.
5. Thomas Mann, *The Theme of the Joseph Novels,* (Washington, D. C., 1942), 16.
6. *Ibid.,* 16.
7. *Ibid.,* 15f.

This remark not only stills our qualms as to the existence of a relationship and, with it, the justification of a comparison of the two books, but it prescribes definitely the method and the scope of our investigation. Laurence Sterne has not influenced Thomas Mann, *Tristram Shandy* is in not a single instance a source of *Joseph the Provider*, but there exists between the two authors and their work a subterranean communication, a similarity of key though not of melody, of attitude though not of expression, and by tracing these we might arrive, not at the establishment of a dependency of one upon the other, but at a clarification of the kindred form of creativeness of the one and the other.

We shall begin with the most elemental substance of a literary work of art: the language and the author's attitude towards it. It was "Sterne's wealth of humorous expressions," Thomas Mann says, which he found stimulating for his own work. And there again, we shall begin with the most elemental comical possibility offered by the language: the sound. It is the onomatopoetic value of the word which fascinates Sterne as much as Thomas Mann, the comical effect achieved by the pure release of sound. Sterne's work is full of it. Who does not remember the "pshaws and "pshis" with which Yorick "would often answer" (*TS*, 24), the Lillabulero whistle of uncle Toby which is his stereotyped reaction to any embarrassing situation, the exclamations of the author, void of meaning, but expressive as imitative sounds? And we find the same device in *Joseph the Provider*: the outbursts of laughter of the villagers, recorded as "hahas, hohos, huhus" (*JP*, 333), the "phis and phois" (*JE*, 472) with which the brothers fall upon Benjamin after the stolen silver cup is found in his possession; the numerous word innovations conceived on the basis of their sound: "phi fellow" for somebody who deserves to be shamed, "aulasaukaulala" (*JP*, 160) as a paraphrase for the foolish stammering of an obsessed person.

It would be wrong to see nothing but a comical effect, and a somewhat primitive one at that, in this linguistic device. If we link it with other stylistic phenomena, it will indicate, on the lowest level, a consummate mastery over the realm of the word. There is a second sympton to be found in both our writers, one which points more clearly in this direction: the cataloguelike, enumerative quality of the language. A single idea or a single impression is circumscribed by a long list of words, all of them having the same or almost the same meaning. Language seems to be driven by an urge to unfold itself, to bring all the possible synonyms into play, to brag, so to speak, with its own richness, evoked by associations of thought or of sound. *Tristram Shandy* is brimful of examples of this stylistic device of which we shall choose only one: "For what hindrance, hurt or harm doth the laudable desire of knowledge bring to any man, if even from a sot, a pot, a fool, a stool, a winter mitten, a truckle for a pully . . ." (*TS*, 177). And we find the same principle in Thomas Mann's long enumeration of the Angels' suspicions as to "matters, steps, undertakings, intentions, manoeuvres, secrets of the widest scope" entertained by God (*JP*, 10). And the same again in the description of the homage paid to Lord Joseph by the courtiers: "They bowed and scraped, they kowtowed and kissed hands."[8] We see that the one thought, servility of the courtiers, is (in the original) paraphrased by no less than seven different verbs, and if we listen closely enough, we shall notice the same acoustic decoration which binds the synonyms together. With Sterne it was an alliteration on the letter *h* (hindrance, hurt, and harm), with Thomas Mann it is an alliteration on the letters *b* and *k* (beugte sich, buckelte und buhlte, kusshandelte, kratzfusste). And if we look for the rhyming effect in these enumerative lists, corresponding to Sterne's "a sot, a pot, a fool, a stool," we shall find a great many examples in *Joseph the Provider* (pp. 47, 333, etc.), although most of them are lost in the English translation. If it be the description of Joseph's wife on her wedding day, adorned with "beads and precious stones, sardonyx, topaz, diamond, jasper, turquoise, amethyst, emeralds and onyx" (*JP*, 262), or the nomenclature of the country where Jacob and his tribe settle in Egypt—"this was Gosen, also called Kosen, Kesem, Gosem and Goshen" (*JP*, 511)—we always find the same effect of accumulative enumeration, of synonymous variety, of catalogue-like listing.

Certainly, it is an old stylistic device. We know that Sterne uses it because he found it profusely employed in his dearly beloved *Don Quixote*; we know that Thomas Mann uses it because it adds a somewhat archaic flavor which is so very appropriate to his tale. The real reason, however, lies deeper. It lies in the degree of consciousness with which language is used by the two authors. Both of them not only tell a story by using language as a simple and naïve tool, but while telling it, they

---

8. *JP*, 240. In the German original the enumeration is still much longer: "Man beugte sich, buckelte und buhlte, kusshandelte, kratzfusste, scharwenzelte und flattierte" (*JE*, 258).

listen to the sounds and meanings of their own words; they, the raconteurs, become listeners who ponder over the words just used, over shades of meaning, the possible implications and associations of their own medium of expression. The language is subject and object in one; it is the creator and the carrier of the story, but at the same time it is creation and object, which can be questioned, analyzed, and interpreted. The author converses with us, but in the midst of his conversation he stops, converses with his own words, inquires into their meanings, their possibilities, their evocative power. Very aptly Walter Watkins puts it this way: "Sterne listens to the sound of his own voice with as critical an ear as he listens to the voice of other people,"[9] and what is true of Sterne is ten times as true of Thomas Mann. Thus we read in *Tristram Shandy*: "Not that this phrase is all to my liking: for to say a man is fallen in love or that he is deeply in love, or up to the ears in love . . . carries an idiomatical kind of implication that Love is a thing below a man" (*TS*, 425), or "by the word *world* I would be understood to mean no more of it than a small circle of the great world of four English miles in diameter" (*TS*, 8). And quite similarly we are told in Thomas Mann's novel what we are to understand when Joseph uses a special word in a specific connection (*JP*, 21), and what is really implied in the phrase that the Governor of the prison, Mai-Sachme, "took nothing on himself" (*JP*, 52).

Thus language ceases to be a simple tool to impart a meaning and a story; it enters as a character in its own right, leads a life of its own, and is allowed all the playfulness which is the privilege of an actor in a play. It has a double face, a double aspect; it *is* the story, but at the same time acts in the story. It is the poet's expression, but he keeps it at a distance as well, and this is, as we shall later see, the true meaning of irony.

This playfulness of the language, the author's playing with the language, manifests itself in a whole series of modes of which Sterne and Thomas Mann are supreme masters. There is, first, the plain juggling with words; Laurence Sterne's: "Of all the cants which are canted in this canting world, though the cant of hypocrites may be the worst, the cant of criticism is the most tormenting" (*TS*, 161); or Thomas Mann's delightful double expression "die Schnur und die Schnurre" (*JE*, 356), an untranslatable twin-formation designating a daughter-in-law and a harlot. There is, secondly, the double meaning, used by Sterne

---

9. W. B. Watkins, *Perilous Balance* (Princeton, 1939), 124.

mainly—and more often than is acceptable to good taste—for the purpose of obscene *double entendre,* but used by Thomas Mann to hint at correspondences to the motions of higher and veiled things. It is simply miraculous how Mann can play with word-roots and their derivations, tying them into a sentence which rests on only one basic syllable.[10]

This double aspect, this double meaning and *double entendre,* bestows a somewhat magic quality upon the language. A word is not only a symbol conveying a clear-cut, well-defined meaning, but it opens up the whole field of allusions, possibilities, associations, reminiscences. Language is not a stable element but dynamic energy, and as such it exerts power. Both our authors testify to this belief, and it is only logical that the magic power of names should play such an important part in their works.[11] A name is more than an arbitrarily chosen designation for a person; it is a shaping force, and name and person form a living, dialectic unity.[12] We remember Sterne's elaborate chapter on names, we remember that the name Tristram was one of the three major catastrophes which befell the newly born Shandy offspring upon his birth, we remember the very stubborn opinion which Mr. Shandy held in this matter and which, in spite of the obvious nonsense, contains the grain of truth which all of Laurence Sterne's nonsense does contain. "His opinion in this matter was that there was a strange kind of magic bias which a good or bad name . . . irresistibly impressed upon our character and conduct" (*TS,* 44). And how many pages does Thomas Mann fill with the meaning and the importance of the name! Joseph's name is no longer Joseph, but it is no longer Osarsiph either, as it used to be during his service with Potiphar. It is now Djep-unt-efonech, and what this name means is explained on over two pages (*JP,* 238 f.). But not only Joseph's name changes; Pharaoh's name is also in permanent flux, because it differs in accordance with the gradual development of his religious efforts;

---

10. Pharao hatte den "Traum *deut*lich gesehen, und dass die *Deut*lichkeit voll von B*edeu*tung gewesen sei, welche nach *Deut*ung schreie" (*JE,* 144).
11. In the case of Thomas Mann there is to an even larger extent a belief in the magic power of numbers; this is noticeable not only in *Joseph the Provider,* but in his other works too. Hermann J. Weigand (*Thomas Mann's Novel 'Der Zauberberg',* New York, 1933, 182) and Harry Slochower (*Three Ways of Modern Man,* New York, 1937, 98) have ingeniously shown the leitmotif-magic of the number 7 in the *Magic Mountain.*
12. Harry Slochower, *Thomas Mann's Joseph Story* (New York, 1938) 25.

and the two courtiers who fall from their height find their names changed by highest decree, and they "are distressed lest these fantastic names which are written in indelible ink in our papers and the proceedings of our trials ... should gradually take on reality and we be so called to all eternity" (*JP*, 72). And quite openly Pharaoh asks Joseph: "So you think that one should not always be called the same but suit his name to his circumstances, according to what happens to him and how he feels?" (*JP*, 187). Of course, we shall not deny that Sterne's joke about names and Thomas Mann's deep brooding about the mythical impact of a name move on very different planes. But even through the Englishman's nonsensical jests shines wisdom: the knowledge of the magic force of the word.

But language does not only wield magic; it is full of demonic terror. Poor uncle Toby's life is almost wrecked by his inability to describe to his friends the exact location of his most heroic military deed, because he cannot get order into the maze of ravelins, half-moons, covered-ways, counterscarps, crosses, dykes, ditches, and all the other devilishly intricate parts of a fortress—an inability that has such a bad influence on his "radical moisture" as to bring him close to his grave. Walter Shandy expresses the situation quite aptly: " 'Twas not by ideas, by Heaven—his life was put in jeopardy by words" (*TS*, 76). And does not uncle Toby's embarrassment remind us, even though again on a different level, of the agonies of the guilty courtier who cannot command his speech, who, in the midst of his asseverations of his innocence, involves himself in such dangerous talk that he himself is deadly frightened and says to Joseph: "Pardon me, I did not mean to say that, at least, I did not intend to say it just like that, I do hope you are not getting the wrong idea ... I talk but when I listen to my own words I am alarmed" (*JP*, 75).

Language is no datum, no given substance to work with; language is a problem that has to be elucidated by permanent analytical discussion, by dialectical reasoning. The same holds true for the raw material of the story, its subject matter. It is not simply presented, but is gradually spun out of the permanent mulling over, the progressive analysis of the "source." With reference to Thomas Mann we can, in this connection, only hint fleetingly at this fact, because the analysis of the myth is for him not only a literary device, but the very philosophical topic of his work. But even in this context we shall have to mention his dialectical play with the information derived from the Bible. Thomas Mann himself admits that his great narrative "often reads like an exegesis and amplification of the Torah, like a rabbinical Midrash."[13] We follow with the greatest amusement the unending discussions and comments on the Biblical text. How was it with the seven fat years and the seven lean years? Were they really seven? Or were they only five? And was the sixth year not rather "partially" fat, or perhaps "partially" lean? But "partial" to such a degree that we might well call it all fat or all lean. And how was it with the seventy children of Israel who migrated from the grove of Mamreh into Egypt? Does this figure include Jacob himself? And does it comprise the womenfolk too? And what does the Bible mean when we read: Pharaoh made Joseph the Overlord of all Egypt? We could go on indefinitely listing examples of Thomas Mann's dialectic attitude toward the "source."

But where is the corresponding feature in *Tristram Shandy*? Actually, there is no source which Sterne could discuss as playfully as Thomas Mann does. But at times we catch the Englishman in an attempt at breaking the simple relationship between the Life and Opinions of Mr. Tristram Shandy and its written record by interpolating an intermediary source which, in fact, has no place in the book at all. The most striking example is in the Second Book where we find this footnote:

> The author is here twice mistaken; for Lithopaedus should be wrote thus: Lithopaedii Semonensis ... The second mistake is that Lithopaedus is not an author but a drawing of a petrified child ... Mr. Tristram Shandy has been led into this error, either from seeing Lithopaedus' name of late in a catalogue ... or by mistaking Lithopaedus for Trinecavellius from the too great similitude of the name (*TS*, 135n.)

How very strange and confusing! Who is making this footnote? We are under the impression that Tristram Shandy is writing his own life story—and then, all of a sudden, there is an editor, another author who adds to and comments on Tristram Shandy's narrative. We are confronted with an amusing sort of picture-puzzle. The effect is one of a strange palimpsest: just as a much older narrative, the original text of the Bible, is sustained beneath Thomas Mann's story, so we find another text, whose author is somewhat mysterious, superimposed upon

---
13. Mann, *op. cit.*, 14.

the autobiography of Tristram Shandy. And yet, this "double" is all-present, not only in footnotes like the one quoted above, but as the "I" of the book who in a good many cases is obviously not Tristram Shandy but somebody looking over Tristram Shandy's shoulder and contributing his remarks *à propos*.

But this is not all. There seems to be an irresistible urge in Sterne to introduce "sources" which the author can discuss and play with. It is impossible to enumerate all of them. But we have only to recall the long insertion of Slawkenbergius' Treatise on Noses, the learned discussions of Messieurs les Docteurs de la Sorbonne as to whether an embryo can be baptized in its mother's womb, the scholastic disputes among Kysarcius, Didius, and Triptolemus as to whether or not a mother is kin to her child—all of them highly amusing outgrowths of a playfully argumentative mind and none of them a contribution to the straight telling of the Life and Opinions of Mr. Tristram Shandy. This dialectic attitude, this tendency to play with sources, with arguments, with meanings, in short, irony, is prevalent in both our authors. The approach to the fable they tell is circuitous; they weave the fabric of a narrative, but while weaving they ask: What is going on here? From the hair-splitting pettifoggery of Sterne's scholastics Phutatorius and Kysarcius and Didius it is only a short step to Pharaoh's question put before Joseph: "All this is very odd. Have you been speaking or have you not? You have been speaking while you did not speak but only let us hear your thoughts, those, that is, which you only think to think. But it seems to me it is the same as though you had spoken" (*JP*, 182). Kysarcius, while weighing the pros and cons with regard to the kinship of a mother to her child, could not do much better than that.

More than once, when talking about the author's attitude towards the language, towards his own subject matter, we have had to use the words *play* and *playfulness*. And now, moving to a higher plane, we shall have to use these words again. For the whole of Thomas Mann's monumental tetralogy is a play, a festival, a festive repetition, as he calls it more than once,[14] a new fulfillment of an old pattern, a pattern as old as the ages, older than the ages. As the author arranges a festive repetition of an old saga for us in order to elucidate our eternal substance and destiny, so God arranges the whole saga as a festive spectacle for Himself in order to elucidate His eternal substance and des-

---

14. *Ibid.*, 3.

tiny. The child Serach, announcing to old Jacob that his son is still alive, epitomizes the meaning of the wondrous and holy story:

> Read it in his laughing features,
> All was but Jehova's jest,
> And in late-believing raptures
> Take him to thy father-breast.[15]

By inviting us to this playful repetition, the author shows us that not only he himself, but also the characters are very much aware of the fact that they are only filling out a prescribed, predesigned pattern, that they live a "story" which they have to shape according to the highest designs. Hardly anybody is more conscious of this fact than Joseph himself; the last words which he addresses to his brothers are full of this knowledge. He could not express it more clearly than he does in his speech to Mai-Sachme: "Truly I find it greater yet to live in a story; this that we are in is certainly a capital one, of that I am more and more convinced the longer I live. And now you are in it with me because I brought you" (*JP*, 262).

In this connection, we can only touch upon the meaning of the "festival" which is the very topic of Thomas Mann's work; we touch upon it only to show that vestiges of a festival, though it is anything but solemn, are to be found in Laurence Sterne's comic *œuvre*. For what is uncle Toby's whole life in the book other than a playful reënactment of an old story, the story here being the campaigns of the Duke of Marlborough which, with the help of his faithful Corporal Trim, uncle Toby duplicates in his little garden behind the house? As Joseph re-lives a story, so does uncle Toby follow his to the minutest detail of the model; and as it is Joseph's highest ambition to adorn his life's story—which is only a mythical repetition—with the beautiful highlights of suspense and dénouement, so it is uncle Toby's highest ambition to adorn his life's story—which is only a historical repetition—with the beautiful highlights of captured fortresses, of heroic deeds and bright strategy. To be sure, Joseph's reënactment is the fulfillment of the timelessly existing, the myth, while uncle Toby's reënactment is just a hobbyhorse. But the highest authority—Sterne calls it Fate—has its hand in uncle

---

15. *JP*, 514. Here, as in some other instances, we have corrected Mrs. Lowe-Porter's translation, since her rendering of *Gottesscherz* by "godlike jest" fails to convey the proper meaning.

Toby's hobbyhorse, too. Although mockingly, it is alluded to as the creator of the pattern which uncle Toby piously fills in:

> When Fate was looking forward one afternoon into the great transactions of future times and recollected for what purpose this little plot (behind Toby's house) had been destined, she gave a nod to Nature. Nature threw half a spade of her kindliest compost upon it with just so much clay in it as to retain the form of angles and indentings—and so little of it as not to cling to the spade and render works of so much glory nasty in foul weather (*TS*, 402).

Reënactment always poses the question of identity—identity of space, of time, of individuality. This problem is one of the most decisive in Thomas Mann's works. If one plays a part, one does not know who one really is: the actor or the part enacted; one does not know to which level of reality one belongs: to the level where the story took place for the first time or to the level where the story repeats itself. The best example is Eliezer, the eternal servant, who is conscious of the fact that he repeats an old pattern. Is he Eliezer, the very old one, who once served with Abraham, or is he the old companion of Jacob, or is he quite another one who is now only called Eliezer, because he plays the part of Eliezer? And this strange confusion of the different layers of reality, the reality of the old story that is being repeated and the reality of the repetition, besets uncle Toby in a most drastic way. The fortress of Dunkirk has to be demolished, so it was enacted by the Treaty of Utrecht. Uncle Toby has to reënact it now. And here this amusing dialogue between uncle Toby and Corporal Trim sets in. Says uncle Toby: " 'We'll demolish the mole, next fill up the harbour, then retire into the citadel and blow it up into the air; and having done that we'll embark for England.' 'We are there,' quoth the Corporal, recollecting himself. 'Very true,' said uncle Toby, looking at the church" (*TS*, 422).

But this strange confusion of time and space caused by the reënactment of something of the past worries not only uncle Toby, but the teller of the story himself. At a certain point he has to ask himself the question: Where am I, during which period of my past am I living?; and having lost his coòrdinates in space and time, he might as well ask: Who am I? "I have brought myself into such a situation as no traveller ever stood before me; for I am this moment walking across the market place of Auxerre ... and I am this moment also entering Lyon with my post-chaise ... and I am moreover this moment in a handsome pavilion ...

upon the banks of the Garonne where I now sit rhapsodizing all these affairs" (*TS*, 467).

We should be very much surprised if Thomas Mann, when reading these lines, had not given a startled jolt of recognition. For this question: On which level of time am I living? must be a very familiar one to the author who revealed for us the "myth" as the sphere in which the ancient and the new are blended in one. This inquiry into the strange medium of our lives, into Time, must be familiar to the one who has probed more deeply and more relentlessly into the abyss of time than any other of our contemporaries, with the possible exception of Henri Bergson. We can understand that Mann found the eighteenth-century Englishman's work "related to his own effort," when happening upon some passages in *Tristram Shandy* which, however fleetingly, ask the question which became one of the most exciting and most decisive themes of the *Magic Mountain*: What is time? In Tristram Shandy's careful calculations as to whether enough time has elapsed between the calling for and the arrival of Dr. Slop to make his appearance on the scene plausible; in his amusing discussions as to whether the five minutes allotted to Mrs. Shandy's eavesdropping have passed—in such instances we can find a parallel, however primitive, to Thomas Mann's profound musings on the relationship between time and the progressive unfolding of a story's material which plays such an important part in the *Magic Mountain*.[16] But not only in the *Magic Mountain*. It recurs in *Joseph the Provider*, in the comments on condensation and excision which "play their part at the beautiful feat of narration and recreation" (*JP*, 230). And is not the insertion of the almost independent *Thamar* novelette[17] an attempt to bridge the time gap between Joseph's elevation to the highest position in Egypt and the arrival of the brothers from Canaan, a great many years later? But even the very modern question: How do we experience time, what determines its duration?—a question profoundly discussed by Bergson and Thomas Mann—is already anticipated in *Tristram Shandy*. It is almost a premature circumscription of Bergson's *durée* when father Shandy tries "to show my uncle Toby by what mechanism and mensurations in the brain it came to pass that the rapid succes-

---

16. A very lucid demonstration of the relationship between time and the unfolding story-material is to be found in Weigand, *op. cit.*, 14-20.
17. How independent this insertion is may be seen from the fact that Thomas Mann published *Thamar* separately in book form (Los Angeles, 1944).

sions of their ideas had lengthened out so short a period to so inconceivable an extent" (*TS*, 167).

However, the main question in the *Joseph* cycle, in *Joseph the Provider* above all, is not "What is time?" but "What is *the* time?"—in which period do we find ourselves and what are this period's demands?[18] To be in accord with one's time, to hear its orders and to fulfill them—that is the socio-ethical message of Thomas Mann in his monumental work. God Himself changes, He lives in time, and

> 'Concern with God' is not alone the creating of God in one's thoughts and determining and recognizing Him, but principally the concern with His will with which ours must coincide; with the demands of the present, the postulate of the aeon, of the world-hour. It is the intelligent listening to what the world spirit wants, to the new truth and necessity.[19]

This is the true greatness of Joseph, that he listens so intelligently to the postulate of the æon, that he turns from the dreaming of dreams to the great political task of a provider for the Continents. He knows what God wants, and he helps Him to achieve it. In this he is Jacob's true son, who knew it too and still knows it. It is this knowledge which makes the old patriarch so undogmatically understanding, so liberal in his attitude towards the modern foppishness of his son, which, although not quite to his taste, is, he well realizes, the demand of the hour. And is not the essence of *Tristram Shandy* something quite similar, although the emphasis is somewhat shifted? If we read the Englishman's novel with something more than a naïve desire for entertainment and laughter, it will not escape us that it represents a hilarious settlement of accounts with the antiquated and obsolete spirit of a bygone æon. Those ghostlike and ghastly scholastics Phutatorius, Kysarcius, Didius, Triptolemus, and the score of others whatever their names may be, with their hair-splitting disputes, their ridiculous arguments which are so logical that they become utterly absurd, are not only plainly comical figures, but revenants from a dead æon, poor wretches who do not know what hour has struck. We laugh at them, because the author wants us to laugh at them; but our laughter is only a faint echo of the Olympic laughter, the mischievous mockery of God directed against those who cannot read the truth of a new

---

18. Slochower (*Three Ways of Modern Mann*, 91) has pointed out that even in the *Magic Mountain* the meaning of time "is in its social contexts."
19. Mann, *op. cit.*, 19.

world-hour. If these cronies, babbling the wisdom of centuries past, are ludicrous, they are ludicrous in the same sense in which Laban is ludicrous, because he, too, is deaf to the new truth and necessity, because he is "stupid before God." For both Sterne and Thomas Mann laughter is the proper answer to so much backwardness, to such a hopeless and abject attempt to keep alive the conceptions of an old age. There is no reason to rage against it (how can one rage against the dead?); and as Sterne heaps ridicule upon the Phutatorii, Didii, Kysarcii, so Joseph states in his very last words: "I could laugh at the thought! For a man who uses power only because he has it, against right and reason, he is ridiculous. If he is not today, he will be so in the future. And it is the future we are interested in" (*JP*, 608).

And what is the demand of the hour? Again, the answers of our two authors are strangely similar: the attitude of irony. Actually Laurence Sterne never bothers to define it, while Thomas Mann's lifework can almost be summarized as the growing and broadening of the conception of irony to an extent where it becomes the basis of human existence, the key to the fulfillment of all human endeavor in the striving towards a "Third Humanism."[20] We used the word "irony" twice before: in connection with the authors' attitude towards the language and with the authors' attitude towards their actual or fictitious sources. We shall have to use it now with reference to the relationship of the author to his own work. Both Sterne's novel and Thomas Mann's Biblical saga seem the highest fulfillment of what Friedrich Schlegel, the theoretician of the German Romantic School, upheld as the ultimate proof of modern artistic greatness: Romantic Irony.[21] Thomas Mann defines Romantic Irony in a parenthetical sentence of his *Joseph the Provider*: "The story teller is the theatre of his story, but the story not his theatre, which circumstance gives him the chance to discuss it" (*JP*, 16). Romantic Irony is the reconciliation of matter and spirit: it never allows the creation, the story, to cut the umbilical cord that links it with its creator, and it never allows the creator

---

20. The best discussion of Thomas Mann's concern with irony as a literary device and as a human attitude is to be found in the chapter "The Ironic Temper" in Weigand, *op. cit.*, 59-95.
21. As to the relationship of Thomas Mann to Friedrich Schlegel, cf. Weigand *op. cit.*, 63-66; Käte Hamburger, *Thomas Mann und die Romantik* (Berlin, 1932), 26 ff.—For Sterne and Romantic Irony, cf. Gertrud Hallamore, *Das Bild Laurence Sternes in Deutschland* (Berlin, 1936), 72; and Alfred Lussky, *Tieck's Romantic Irony* (Chapel Hill, 1932), 135-58.

to fall into imageless introspection. Romantic Irony is the reconciliation of the Infinite and Finite; for while the Infinite materializes itself in the cosmos of a narrative, the single narrative transcends itself by its conscious participation in the eternal. This Romantic Irony manifests itself by the permanent interference of the author in the course of his story, by his conversations with his audience, by his discussions of the mechanism of his narrative, by his comment on the events of his tale, in short, by a constant and most conscious omnipresence of the creator in his creation. And here we discover one of the main reasons why *Tristram Shandy* could become Thomas Mann's steady companion, here we recognize the sign which stamps the two authors as brethren of the same spirit. The similarity in the epic technique is striking. We consider first the relationship of our two authors to their audience, and we find almost a duplication of attitude: the same cajoling, the same announcements of what the reader is to expect, the same seemingly angry exhortations about his impatience and bad manners. We are allowed to look into the workshop of the author by being told what the next chapters have in store for us, be it Sterne's very elaborate enumeration of what he wants to deal with in the volumes in preparation (*TS*, 303), or Thomas Mann's announcement of the exciting events he still has to narrate before he can finish his saga (*JP*, 462). We are told how we ought to react and how we probably do react in a specific instance (*TS*, 7, 95; *JP*, 289, 324); we are scolded for our impatience, for our refusal to follow the road which the author has chosen. Sterne, too, is strict with his readers, and he has no compunction about inflicting the following punishment: "The lady has to read the whole chapter over—'tis to rebuke a vicious taste which has crept into thousands besides herself of reading straight forward, more in quest of the adventures than of the deep erudition . . . which a book of this cast . . . would infallibly impart" (*TS*, 50). And in very much the same scolding vein Thomas Mann talks to his readers: "It would be a pity if now, having heard all these things, our audience were to disperse or turn away its ears thinking: Well, . . . the climax is reached, nothing better can be coming, there is only the end of the tale and we already know how it turned out, we cannot get excited. Take my word for it, you are wrong. Let me advise you and remain seated, all of you!" (*JP*, 462).

Again and again the author converses with us, again and again he converses with his own story. He keeps it at a distance, he detaches himself ironically, and this distance gives him an opportunity to discuss his own creation. Thomas Mann tells us about the necessity of epic condensation and omission (*JP*, 230), and this admission sounds like an echo of Tristram's regret that he cannot tell everything, because, having recorded thus far only one day of his life, he finds himself already in the middle of the fifth volume (*TS*, 255). The author keeps his ultimate freedom in the handling of his story, he directs it and arranges it as he sees fit; and as Tristram Shandy suppresses some of his thoughts because it would not be proper to mention them (*TS*, 95), so Thomas Mann assures us: "The names (of the other daughters of Pharaoh) I could easily tell you, but . . . I feel no inclination to put them down" (*JP*, 284).

At each point we are reminded of the presence of the author, nowhere are we allowed to take his tale as naïve reality. And if we are not allowed to take the epic as strict reality, neither are we allowed to take it as a conscious piece of fiction, because all at once the authors address their own characters as if they were real existing beings; and while Tristram Shandy makes his straightforward declarations of love to uncle Toby and Corporal Trim (*TS*, 200, 330), Thomas Mann talks to his Joseph and assures him that soon enough he will be deeply in love with Asenath, the girl whom he has just married (*JP*, 278). Is there a more charming example of Romantic Irony than the short passage in *Joseph the Provider* where Thomas Mann pretends to suppress some aspects of Joseph's wedding ceremony—out of deference for old Jacob who would disapprove of this heathenish orgy.

> That we do not go into them with the last degree of exactitude is due to a kind of consideration for old Jacob back there at home . . . Jacob would assuredly have flung up his hands at the sight of much that happened at the wedding. It would have confirmed him in his honest prejudices against Mizraim . . . prejudices which we would wish to respect, and so do not describe the occasion with such particularity as to imply that we approve of what went on (*JP*, 272).

This illusion that a character in the book leads a life apart from his fictional existence, that he could hear what the author tells him or tells about him or about others, that, though disappearing from the pages of the book, he is still alive and around, is overwhelmingly reflected in Sterne's hilarious remark:

> Dr. Slop is engaged with the midwife and my mother upstairs. Trim is busy in turning an old pair of jack-boots into a couple

of mortars to be employed in the siege of Messina next summer
... all my heroes are off my hands, 'tis the first time I have had
a minute to spare (*TS*, 170).

We shall not have exhausted the demonstration of Romantic Irony in Sterne and Thomas Mann until we mention the playful arbitrariness with which the authors arrange and present their subject matter, with which they interrupt and mend again the continuity of the story proper. This is not the place to analyze the structure of *Tristram Shandy*, if indeed anybody would call this hodgepodge a "structure." Whoever would look in *The Life and Opinions of Mr. Tristram Shandy* for the life and opinions of Mr. Tristram Shandy would be badly disappointed. He will find an endless sequence of what the author calls "digressions" (digressions from what? we have to ask), a wild mosaic of disconnected stories, anecdotes, arguments, insertions, sermons, drawings, footnotes, reminiscences, bits of erudition, so wild that we can rightly call them paranoiac. There is no continuity: in the midst of Book VI the author tears out a page; the Author's Preface follows Chapter 20 of Book III; in Book IX Chapters 18 and 19 are omitted, only to be inserted after Chapter 25; a good number of chapters are begun, interrupted, and started all over again—to mention only a few of the crudest antics of Sterne's epic technique which mirrors the utter and boundless arbitrariness of the creative spirit. Surely, there is nothing comparable to be found in Thomas Mann's conscientious and painstaking method of storytelling. But in his case, too, the real value and greatness of the *œuvre* do not lie in the simple presentation of the story material, but in his philosophical meanderings, in his profound marginal discussions, in his lucid ponderings *à propos*. And the long interruption of the main course of action by the insertion of the *Thamar* novella testifies to Thomas Mann's inclination towards digression, points to the poet's supreme sovereignty over the crude subject matter.

But irony as a stylistic device is only an outgrowth of a much more profound ironical attitude, an attitude in which Thomas Mann recognizes the realization of the eternally—and therefore truly—human.[22] Irony he calls it, but it is strangely reminiscent of what Aristotle called the "metotis," of what Nicolaus von Cues called the "coincidentia oppositorium," of what Goethe called the "die and grow." It is a synthesis, but a synthesis in

---

22. For the connection between Romantic Irony and the "Third Humanism," cf. Käte Hamburger, *op. cit.*, 92 ff.

which both positions, the "yes" and the "no," are still autonomously alive. To achieve this irony is the highest task of man. Thomas Mann's work is a monumental clarification of this truest fulfillment of the human mission and destiny: in the realm of existence the reconciliation of Life and Death, in the realm of philosophy the reconciliation of Matter and Spirit, in the realm of psychology the reconciliation of the Conscious and the Unconscious, in the realm of ethics the reconciliation of bourgeois virtues with artistic daring, in the realm of historic development the reconciliation of tradition with the demand of the hour, in the realm of politics the reconciliation of conservatism with social progressiveness. There is no more beautiful realization of this truly human attitude than Joseph: the dreamer of dreams and the shrewd economic reformer of a world empire; the man who is faithful to his invisible God and faithful to the demands of this world, who is a stranger in Egypt and a father to his country, who lives in Menfe, the city of Death, as a provider of life for the Oikumene. And in all this he is the true son of the great father Jacob, the moon-shepherd, the glad-sorry man, whose attribute is "tam" (*JP*, 259), which means yes and no, the light and the dark, the relentless and holy seeker and finder of God, and the roguishly shrewd founder of a people.

But what has all this to do with a certain "plain and simple humorist" called Laurence Sterne and his brain child *Tristram Shandy*? Yet, is not *Tristram Shandy* full of the same irony: the story of a poor wretched creature whose entrance into this world is marked by a succession of catastrophes, and who, both willingly and unwillingly, becomes the donor of so much mirth, a true "glad-sorry" man? One may argue that Tristram Shandy has to be eliminated because he can hardly be called the hero of the book. But who is the hero? Is it father Shandy or is it uncle Toby? Or is it not rather the relationship, the equation between father Shandy and uncle Toby, the touching and adorable tie between the cold and painfully barren intellectualism of Walter Shandy and the warm and naïve simplicity of uncle Toby, this unforgettable relationship (and irony means basically relationship) between the two brothers, one of whom is dark and the other light, one of whom is "no" and the other "yes"? This sympathy seems to me the very basis of Sterne's book, and when reading it, we cannot help recollecting Friedrich Schlegel's beautiful definition: "True irony—for there is a false one too—

is the irony of love."[23] And as a sort of enlargement of this statement we read in Thomas Mann:

> For sympathy is a meeting of life and death; true sympathy exists only where the feeling for one balances the feeling for the other. Feeling for death by itself makes for rigidity and gloom; feeling for life by itself for flat mediocrity and dull-wittedness. Wit and sympathy can arise only where veneration for death is moderated . . . by friendliness to life, while life, on the other hand, acquires depth and poignancy. This happened in Joseph's case (*JP*, 258).

And this, we may add, is exactly what happens in the case of the Shandy brothers. Irony, as the truly human, is not the either-or, but the one-and-the-other; it is the permanent blending of the antinomies which beset man, and which he is called upon to integrate in an ever-precarious balance. Irony means living in two realms at the same time, in those "two beds" in which Walter Shandy arrives at all important decisions of his life: the bed of sobriety and the bed of spirit (*TS*, 395).

The meeting place of the opposites is wit and sympathy—we read in Thomas Mann. And wit is the ultimate meeting place of our two authors. This wit, or we might call it more properly humor, is the very essence of the two books. We do not mean the very obvious and quite often revoltingly indelicate jokes of Sterne, although these may draw the most boisterous laughter. It is rather the "merry heart" of which Yorick says that there is no danger in it (*TS*, 23); it is that "betwixt the fullness of the heart and stomach and the severe fasting" (*TS*, 396), which, as Sterne tells us, make up the very essence of his writing; it is, in short, Shandyism, this tender though whimsical, respectful though intimate, natural though inconceivable relationship between the two Shandies who are as far apart from each other as fire and water. In this strange friendship there is sublime wit, which Thomas Mann defines in his *Joseph the Provider*:

> Quite early (in our tale) it was said that wit is of the nature of a messenger to and fro and of a go-between betwixt opposite spheres and influences: for instance between the power of the sun and the moon . . . between the blessing of the day and the blessing of the night, yes, to put it directly and succinctly, between life and death (*JP*, 535).

Wit is the most genuine expression of the human being, his in-

---

23. Friedrich Schlegel, *Philosophie der Sprache und des Wortes*, in *Sämmtliche Werke* XV (Wien, 1846), 56.

alienable fatherland. And being this, it is the true guide to humaneness. It is the power that strengthens our lives, the great comforter which accompanies us through the darkness encroaching upon us. "True Shandyism," Laurence Sterne tells us, "opens the heart and the lungs; it forces the blood . . . to run freely through its channels, makes the wheel of life run long and cheerfully around" (*TS*, 305). This mirth is the soil which nourishes us, it is the only solution that is given into our hands to free us from the burden which our mortal existence places upon our shoulders. I could not think of a more beautiful and more deeply moving praise of this divine mirth, of a more profound interpretation of its redeeming function than Joseph's words:

> For lightness, my friend, the artful jest, that is God's very best gift to man, the profoundest knowledge we have of this complex, questionable thing called life. God gave it to humanity so that life's terribly serious face might be forced to wear a smile. My brothers rent my garment and flung me into the pit; now they are to stand before my stool—and that is life. And the question whether we are to judge the act by the result and approve the bad act because it was needed for the good result—that is life too. Life puts such questions as these and they cannot be answered with a long face. Only in lightness can the spirit of man rise above them: with a laugh at being faced with the unanswerable, perhaps he can make even God Himself, the great Unanswering, to smile (*JP*, 357 f.).

In this art of jest, which seems to us the wisest answer to the insoluble problem of human existence, Laurence Sterne and Thomas Mann show their basic kinship. We have tried to demonstrate their affinity in more than one respect, in spite of the discouraging verdicts of official Sterne experts. Their interpretations of Sterne did not point in a direction where we could have hoped to find common ground. But there exists another verdict on Sterne, a much older and, it seems to us, a much wiser one. It not only characterizes Sterne's human attitude, but it stresses at the same time Sterne's "message," the elements of his work which are helpful to us in our own life struggle. I quote these words, written sixty years after Sterne's death, as an evaluation of the English novelist—words which miraculously characterize Thomas Mann as well:

> This noble benevolent irony, this consideration for the part combined with the view for the whole, this equanimity in the midst of all contrarieties, this steadiness in the midst of all fluctuation and as all other related virtues might be called, were to me a

permanent source of education and ennoblement, and these are, in the last analysis, the sentiments which lead us back to the right path after all the errors and pitfalls of life.[24]

The voice just quoted is one of the dearest and most venerable in world literature. It is the voice of Goethe.

---

24. Goethe, Letter to C. F. Zelter, December 25, 1829.—About Goethe's attitude toward Laurence Sterne, cf. Wilhelm Pinger, *Laurence Sterne und Goethe* (Berkeley, 1920); Harvey W. Thayer, *Laurence Sterne in Germany*, (New York, 1906), 97-107; Gertrud Hallamore, *op. cit.*, 42-45 and 57-59.

# HERMANN HESSE:
# THE EXORCISM OF THE DEMON

The conferring of the literary Nobel Prize for 1946 upon Hermann Hesse has brought into the international limelight, however briefly, a figure whose features were unfamiliar to the literary world at large. It has also illuminated the perplexing fact that our notions of literary greatness and fame are both arbitrary and relative in that an author, whose merits and standing are solidly confirmed at home, may be found "obscure" by foreign literary critics. The question that was being asked somewhat mockingly "Who, after all, *is* Hermann Hesse?" must be disquieting to anybody familiar with contemporary German literature. And the fact that second and third rate German novelists and biographers gained easy admittance into our country, while only a few of Hesse's books were translated (and are now being gradually re-issued), sets one thinking about the strange selective process at work in the establishment of a world-literature. This phenomenon would lose its awkwardness if Hesse's talent, themes and problems were such as to appeal primarily to a narrowly defined home audience. But this is not the case. One cannot easily dismiss the fact that two such discerning and different writers as Franz Kafka and André Gide have counted Hesse among their favorites, that a true citizen of the world, Romain Rolland, has not only found him worthy of personal friendship but considered him one of his most interesting literary contemporaries. This, and the adoration which Hesse's *Demian* (published anonymously in 1919) enjoyed among the élite of German youth who clasped this book as if it embodied a new Revelation emerging from the apocalypse of the World War, may justify a closer analysis of Hermann Hesse's literary work. This evaluation will not deal with the obvious ties connecting Hesse with the poets of German Romanticism; it will not focus upon the socio-political concerns as expressed in his pacifist manifestos published during the first World War. Rather it will concentrate on Hesse's ruthless and self-tormenting exposure of the *condition humaine,* his metaphysical anxiety, his struggle with the demon and yearning for redemption which make him both a "modern" in the truest sense of the word and an ally of those who, by self-dissection, have made us painfully aware of the fate of man under the Sign of the Crisis.

## I. Awakening

"In the beginning was the myth"—these are the opening words of Hesse's *Peter Camenzind* (1904), the novel which carried an almost completely unknown author to fame, rather incongruous opening words; for the story of the Swiss peasant lad who, after years of struggles, disappointments, self-deceptions and frustrating experiences in the literary world finally returns to his native village, is much more closely related to the poetic realism of the late 19th century than to the myth-creating and myth-recreating efforts of our generation. Still, that these words introduce Hesse's first full-fledged literary achievement, that they stand as watch-words over his career, is no accident. The myth which is "in the beginning" will be forever the subsoil from which Hesse's works grow.

The myth is man's first answer to (or rather his first groping visualization of) the problems with which his own existence and his position in the cosmos confront him. It is man's awakening to himself, and it has all the landmarks of an awakening: the lingering on in the twilight region between night and day, the shock at the immediate directness of the new light, the courageous attempt to transpose experiences of a primeval nature into the language and symbols of reality. In just this way Hesse's stories are myths; his entire work seems an endless recording of the process of awakening. The very word fascinates him, and in his last work, the monumental *Glass Pearl Game* (1943), published in this country under the title *Magister Ludi*, we find the protagonist's admission that "awakening was to me a truly magic word, demanding and pressing, consoling and promising." The process of waking in the morning was described with terrifying minuteness in *Kurgast* (Diary from a Health Resort, 1925), as memorable as the similar analysis in Proust's *Du côté de chez Swann*, but intensified by the horror of facing the light again, by the deadly desire not to venture across the threshold of a new day. A painful exercise in trespassing the threshold: this, and nothing else, is the essence of Hesse's works.

In the early novels, *Peter Camenzind* and *Under the Wheel* (1906), this "exercise" was still so much shrouded in psychological realism that Hesse appeared to be one more of the many sensitive and delicate anatomists of puberty. Hans Giebenrath, hero of *Under the Wheel,* falls all too clearly into the well-established type of the languid adolescent: troubles with an antagonistic father, endless conflicts with a cruel and impersonal school-system, vague wanderings into the thoroughly bewildering realm of eros and sex, and finally the only half-intended suicide after some cheap carouse. Yet, in the light of Hesse's later development, it becomes quite obvious that the psycho-biological "case histories" of Peter Camenzind and Hans Giebenrath are only timid approaches to the painful process of awakening, timid even to the extent that both heroes shy away from passing through *la porte étroite*: Hans Giebenrath lets himself half-wittingly glide into the river, while Peter Camenzind returns to the quiet shelter of his home village where the "light of the day" does not penetrate. (The fact that in both cases the return to the dark is caused by failure to establish satisfactory sexual relations opens the door to psychoanalytic interpretations to which Hesse has been only too often subjected.) There is, in these early books, still a wall barring the adolescent hero from the open road, the same wall which separates young Hesse from the realization of his own inner self and of the problems which beset him and his time. A shock was needed to break down the barrier and bring an awakening which would force upon Hesse the reëvaluation of all values, and open the road before him. The shock came in the form of the first World War.

From this time on, the veil which so strangely shrouded Hesse's earlier productions is ruthlessly drawn away. No longer does the poet shrink from tasting the "forbidden fruit," from trespassing across the threshold between the stage of innocence and the acceptance of man's fate. No matter how painful this step might be, it has to be taken. In one of his short stories, *Klein and Wagner*, written immediately after the War (1919), we read: "In reality there was only one thing which man feared: letting himself fall, taking a step out into the Unknown, the little step beyond all existing securities. But who has once, just once abandoned himself, has just once given himself into the hands of fate, he is free." Klein, the hero of our story, has set himself free. After a secure life as a bank clerk he suddenly woke up and saw the humiliation caused by his daily routine, by his marriage to a woman he had never loved and finally learned to hate, by the suppression of all noble and strong desires. This awakening was his "original sin": the little bank teller, before embarking on his road to freedom, defrauded his institution of a considerable sum: he had fallen, but he was free. It would be hard not to see in this story, this little anecdote lifted from the every-day criminal register, a paraphrase of the story of the fall of man.

Protestant to the core, haunted by the consciousness of original sin, Hesse has circled again and again around man's tasting of the forbidden fruit of the tree of knowledge, his awakening amidst fear and trembling. The Forbidden which has to be faced exerts a dangerous but promising fascination. Already in *Under the Wheel* there was a dark and slimy alley which exuded "together with a strangely foul air a blissfully uncanny anguish, a mixture of curiosity, anxiety, bad conscience and heavenly premonitions of adventures." All of Hesse's heroes are simultaneously repelled and attracted by this dark alley, none more strongly than the young protagonist of *A Child's Soul* (1919) whose story becomes one of the most terrifying records of mental anguish in contemporary literature. Drawn to his father's room, where he has no business to be, he rummages in all the corners and drawers of the study "only to follow a compulsion which almost choked me, the compulsion to do evil, to hurt myself, to load myself with guilt." When the Serpent whispers, Adam will not resist, the sin has to be committed. And so the youngster in *A Child's Soul* steals fruit from his father's drawer, not an apple but a few dried figs (and that the fig-tree is introduced makes the "mythical" impact of the story perhaps more obvious than necessary).

The urge to find out the "secret" about one's self and the hidden corners of life, curiosity in the widest and most dangerous sense, is the driving force behind Hesse's work. It is a ruthless curiosity, shameless and without mercy, and it will not rest until the last veil is drawn back. For this reason then, and not for the sake of psychological subtleties, Hesse has delved again and again into the minds of vagrants and adolescents, since for them everything is unknown and without name before they have "found out." They are all spies tracking themselves down, excited by the scent of the Unknown, hankering after secrets. They are all very much akin to the Kierkegaard who admitted that it would have given him great satisfaction to be a member of the Copenhagen criminal police force. They are all brethren of Gide's protagonists, the ruthless exposers and explorers, the snoopers through *Les Caves du Vatican,* living embodiments of a curiosity which never seems to exhaust itself so that the very last sentence of *The Counterfeiters* can start with the words: "Now I am curious . . . " In one of his early writings, a collection of fairy tales, short stories, diary pages and poems entitled *Hermann Lauscher* (1901), Hesse calls Lauscher's most characteristic feature a "self-tormenting love for truth," and he could have hardly found a more appropriate self-characterization. He is consumed by an uncontrollable and at times embarrassing desire to be naked, to show himself in so merciless a light that even the "private parts" of body and soul will not be spared exposure. In his story *Klingsor's Last Summer* (1919), the painter Klingsor gathers in his final hours the strength to do his self-portrait. And this is what his friends see when, after Klingsor's death, the picture has been found: "It is Man, Ecce Homo, the tired, rapacious, wild, child-like and overrefined man of our late period, homo Europaeus, dying and desiring to die: purified by every longing, sick with every vice, enthusiastically elated by the knowledge of his destruction, ready for every progress, ripe for each regression, all glow and all fatigue, devoted to fate and pain as the morphinist is to his drug, lonesome, hollowed out, old as the ages, at the same time Faust and Karamasov, animal and sage, all bare, without any ambitions, all naked, full of a child's fear of death and full of the weary readiness to die his death." It is Klingsor's portrait, but not Klingsor's alone. It might be Nietzsche's portrait of Man on the Eve of the Superman—if it were not Hesse's portrait of Hesse. To find the same merciless exposure in the "first person," one has only to leaf through the *Diary from a Health Resort,* the abysmal record of a sick man who, with masochistic satisfaction, watches the deformations, pains and ridiculous motions of his sciatica-ridden body.

But this violent urge for confession is mixed with a stubborn secretiveness, a bashful hiding behind the "fig-leaf," an obstructive silence opposed to the asking and demanding voice: "Adam, where art Thou?" Guilt cries out for confession, but guilt breeds a dark recalcitrance as well. In the first story of the Lauscher-collection, written as early as 1896, we meet for the first time this bliss of confession mixed with the stubborn refusal to admit one's wrong which will shake the Steppenwolf no less than Emil Sinclair, hero of *Demian.* The conflict of remorseful desire to do penance and of rebellious self-assertion in the face of the power which demands submission is being incessantly fought on the battlefield of the soul, and vests Hesse's works with an urgency and tension truly religious. In the very signature which Hesse puts under his writings we can trace this bewildering spectacle of confession and hiding. Is it not revealing that one of his very first works presented itself to the audience as *The Posthumous Writings and Poems of Hermann Lauscher, edited by Hermann Hesse*; that his latest one is entitled *The Glass Pearl Game, the Attempt of a Life Chronicle of Magister Ludi Joseph Knecht, edited by Hermann Hesse*; that his *Demian* appeared anonymously with the subtitle *The Story of Emil Sinclair's Youth*; that *Steppenwolf* (1927) pretends to be the autobiography of a certain Harry Haller, found in his room after he has mysteriously left the town where he lived for a few months? There is a permanent hiding behind pseudonyms, behind a mere editorship—in short: a recalcitrance to "admit" which is ironically counteracted by the urge to expose himself, to "confess." Lauscher's first name is not Hermann by chance; the initials of the Steppenwolf are not incidentally H. H. (which, by the way, are the initials of the hero of *Journey into the Orient* [1932] as well), and for good reasons the first Magister Ludi, the inventor of the *Glass Pearl Game*, is called Calwer, the man from Calw, the little town in Swabia where Hesse was born in 1877, and which with its old houses, narrow streets and murmuring brooks appears in so many of Hesse's stories. These are more than playful attempts to mystify the reader. They are true symptoms of this bliss of confession mixed with the stubborn refusal to admit one's wrong. And it seems quite characteristic that Hesse has never called any of his books a "novel" but has rather chosen the non-committal term a "narrative," which leaves the question between "confessional" authenticity and "impersonal" fiction in an ambiguous balance.

## II. Father and Mother Image

A balance? Rather an indication of the basic polarity which runs through all of Hesse's works. Except for the two "narratives" which present Harmony Regained, *Siddhartha* (1922) and the *Glass Pearl Game*, it will be obvious even to the casual reader that each of Hesse's major books has a double focus, has two heroes which are "two" in the sense in which a schizophrenic is "two": in *Under the Wheel* Hans Giebenrath and Hermann Heilner; in *Death and the Lover* (1930) Narziss and Goldmund; Demian as the companion of Emil Sinclair, the narrator; and finally the Steppenwolf, who is equally two, if not many more, in one. This cleavage of personality symbolizes the two elements which constitute man and his world: the father-element and the mother-element. It is only during the war years that the metaphysical polarity of these two worlds finds its full and unambiguous expression in Hesse's work. While the mother, embodiment of all sensuous, vital and elemental principles, remained inconspicuous and pale in *Peter Camenzind*, she was totally absent in *Under the Wheel*. In *Rosshalde* (1914), the story of an artist's unhappy marriage, man and woman are pitted against each other, but they are seen from the "wrong angle," as husband and wife rather than as father and mother. The war is still waged on the physical and psychological front; it is only after the "awakening" that it will be shifted to the mythical level, that father and mother will emerge as archetypes, as the embodiments of the spiritual and vital energies fighting in and for man.

In *A Child's Soul* the two worlds are seen as opposite polarities. "Downstairs in our house mother and child were at home, a harmless air pervaded the place; but upstairs power and spirit were dwelling, here was tribunal and temple and the realm of the father." This Upstairs (we cannot help associating the structure of the Christian cosmos) "smelled of sternness, of law, of responsibility, of father and God." The rule and suppression which the father-God imposes upon Hesse's heroes are responsible for the wild outbursts of rebellion with which his books, written in the late teens and early twenties, are swarming. No psychoanalyst is needed to diagnose the neuroses and violent traumas of the patients. Oedipus is at work in Emil Sinclair's frightful dream in which he sees himself hiding behind the trees, armed with a glittering knife which the seducer has put into his hands, ready to jump upon the tall figure walking down the alley: his father. Oedipus is at work in the blasphemous and delirious ravings of the youngster in *A Child's Soul*, after the sin has been committed: "I have killed, I have burned down houses, because I had fun doing it and because I wanted to mock at you and rile you. See, I hate you, I spit at your feet, you God. You have tortured and flayed me, you have given laws which nobody can obey."

Even though these and similar quotations point strongly in the psychoanalytic direction, it would be wrong to tag Hesse too ostentatiously with the ever-handy Freudian label. Hesse's concern is a truly religious one, the groping and hoping for personal salvation, and Freud's secularization of God as a pure magnification of the individual father, his interpretation of the religious emotion as a disease-symptom, would seem to Hesse no less unacceptable than they were to Kafka. It is characteristic enough that in the earlier works, in which the father-son conflict is at its highest pitch, the mother is totally or almost totally absent. It is only in *Demian* that "the mother" plays a decisive role in the development of the hero. Yet, her very name, Mrs. Eve, identifies her as the mythical All-Mother, the great womb in which life rests,—and not as the individual Freudian libido-object. Those who have tried to fit Hesse to the Procrustean bed of Freudianism overlook the fact that Mrs. Eve is not "mother" but "mother-image," not a psycho-physical reality but a myth, clearly evidenced by the fact that she is not Sinclair's mother (who does not appear in the book at all), but the mother of Sinclair's "double," Demian. To be sure, she is sex-object, too (the gossip about the incestuous relations between her and her son Demian is revealing). But the emphasis lies on her relationship to and meaning for Sinclair, and in this relationship the Oedipus-Jocasta motif is entirely lacking. Sinclair's long and painful pilgrimage to the "mother" does not describe the process of emerging from a dark individual neurosis to the unmysterious and rational daylight, but rather a descent into the dark mysteries of the "essence," into the procreativeness of motherly life. A Freudian interpretation would achieve here what it always achieves: the reduction of a symbolic image to its purely psycho-physical elements, and, by the very rationalistic process of this reduction, the destruction of the ontologic authenticity of the symbol. (It is not surprising that for many years Hesse was under treatment by a disciple of C. G. Jung whose objection to Freud is mainly based on Freud's rationalistic destruction of the super-individual myth, and that *Demian* was written as part of his psycho-therapeutic cure).

It is in *Steppenwolf* that the two elements clash most violently: man, the detached and cool evaluator of values, the rational and demanding law-giver and judge locked in deadly battle with the animal, whose ambition it is to break all "civilized" fetters by the assault of his vital instincts, sneering triumphantly at the hopeless attempt to keep the mother-world, the drives and desires of the amoral natural forces of life, in chains. This schizophrenic duel finds its most nightmarish expression in the double-taming scene which Harry Haller witnesses in the "magic theatre," the place where his inner turmoil is externalized on an imaginary stage in a series of wild spectacles. In a merciless mirror, Harry Haller sees himself cracking the whip over the well-trained, emasculated wolf, until the wolf takes over and now, whip in his paws, forces Harry to walk on all fours, to debase himself to the lowest animal level.

These shrill and cacophonous tones, which remain unresolved in *Steppenwolf,* find their harmonious resolution in *Death and the Lover.* Clearer than ever before, father and mother principle, Spirit and Life, are confronted: Narziss, abbot of the monastery, the thinker who lives in the self-sufficient loneliness of the intellect, and Goldmund, the young novice whose very name (Golden Mouth) indicates his hunger for life, the joyful exuberance of pouring himself into the stream of being. It is Goldmund's story which is being told, his tours and detours in search of the Great Mother. "Strange haunting dreams of delight and triumph, visions of her in whom all his senses had his share, and then, with its scents and longings, the mother world would be about him: its life calling enigmatically; his mother's eyes were deeper than the sea, eternal as the gardens of paradise. Life would taste sweet and salt upon her lips; his mother's silky hair would fall around him, tenderly brushing his mouth. And not only was this mother all purity, not only the skyey gentleness of love: in her, somewhere hidden between enticements, lay all the storms and darkness of the world, all greed, fear, sin and elemental grief, all birth, all human mortality." With these visions before his eyes, Goldmund breaks out of the cloister and starts upon his enraptured dance of love. An endless chain of sensuous and sexual experiences: the gypsy girl, the peasant's wife, the two high-born sisters, the servant maid, the Jewess Rebecca, the count's mistress. If Hesse avoids monotony in this merry-go-round of the senses, it is due to the fact that with each new beloved Goldmund becomes a new lover. He is a true vagabond, a true explorer of the delights and ills of the mother world, an artist not only when he tries to carve in wood the faces and bodies he has loved, but also when he becomes one with them in flesh. His vagrancy is in truth an earnest and pious quest, his hunger for life does not taste of the nihilistic attempt to plunge headlong into life out of fear of death. In Klingsor's hectic vitality the panic of the "last summer" still reared its ugly grimace. His craving for burning and intoxicating colors was nothing but a running away from death already waiting at the gates. There is no panic in Goldmund's rovings. The Black Death, which hits the country while Goldmund's roaming is in its height, and which throws the world around him into a delirious frenzy of lust and greed, only helps Goldmund to strengthen his equilibrium and to withdraw into an idyll, one of the very few that the vagabond finds in his restless wanderings. Goldmund's pilgrimage is an act of self-realization, not of self-defence. His indulgence is not born out of the dogmatic, purposeful opposition of an anti-intellectual intellectual, as is the case in so many of D. H. Lawrence's writings with which *Death and the Lover* has been quite unjustifiably linked. *Lady Chatterley's Lover* is repellent for the very reason that it represents a "gospel" (though it is the resentful gospel of an Anti-Christ) which by its very opposition to the values it wishes devaluated, destroys the innocence of the flesh it strives to celebrate. Goldmund's exuberance is free of the corrosive gnawings of an anti-intellectual revelation; his devotion to the All-Mother is borne up by the all-embracing pantheism of a St. Francis of Assisi. (It is not without interest that very early in his career [1904] Hesse published a short monograph of the child-like saint whose exalted love for all beings flowed into the dithyrambic Song to the Sun.)

The violent tension of *Steppenwolf* is overcome. Father and mother worlds have ceased to be irreconcilable enemies. In *Death and the Lover* the two worlds are conceived from the outset as opposite yet complementary poles between which man's existence is suspended. No longer is the father the exacting and punishing authority set over life as a stern and hostile ruler. As a monk, and later abbot of the cloister, Narziss is at the same time "father" and "brother" to the mother-child. From his face all the threatening and antagonistic features have vanished. Brooding in monastic loneliness over the timeless rules and patterns, he is the embodiment of the pure Spirit, remote from ever-changing life with its organic rhythm of birth, growth and decay. He is the *logos* which was "in the beginning" (it is not by chance that he is presented as a distinguished logician and mathematician), in him rests the dead eternity of the Spirit. But this father, "Father" Narziss, is no longer hostile to life, to the world of fleeting phenomena. It is Narziss who opens for Goldmund the door into life; it is he who takes him back to his heart after the lost son has spent strength and life in his search for the Mother. Goldmund was in his mind during all the years of separation, but he was no less in Goldmund's life during all the stages of the wild pilgrimage. For to Goldmund, the artist, who, in his creations, immortalizes the mortal moment, snatches lasting images from the ever-changing stream of life, the world of the father is always present. And it is highly fitting that, when Goldmund carves his first sculpture, the figure of St. John the Baptist, it is Narziss' face which takes shape under his hands. In art the two poles, the world of the father and the world of the mother, seem to merge into a synthesis. And yet, a full and permanent union is impossible. The Matrix which is the chaos will always elude the grip of the logos. The supreme image, the statue of Eve, the All-Mother, which Goldmund has carried in his heart all his life, he will never be able to finish. Death, the world of the father, in which there is no growth, no form, no dream, where there is only the imageless stillness of the thought, will overcome Goldmund before the supreme achievement is even begun. But where, Narziss, is your victory? The last words of Goldmund, ringing forever in the Father's ears long after the beloved vagabond has died in his arms, are a last and paradoxical defiance of the mother world: "But how will you ever die, Narziss? You know no mother. How can we love without a mother? Without a mother, we cannot die." In this last scene in which Narziss sees life slowly fade out of the eyes of his beloved one, there is a gleam of the Beatific Vision in which the word has become flesh and the flesh has become word.

## III. The Great Exorcism

There is only a gleam of the Beatific Vision, and to achieve even that much, one has to "travel through the hell in myself," a phrase by which Hesse has summarized the substance of his *Demian*. And this phrase is the theme of all of Hesse's works, at least up to *Death and the Lover*. What is this hell in myself? It is the religious term for the conflicts arising from man's divided nature, for the chaos of chthonic, inchoate forces in us which, as long as they are not integrated in a controlled and controllable order, exert a subterranean but no less tormenting tyranny over us. In the exposition of this chaos and of the anxiety which it breeds in us, Hesse has been untiring. *Glance into Chaos* he called a series of essays on Dostoevsky (1919) whom he has rightly considered his closest fellow-traveller into the abyss of the human soul, and "glance into chaos" might well be the general title of all his works from *Rosshalde* to *Steppenwolf*. No Freud was needed to open his eyes to the "dark aspects of the soul," he had learned from the "original" masters, the German Romanticists, Dostoevsky, Nietzsche. At the age of 23 he wrote in his diary (later included in his *Hermann Lauscher*): "At that point I began to feel that the hour of a long-postponed battle had inexorably come, that everything suppressed, chained, half-tamed in me was tearing at the fetters, exasperately and threateningly. All the important moments of my life in which I had deprived the feeling of the Eternal, the naïve instincts, the innate unconscious life of some of their territory, gathered before my memory like an enormous, hostile host. Before their onslaught all thrones and columns trembled. And now I knew suddenly that nothing could be rescued. Unloosened, the lower world in me was reeling forth, it broke and sneered at the white temples and favorite images. And still I felt these desperate rebels and iconoclasts related to me, they wore the features of my dearest memories and childhood days."

It is this division in us that is the source of all our anxieties. "And why are they frightened?" asks Demian. "One is frightened when one is not in self-agreement. They have fear because they have never said 'yes' to themselves. A community of human beings who are afraid of the Unknown in them." To cure this disease no short-cut is available. The first therapeutic step is to decompose by relentless probings the easy securities which tend to divert our attention from the schism which rages in us. The first duty is the confession of the disease, the almost proud admission that we are psychopathics. Such was the courage of Dostoevsky: he was a prophet, a messenger of a higher and truer life because he was a hysteric and epileptic (*The Brothers Karamasov or the Decline of Europe*); such was the courage of Nietzsche who had dared to ask the "terrible and harassing question whether under certain historic and cultural conditions it was not worthier, nobler and more proper to become psychopathic than to adjust oneself to these conditions by sacrificing one's ideals" (*Diary from a Health Resort*). This, so Hesse continues at this point, "has been the topic of almost all of my writings." It has indeed. And it was this very courage to "become psychopathic" which, in the eyes of post-war German youth, raised his *Demian* to the level of a revelation. Here was a man who, after all the false securities had broken down, did not offer them a new program by which to adjust themselves, by which to join quickly the broken pieces into a new but certainly not firmer structure. Here was a man who showed them that there was only one thing left: to be glad that all the deceptive supports and props had gone, that the road was clear now for the investigation of the disease and for its possible cure. The message that resounded from *Demian* echoed forth even more strongly from Hesse's philosophical essay, *Zarathustra's Return* (1920). It was Nietzsche's message, but already the literary presentation—the sage walking with his disciples at the outskirts of the town, provoking questions and answering them—made it clear that it was another philosopher's message as well, Socrates' message: Know Thyself.

To know oneself, to explore the hidden corners in one's soul, not to flinch even if one finds these corners populated with beasts and demons, this is the purpose of Emil Sinclair's, Steppenwolf's, Goldmund's travels. These descents into the subconscious, into the lower world, may, at times, read like samples from a psychoanalyst's handbook; but again, the direction of Hesse's genius was established long before he was ever exposed to Freud. It is the following program which, in 1900, Hesse outlines in "Lauscher's" diary: "To lift everything to the surface, to treat oneself to everything Unspoken and Unspeakable as to an unveiled mystery!" And not knowing Freud yet, he continues characteristically enough: "I know very well, this is Romanticism." If *Demian* and *Steppenwolf* are applied Freudianism (we have made our qualifications above), they are at least as closely related to the great "midwifery" of Socratic dialogues; they are records of a merciless exorcism and conquest of the dark powers which we have "to lift to the surface" in order to know ourselves. It is Narziss who quite consciously formulates the principle of midwifery: "Some demon must be at work in Goldmund, a hidden fiend to whom it was permitted to divide this noble being against itself . . . Good then, this demon must be named, exorcised and made visible to all and, when this was done, he could be conquered."

As every patient has his analyst, so every one of Hesse's travellers on the *Road into the Interior* (under this title Hesse collected a number of his shorter stories) has his midwife Socrates: Hans Giebenrath his Hermann Heilner, Emil Sinclair his Demian, Goldmund his Narziss, the Steppenwolf a whole group of them: the mysterious author of the inserted "Treatise Concerning the Steppenwolf," the girl Hermine who is only a female materialization of his schoolmate Hermann, and the strange musician who is Pablo and Mozart in one. They are all externalizations of the inner teacher who leads the hero on his way; and that the name "Demian" resembles in sound so closely to "daimon," the voice which, according to Socrates, guides and awakens the soul of the disciple, is certainly not accidental. (It may be mentioned in parenthesis that the name of the hero of *Demian,* Emil Sinclair, equally evokes in the German reader the association with Greece. Sinclair was the closest friend of Germany's most exalted and tragic spiritual traveller to Greece, Friedrich Hölderlin, whose main work, *Hyperion,* represents the most magnificent transplantation of the Greek "paidaia" unto German soil.) What these "midwives" impart to their disciples is the "viper bite of philosophy" of which Alcibiades speaks in his eulogy to Socrates, this festering sting driving to self-realization. It is the supreme and most subtle form of seduction because it does not quench the thirst but heightens it, the thirst and longing to know oneself. And when Sinclair calls his friend Demian a "seducer," he is as clairvoyant as were the archons of the city of Athens who condemned Socrates to death for seduction of the youth. For he who has learned to know himself will no longer bow to the lures and threats of authority. He has become free.

On this road to freedom travels Emil Sinclair, driven on by Demian's voice, the permanent and catalytic mobilizer of "anamnesis," although here we are not faced with the remembering of innate "ideas" but with the rediscovery of all the emotional and vital urges which are lurking underneath the surface and have not yet become "members" in the chain of Sinclair's being. "You know that 'your permitted world' was only half of the world, and you have tried to suppress the other half as the priests and teachers are doing"—this is Demian's "viper bite of philosophy," and it tears open the wound through which Sinclair's lower world will tumble into the light of day: a series of dreams, drawings and paintings welling up from the unconscious, haunting reminiscenses of images which he has seen in his childhood. And there will always be Demian or one of his mysterious messengers who will interpret these symbols for him, will throw open the door to a world which "the priests and teachers" laboriously try to camouflage, until Sinclair finally reaches Mrs. Eve, the source of all life, until he finds and learns to know—himself.

It is in much wilder and dissolute stages that the Steppenwolf is exorcised. Already the composition of the book makes it plain that we are again on the "road into the interior." The first observation point is still far outside; the anonymous young man in whose house the Steppenwolf used to live and with whom he had an occasional talk. The second step brings us closer: the Steppenwolf's diary, by which Harry Haller introduces himself, has been found. The third step takes us inside: it is the inserted "Treatise Concerning the Steppenwolf" ("For Madmen Only"), a mercilessly rational exposition of the "case" drawn up by a mysterious, completely detached observer. The fourth step: Harry Haller's life as the concrete presentation of the problems which the Treatise has analyzed theoretically, and finally, the fifth step, the initiation into the "magic theatre" where the pandemonium of his soul materializes itself before his eyes in a series of punch-and-judy shows. It is a boring beneath the surface until at the end the hidden demons appear in a frightening and unbridled mummery. So complete and ruthless is the unmasking of the subconscious powers and drives that a realistic frame, which still existed in *Demian*, can no longer accommodate them. Only a "magic theatre," working with all the ghoulish tricks of a Grand Guignol, can furnish the proper stage for this supreme exorcism.

However, the heightened frenzy of this raising of the demons does not only indicate that the schism between the two worlds has become deeper and more dangerous; it points toward a much more serious affliction: the raging against the principle of "personality," of individuation as such. Emil Sinclair was groping for the road to himself, for self-encounter which would lead to self-realization and freedom for himself. What Harry Haller is after is freedom from himself, the complete destruction of the bond which holds the particles of the Ego together and establishes the unity of the person. It is an "analysis" whose aim is no longer integration but utter dissolution of the Ego. Harry Haller does not suffer from a "split" personality, but from the individuation of man in personality as such. The "Treatise Concerning the Steppenwolf" describes the situation aptly: "The body is always one, but of the souls that live in it, there are not two or five, but innumerable ones. Man is an onion consisting of hundreds of layers . . . The old Asiatics realized and knew it very well, and in the Buddhist yoga they invented an exact technique for unmasking the delusion of personality." Harry Haller is afraid of self-encounter (again and again suicide seems to him the only possibility of deliverance), his descent into the hell is not guided by the demand for re-membering, but by the desire for complete dis-membering. His watchword is no longer "find yourself," but "dissolve yourself into nothingness": his exorcism is yoga. It is only at the end of the self-annihilating magic-theatrical performance, which Haller watches with masochistic desire to punish himself for his individuation, that he is called to order by Mozart: "Of course, you'd fall for every stupid and humorless arrangement, generous gentleman that you are, for anything full of bathos and devoid of wit. Well, I shan't fall for it, I won't give you a nickel for your whole romantic penitence. You want to be beheaded, you want to have your head chopped off, you madman. For this idiotic ideal you might commit another ten murders. You want to die, coward that you are, but not live. But in the devil's name: live—that's just what you are to do." The road into the interior, which threatened to become a road into nothingness and dissolution, has led once more to the self. The mirrors of the magic theatre, which might have refracted the rays of the personality into infinity, have merged into a lens where the beams are gathered again in a cone. Analysis has resulted in *Gestalt,* the unleashing of the demons in a conquest over them. At the end of the exorcism the door of the magic theatre leads into the open and Harry Haller knows: "Mozart is waiting for me."

### IV. Individuation, Time and Irony

It is in *Steppenwolf,* which again and again has been proclaimed as plainly "psychoanalytic," that the decisive difference between Hesse and Freud becomes apparent. What Freud tries to repair is the disturbance of man's functional existence in the world; the malady which Hesse exposes time and again is the disturbance of man's authenticity, his *Eigentlichkeit,* as Heidegger puts it. Freud is a reformer who points at curable diseases, Hesse is an existentialist who points at the malaise inherent in the *condition humaine.*

Before Harry Haller enters the magic theatre, his psychogogue Pablo (who will later appear as Mozart) opens his eyes to the real root of his sufferings: "Undoubtedly you have guessed long ago that the conquest over time, the deliverance from reality is nothing else but the desire to get rid of your so-called personality. This is the jail in which you are sitting." The true (and incurable) plight of man began with his individuation, with his separation from the All-ness, with the beginning of time. Time is the horrible proof that paradise is lost, that man is no longer living in his *Eigentlichkeit,* but in the all-powerful and tormenting sequence of moments (this is what Heidegger calls *die Geworfenheit*), the permanent transiency of all things and of his own existence. It is man's curse that he can no longer live in the simultaneousness of his experiences, that he is suspended between eternity which knows only past and future, and time which knows only the transitory moment. Now it becomes evident that the great exorcism which we tried to analyze above means more than the schism in the individual soul: it is the paradoxical attempt to mobilize all the powers, actions and reactions of the soul into an ever-present simultaneity (Heidigger calls it *Zuhandenheit*) which will be capable of outwitting the deadening course of time. Klingsor's desperate cry "Why does time exist? Why always only this idiotic one-after-the-other and never an effervescent, satiating at-the-same-time?" rings through all of Hesse's writings up to *Magister Ludi*. If one could keep the moment alive, if one could rescue all one's yesterdays, then the suffering would be gone. And in this attempt to conquer time, Hesse's heroes are the true companions of Proust's, Joyce's, Thomas Mann's protagonists. They are all *à la recherche du temps perdu* (although their tensions and their revolts against the "idiotic" one-after-the-other are much more violent than Proust's, and much more akin to James Joyce's); they are all in the process of a re-membrance of things past (which, however, is a suitable title for Proust's *oeuvre* only when the word "remembrance" is taken in the special sense suggested here.)

But how is the eternalization of the moment possible? Hesse does not attempt to give an answer to the unanswerable question. In none of his "solutions" is finality. But in every single one of his books there is the attempt to face the insoluble bravely and honestly. There are the attempts of the "artists," of Klingsor and Goldmund, who give themselves to the moment so unreservedly in the hope that the very intensity of living will save it from destruction. But in the case of Klingsor the insatiability is nothing but an outgrowth of the horror vacui, and Goldmund must realize that his life is spent before the ultimate task, the sculpture of Lady Eve, can take shape. Still, art seems to hold a promise, it might become the powerful weapon which can defeat the dance of death. And Goldmund ponders: "When as craftsmen we carve images or see laws to formulate our thoughts we do it all to save what little we may from the linked, never ending dance of death." In music, above all, the solution seems to be reached. In *Steppenwolf*, and particularly in *Magister Ludi*, music appears as deliverance from the curse of the one-after-the-other. On one of the mysterious streamers over the different show-cases in the magic theatre, Harry Haller reads the inscription: "The Essence of Art. The Transformation of Time into Space through Music." And even before he entered the magic theatre, he had come to the realization: "Yes, that was it, this music was something like time frozen to space and above it hovered a superhuman serenity, an eternal, divine laughter." To "live in music"—that might be the answer, to develop in time but not to be subject to the law of succession and transiency, to transcend each moment by fitting it into a timeless harmony, in short, to live in humor. "To live in the world as if it were not the world, to respect the law and yet to stand above it, to possess as if one did not possess, to renounce as if it were no renunciation, all this only humor is capable of achieving." (*Steppenwolf*). It means what one might call to live symbolically, to be in the things but to be beyond them at the same time, to analyze while experiencing and to experience while analyzing. It is exactly what Thomas Mann has defined again and again as the attitude of irony. It is, in terms of Heidegger's Existentialism, the permanent blending of *Geworfenheit* with *Vorlaufen zum Tode*. In his *Diary from a Health Resort,* Hesse has given, with the help of a clinical case, an example of how the ironic solution can lift us beyond the tormenting pressure of the "moment," of the cage in which we sit. By living in irony, by living as if he were playing a rôle which he can watch and analyze as an outsider, the sciatica-ridden guest of the health resort has cured himself, perhaps not from the disease of his swollen and creaking joints, but from the much deeper disease which made the physical illness unbearable. One day, after having dragged for many weeks his painful limp through the deadly monotony and the dead-earnest healing routine of the sanatorium, he lifts himself above his miserable existence and looks at himself from the outside. And seeing a ridiculous hypochondriac, worried about every motion that might cause him pain, shuffling down the staircase, putting the chair in the right angle so that sitting down will become easier, he bursts out into laughter which opens the road to recovery. It is the salvation through irony, the annihilation of the moment by transcending its laws and conditions, it is the being oneself and not being oneself at the same time which, on the intellectual level, is expressed in the patient's ironic statement: "I have the misfortune that I always contradict myself."

It is the very attitude which Kierkegaard scorned in his *Either-Or* as the "aesthetic" one because it lacks the absoluteness, the firm conviction that time and eternity are irreconcilable antipodes, that we cannot save ourselves under any circumstances. It is man's sinful attempt to play God, to bridge the unbridgeable gap between here and there, to "communicate" without undergoing and reliving the stages of Christ's Passion. And Kierkegaard would have been seized with rage, had he been able to read in *Demian*: "Instead of crucifying oneself or somebody else, one can with solemn thoughts drink wine from a chalice and while doing it think the mystery of sacrifice." For Kierkegaard this substitution would have been stark paganism, as would be the Franciscan mysticism which we so frequently encounter in Hesse's works, the attempt to break the cage of individuation by expanding the soul so that it will become the lost All-ness again. It is quite characteristic that the Christian Hesse again and again substitutes for Christ's words "Love Thy neighber as Thyself" the Buddhist's *"tat twam asi,* Love your neighbor for he is yourself."

His yearning for deliverance from the Ego, from the tyrannical dictate of temporality, has frequently led Hesse onto the road to India. The atmosphere of the Orient was familiar to him from his earliest childhood (both his father and his maternal grandfather were leading figures in the German-Swiss Indian Missionary Association; his mother, in fact, was born in Malabar), and this made access to the wisdom of the Orient particularly easy. But even without this stimulating heritage, Hesse would have found the way to Buddhism. For Buddhism offers the most radical possibility of undoing the curse of individuation, of annihilating the "idiotic one-after-the-other" by the postulation of the eternal simultaneity of Nirvana. What the East means to him, Hesse has expressed in his *Journey to the Orient*: "not only a country and something geographical, but the home and the youth of the soul, the everywhere and nowhere, the oneness of all times." However, it should be made quite plain that Buddhism (at least the Mahayana Buddhism with its extreme vision of the Universal Void) remains for Hesse a radical possibility, but by no means the solution to the problem. The extinction of the Ego, of the will to be, the kingdom of a lifeless and motionless eternity, in short: the realm of the Father, is only one station of the road to redemption, only one pole in the basic polarity of man's existence. Mozart's angry exhortation in *Steppenwolf*: "in the devil's name: live—that's just what you are to do" has rung down the curtain over the Nirvana, over

Harry Haller's suicidal attempts to break out of the cage of individuation. But even in his Indian legend *Siddhartha* (Siddhartha, of course, is the historical name of the Gautama Buddha), which to many seemed a complete affirmation of the Buddhist faith, the dividing line is quite sharply drawn. It is again a quest for self-realization and salvation, and Siddhartha's travels lead through all the stages of self-fulfillment: life among the ascetic brethren who kill the desires of the flesh by flagellation in order to approach the "atman," life among the courtesans and nabobs of the big cities who, by draining the cup of pleasure to the last, hope to enter into the essence. But early in his travels Siddhartha has grasped the "ironical" solution: "Both, the mind and the senses, were pretty things behind which the last meaning was hidden, both had to be listened to, with both one had to play, neither of them was to be despised nor overrated." And when Siddhartha finally meets the great teacher Buddha, it dawns upon him that he cannot become his disciple either. For Buddha's division of the world into Samsara and Nirvana, deception and truth, phenomena and essence, time and eternity, is in Siddhartha's eyes no more than a pedagogical device. The true wisdom Siddhartha finds as a ferryman, as the link between the shores while watching the water and realizing "that the river is the same at all places, at its origin and its mouth, at the waterfalls, at the ferry point, at the rapids, in the ocean, in the mountains, everywhere, always simultaneous, and that for it there exists only presence, not the shadow of the past, nor the shadow of the future." This, then is the solution: the stream itself is the coeval unity, the rhythm of fleeting moments is the everlasting presence.

This paradoxical oneness of the opposites, of time and eternity, individuation and Universal Self, life and death, mother and father, the apparent two which are essentially one, will show us again how wrong it is to interpret the polarity of Hesse's heroes in terms of narrow Freudianism. (It would be about as fitting to discover in the Indian gods Shiva and Vishnu "neurotic cases of split personalities"). That the tension between the poles is insoluble, that a definite fixation of the "condition humaine" is impossible, that the problem of man is beyond solution, can be learned from the very rhythm of Hesse's works. His books bear the relationship of complementary colors to each other. A great many of his readers found it baffling (and many even shocking) that *Siddhartha*, the serene Oriental legend in which all doubts seemed to be stilled, was followed by the weird Grand Guignol of the *Steppenwolf*. But the extreme amplitude of the pendulum's swing is just Hesse's unmistakable rhythm. "I have the misfortune that I always contradict myself"—*Demian*, the travel through "the hell in myself," is followed by *Siddhartha*. The companion piece to Siddhartha's saintly pursuit is the Witches' Sabbath of *Steppenwolf*. From Harry Haller's shrill dissonance, the pendulum swings to the tense but harmonious duo of Narziss and Goldmund. But "since the paradox has to be risked again and again, the essentially impossible undertaken always anew," Goldmund's story, the love song to the fully experienced moment, to the intoxicated dance of life, required as a complementary color the lofty kingdom of Nirvana, the dead Void of eternity. It presented itself as the life story of Josephus Knecht in *Magister Ludi*.

This, Hesse's last work is—not only in volume—his most ambitious achievement. That it does not quite succeed has nothing to do with his artistic skill. The kingdom of eternity, "the extinction of the individual," cannot manifest itself in the framework of a realistic prose narrative however esoteric and legendary it may be. Without the help of a "magic theatre", the attempt to render visible the place which is beyond space and time must end in failure, although, in Hesse's case, it is a most magnificent and noble failure. The story of Joseph Knecht takes place at a nowhere, in a completely secluded statehood of laybrethren whose only pursuit is learning and research. It takes place at no-time, at a period hundreds of years after the "age of wars" in which European civilization went to pieces. And the highest symbol of this citadel of the Spirit is the glass pearl game, "the sum total of everything spiritual and artistic, a sublime cult, an Unio Mystica of all the shattered branches of the Universitas Litterarum," a strange device by which, according to the highest rules of mathematics and musical harmony, one can "play" and vary all the distraught contents and values of mankind's spiritual manifestations into an all-embracing synchretism. If it can be fathomed at all (and it is Hesse's great achievement that it can—almost—be fathomed) it might be the invention of Chinese sages helped along by the great German mystic Jakob Boehme. In the glass pearl game the Spirit has— to use a Hegelian term—come to itself, it no longer creates but hovers in the immobility of self-meditation, introspection and auto-association. And its purest vessel is the Magister Ludi

Josephus Knecht whose very name (Knecht-bondman) indicates that he is a function and not an individuality. (There has probably never before been written a "biography" which is so drained of *bios* and any individual psychology). Here is the austere world of the father—until shortly before the end not a single woman appears on the pages of this book—and it is quite fitting for "life" in the Nirvana that Knecht refers to his own development as a succession of "awakenings" and "transcendencies." But this fortress of eternity, in which Knecht rises to the highest office, is only part of his "home." Against the advice of his superiors and colleagues he indulges in the study of history, the concern with the living moment, and at the height of his career he renounces his lofty office and leaves the world of the pure Spirit in order to dedicate himself to the modest service of an educator of a young man of the world. As Goldmund returns to the Father Narziss after he has plumbed the depth of the mother-world, so Knecht, who is Narziss reborn, finally finds his way into life after he has plumbed the depth of the father-world. The "ironic solution" is found again. And highly ironic is the end of the book. The very day Knecht enters into the service of life, he dies by drowning in a mountain lake. He, the unrivaled and idolized master of the great game, dies in the services of an immature youth who seems hardly worthy of this extreme sacrifice. But there is no futility in this irony. When the boy sees the master perish in the waters, the moment of his awakening has come: he knows that from now on he will have to live a life which will not only be his but that of the Magister Ludi as well. The transiency of man's existence, the fleeting instability of the moment, does not mark the victory of death but the triumph of eternal rebirth. Time, the one-after-the-other, is in the ironic vision eternity, the everlasting at the-same-time. The "idiotic" rhythm of birth, unfolding and decay is the very heartbeat of the eternal, the great law of Hegel's dialectics: *Aufgehobensein* with the threefold meaning which the word *aufgehoben* carries in the German language: annulled, preserved, and raised to a higher level.

\* \* \*

In the summer of 1947 Hermann Hesse reached the biblical age. His latest work, magnificent in spite of its failures, seems to indicate that the storm has subsided. But we should not be unduly surprised if, provided that his almost complete blindness should ever allow him to return to writing, he were to continue to "contradict himself." He who has glanced so deeply into the chaos, who has felt so closely the grip of the "daimon," is not likely to catch more than a glimpse of the great calm in which the antinomies are resolved and reconciled. The balance is too precarious to be upheld, and even in the serene and austere pages of *Magister Ludi* we find confessions like the following: "There is no noble and lofty life without the knowledge of the devils and demons and without a perpetual battle against them." He is of the family of Dostoevsky, of those who tear out their hearts so that grace may be bestowed upon them. Peace in God, that is the goal, but the price they have to pay is tremendous. "Serenity"—this word sounds like an echo from the celestial city through Hesse's later books, and in his last work he has tried to catch its sublime reflection: "This serenity is neither frivolousness nor self-complacency, it is the highest wisdom and love, the affirmation of all reality, the wide-awakeness at the brink of all depths and abysses, the virtue of the saints and the knights." But only the one who is willing to recognize and confess his sinfulness has a slight chance to become a saint. Exactly that Hesse has done all through his life: he has beaten his breast praying for grace. "There are two roads to salvation, the road of justice for the just ones, and the road of grace for the sinners. I who am a sinner have again committed the mistake of seeking the road of justice" (*Diary from a Health Resort*). Only by an act of grace can serenity be envisaged; man cannot deserve it, he can only hope for it. The ironic attitude itself is not man's achievement, but the highest blessing that sainthood can bestow.

Again and again, Hermann Hesse has been compared and linked to Thomas Mann. To be sure, they are contemporaries. But the human attitude and the emotional climate of the two are vastly different. Hesse himself felt it very clearly when he drew in *Magister Ludi* the loving and astute portrait of Thomas von der Trave. (The Trave is the river on whose banks Lübeck, Thomas Mann's birthplace, is situated.) A sketchy comparison must of needs work injustice upon both of them. Thomas Mann —at least the mature Thomas Mann—is the apex of civilization; the demons, who are by no means alien to him, are subdued and neutralized. In this he is a true heir of Goethe. Hesse is the heir of Dostoevsky, whose concern is not man's autonomous dignity but man's saintliness, not justice but grace. The demons are on the loose in Dostoevsky as well as in Hesse. Thomas Mann is, if these geospiritual generalizations be taken with a grain of salt, a Westerner, Hesse an Easterner. For Thomas Mann, the East is the danger zone which has to be warded off if man wants to live (Tadziu in *Death in Venice,* Mme. Chauchat and Naphta in the *Magic Mountain*), while Hesse has again and again seen the light arising from the East. Hesse has loudly proclaimed his love for Dostoevsky; Thomas Mann has published a beautiful essay on the great Russian with the characteristic title: "Dostoevsky—but in Moderate Doses." And the heroes of Thomas Mann's greatest *oeuvre* are Abram, Jacob and Joseph, proud men who have concluded a covenant with God, a Magna Charta of almost equal partners; the hero of Hesse's greatest *oeuvre* is Josephus Knecht, the humble servant. If the serenity for which Hesse so fervently strives is the "virtue of the saints and knights," Thomas Mann's serenity is knightly, Hermann Hesse's saintly.

There is nothing in Hesse's work to remind the reader of Thomas Mann's superior and, at times, olympic equanimity, the smoothness and ease of his transitions from one phase to the next, even in political matters. And if Thomas Mann's supreme vision is the Third Humanism, Hermann Hesse's is the eschatological Third Kingdom. Thomas Mann's work is undoubtedly wider in scope, richer with meaning and purer in outline; yet his heart never pulsates so visibly, audibly and close beneath the surface as does Hesse's. It is a tormented and struggling heart, beset by the tragic upheavals of our times, but much more thoroughly beset by the unalterable and timeless tragedy of man's existence. With the single exception of Franz Kafka, there is in contemporary German literature hardly anyone who has so valiantly and incessantly struggled with the angel as Hermann Hesse. Out of these struggles cries arose, but some of the purest and most beautiful poetry as well, some prose reminiscent of Mozart in its graceful serenity, short stories like *Knulp, In the Old Sun, How Beautiful Is Youth,* where tensions and conflicts only grumble on in the bass accompaniment while the leading melody rises to lofty mirthfulness. These are the short moments of paradisiac bliss which grace bestows upon the sinner. But the battlefield remains always close, the demons are lurking, smashing the peace so hardly won. And it is as deeply moving as it is revealing to read in one of Hermann Hesse's late poems:

> Heaps of shards and shambles far and wide:
> Thus ends the world, thus ends this life of mine.
> And I wished but to cry and to resign—
> If there were not this stubbornness inside,

This stubbornness to ward off and to fight,
Defiance deep deep in my heart below,
And then my faith: that what torments me so
Must, must one day turn into light.

## THE SHROUD OF SILENCE

This paper does not attempt to be more than a first and perfunctory glance at some haphazardly collected colors for a large tableau, for a landscape which transmits, through the medium of German literature within the last sixty or seventy years, the image of the agony and the forlornness of modern man. I have chosen as the startling symptom of this plight the muteness of man and the muteness of the poet who, in the days when the world was still whole, experienced himself proudly and modestly as the mouthpiece of mankind.

As a symbolic landmark I should like to evoke at the beginning the image of two great German poets who, shaken by the horror of their own sufferings and of the sufferings that had befallen the world around them, lost their voices and grew silent: the image of Rainer Maria Rilke and Franz Kafka. Rilke, who felt that the cataclysm of the First World War had buried under ruins his existence as a poet—and I think we are entitled to take as genuine truth his own assertion, although we know that his work did not cease quite as radically as he himself has claimed—and Kafka, who, despairing at the futility and inconclusiveness of his life's struggle, besought his friend to see to it that none of his unpublished writings would survive him. The poet who finds himself divested of the gift of communication, who, like Rilke, can no longer find the word that would transmit his inner life, or who, like Kafka, wants to call back posthumously into the night of silence the word once uttered—this indeed is a frightful symptom of the desolation which is visited upon our age. That the poet suffers more acutely, that the plight of the world and of his own soul presses him harder than us, the average man, this is not new: in fact, it is quite proper and in order, it is his specific, painful privilege. But it is new that the suffering has become ineffable, that it cannot solve and absolve itself through the word, that the one whose highest function it was to be the mouthpiece of mankind, lapses into impenetrable silence. To lament, to voice the woe of the world: this has been the poet's office since time immemorial, his authentic mission and nobility—and how proud, how victorious sounds to us, the children of a harsher age, Tasso's confession:

> Nur eines bleibt—
> Die Träne hat uns die Natur verliehen,
> Den Schrei des Schmerzens, wenn der Mann zuletzt

> Es nicht mehr trägt—und mir noch über alles,
> Sie liess im Schmerz mir Melodie und Rede,
> Die tiefste Fülle meiner Not zu klagen.
> Denn wenn der Mensch in seiner Qual verstummt,
> Gab mir ein Gott zu sagen, wie ich leide.

What a blessed world in which the poet still finds the word that will express his sufferings, in which he can still speak through the despair and above it. How grim, as compared to this brightness, no matter how heavily paid for, must an age appear in which the despair looms so large that even the poet cannot articulate it any more. And this very fact, the fact that the word has become suffocated, seems to me the frightening signum of our present cultural era.

We shall collect a few samples at random. There arose, in the middle nineties of the last century, the voice of a youth who, with a handful of verse, seemed to awaken German poesy from a long and only sporadically interrupted spell of hibernation. His name: Hugo von Hofmannsthal, and his voice of such a splendor and richness, of such subtlety and sweetness that a highest goal seemed to be attained. What could one not expect of one who had begun thus? And yet what happened? The voice which had hardly asserted itself breaks off, silence spreads, and out of this silence grows eventually the soul-searching document by which the poet confesses his allegiance to silence, *Der Brief des Lord Chandos,* in which Hofmannsthal, only thinly disguised as a young littérateur of the Elizabethan period, proves to us and to himself that the word endowed with the power to communicate is irretrievably lost. For the primeval images of his soul hover in such remoteness that the word cannot find them, yes, that they grow pallid when the word tries to approach them, "because the language in which I might be able not only to write but to think is neither Latin nor English, neither Italian nor Spanish, but a language none of whose words is known to me." In all of Hofmannsthal's work language, the self-expressive word, proves to be a most problematic conductor of the vibrations of the soul. Music is needed to bridge the chasm of silence; the mute gesture, as for instance in his poem "Die Beiden," becomes the only possible medium of communication, and his final view of our world is represented by the *theatrum mundi* on whose stage man lives and recites a rôle, enacting a supra-empirical *ludus* whose dialogue is pre-existent, and whose language is a strange form of muteness of man as an individual. We may point, within this much too general vista, to one of Hofmannsthal's most beautiful creations, his melancholy comedy *Der Schwierige* whose hero—indeed, a very ill-fitting term—is afflicted by a chronic inability and reluctance to communicate, a play whose high points are moments of silence, and whose happy ending consists in the execution of a gesture, hallowed by tradition and carried out *sans mot dire*.

Today we know how mistaken those of Hofmannsthal's contemporaries were who ascribed the poet's lapse into silence to a lack of vitality, of robustness, to a decadent hypersensitivity which exhausted itself in the first effort. Today we know that *Der Brief des Lord Chandos* testifies to a supra-personal malaise. For in quite different quarters, in the work of Gerhart Hauptmann, whose earthiness and unesoteric vigor can hardly be disputed, the tragedy of man's muteness unfolded itself no less powerfully even if springing from very different motives, from social, psychological, characterological factors which are indeed quite alien to Hofmannsthal. To be sure, the theme was to be fully developed by Hauptmann only in one of his later plays, one of his greatest, it seems to me, in *Rose Bernd*. In the gallery of Hauptmann's dramatic characters she is by no means unique, and her speechlessness, the stony silence which she opposes to the voice that so gently and helpfully asks the delicate question, are conditioned by the social atmosphere which envelops Hauptmann's human beings, and by the basic tenets of naturalistic style. Yet Rose's inability to talk at the decisive moment, this silence growing from a sense of shame, from remorse, fear, and boorish obstinacy, makes her, beyond all the social and stylistic specifications, a general symbol of the helplessly exposed *stumme Kreatur* of whose awkwardly speechless bafflement Hauptmann has been the most moving chronicler. Earlier in his career, he fashioned out of this human muteness some of his most profound and convincing effects, for example at the end of the second act of *Die Weber* when old Baumert, stammering like a child, repeats the words of the "Weaver Song" which the citified soldier Jäger recites for him, touchingly and pathetically clinging to the words which he himself is incapable of formulating in the bleak desolation of his soul. And still earlier, in Hauptmann's very first plays, this speechlessness seemed to transform itself into a dramaturgical device noticeable both in *Vor Sonnenaufgang* and *Ein Friedensfest*. Here we find a strange propensity to what we might rightly call the pantomimic, a fading out of the voice at the very dramatic climax, a long musical pause during which the action is carried on by mere mimicry and gestures, replacing and suspending the spoken word. The great reconciliation scene of *Ein Friedensfest* is reduced to a sequence of gesticulations, and reduced to pantomime is the last scene of *Vor Sonnenaufgang,* in which Helene learns that the beloved one has left her, and that now no other issue is open to her but suicide.

No longer is it given to man, no longer is it given to the poet to say how he suffers. And man lives in the darkness of his solitude, at the fearful brink of destruction and self-destruction, because he cannot entrust himself to his fellow by speaking up. The shroud of silence actually transforms itself into the Nessus shirt of fate in Arthur Schnitzler's work where silence and secretiveness generate a most explosive power. Schnitzler has become the supreme master of concealment, the great manipulator of marionettes who, through their silence and in silence, enact their tragicomedies. Christine in *Liebelei* driven to suicide because she was not told the truth; young Medardus' heroic exploit thwarted because Helene kept silent; *die Gefährtin* concealing her real emotional attachment through the many years of her marriage, and her husband silently knowing all the time what she had so cleverly contrived to hide from him; Rademacher in *Die letzten Masken* patiently waiting for the supreme hour of his life when he would be able to speak up, and, when the moment finally came, swallowing his words and taking the unspoken truth into his grave; the bachelor in *Der Tod des Junggesellen* maliciously hoarding secrets as a miser hoards gold; *Die Frage an das Schicksal* not being asked, since the spoken word might shatter the illusion on which Anatol's life is built.

If Hauptmann's pantomime demonstrates the powerlessness of the word proving too feeble to convey adequately the state of tension in a human soul, a glance at Schnitzler's work should convince us that the step from powerlessness to senselessness is small indeed, that the bridge from man to man—and this is, after all, the holy function of language—no longer exists. Then the time has come to turn one's back silently on the laughter and chatter of life, as Thomas Mann's Tonio Kröger turns his back, and, while the Hans Hansens and Ingeborg Holms are dancing and frolicking, stares into himself, wordlessly. The silence will grow in Thomas Mann's human beings until it finds its first culmination in the lonesome traveler to Venice who can only follow with his eyes the boy he loves, and will not once, not a single time, address him by word. Gustav Aschenbach is suffocated by cholera, but we might as well say that he is suffocated by the word not uttered, the word that could have paved for him the road back into life. The deadly disease approaches under a cloak of silence, and Gustav Aschenbach himself becomes its most powerful accomplice by challenging all the warning and life-protecting voices with his imperious dictum: "One ought to keep silent." The word as the carrier of free communication, as the redeemer of man's forlornness will return in Thomas Mann's work to the degree in which he overcomes the hopelessness of his times, and his own hopelessness in facing them. To be sure, the word returns first somewhat timidly and hesitatingly, like something that has to be won by detour and circumvention, circumvention in the quite literal sense. For it is assuredly very significant that the great love dialogue in *Der Zauberberg* is conducted in French, in a half-language, so to speak, in an unauthentic, ungenuine language in which Hans Castorp takes refuge to escape the prison of silence. It is in this chapter that one of the deadly fascinations that stalk Hans Castorp in *Der Zauberberg* becomes most acute, but at the same time neutralized and disarmed, because the spoken word has the power to break the dangerous spell that hovers around Mme. Chauchat. Yet it is only in the Joseph novels, this hopeful, optimistic, self-reliant confession of the humanist, that man will be able to speak again fully and richly. For precisely this is Joseph's unconquerable charm, the sign of his God-kinship and of his ultimate triumph, that he knows how to speak fluently and convincingly, that he demonstrates the victorious power of the human and the humane by talking and talking again. Man in the bright light of day—that is man who talks, Joseph, who, through the beautiful discourses at the rim of the well, communicates, though in a somewhat mischievously coquettish fashion, even with the moon, the star of the night. Surely it is not accidental that, in his preface to the new American edition of the Biblical cycle, Thomas Mann calls his narrative a "gigantic work of speech," and although he does not tell us why he has chosen this term, it is quite evident that, from the Tales of Jacob to the last farewell speech of Joseph, man's promotion and humanization as recorded by the great novel is indeed brought about by his glorious ability to communicate through the word.

Yet this bright scenery of happiest and most successful communicativeness Thomas Mann follows up with a very different image, the image of the most extreme human forlornness, the portrait of Dr. Faustus, petrified in loneliness. Nowhere in modern literature have the horror and agony of silence found as overpowering an expression as in Thomas Mann's last great novel. Man under the heavy cross of silence, poisoning with his bedeviled breath the word which dares venture into his atmosphere—this is the culmination of the tragedy of the German composer Adrian Leverkühn. So cursed is this man that he must bury under the shroud of silence the most beloved being, the young flower of life which, cheerful, guileless, and unsuspecting, strays into his orbit. The most beloved creature, the little son of Adrian's sister, breaks into the chilly loneliness of genius, laughing and gaily chattering away, but he must pay with his life for the boldness of penetrating into the realm of the great silence. Most appropriately the little nephew's nickname is Echo, he *is* the echo, the answer, the communication which man establishes with the world around him, the voice which calls back what we call into nature, and this voice must perish in an atmosphere which no longer carries and supports the word. In Adrian's icy universe the voice cannot be sustained and transmitted, there can and must be—no echo.

But the end is not yet. The word has no future, no echo which could spread it and carry it on; but even the human voice of yesterday is engulfed and annulled by the deadly silence. The word through which man declares his allegiance to his status of man and to all mankind is revoked. This is the terrible meaning of Adrian Leverkühn's last composition, *Dr. Fausti Lamentation*. It is Adrian's cancellation and revocation of Beethoven's *Ninth Symphony* in whose last movement the human voice jubilantly bursts forth with the exultant cry of joy in which, through Schiller's words which rise over the mere instruments, the loving communication with all the millions, the embrace of all mankind, is celebrated. This triumph of the human voice, this redemption through the word is now reversed and cancelled in *Dr. Fausti Lamentation*. For the agonizing effect of this composition consists in the fact that the voice gradually dies away, is smothered by the weight of muteness until nothing remains but a painfully wailing tone which, helplessly doomed, hovers in the air. The abysmal end has come, for Adrian the dull night of a wordless insanity, for the world around him the crashing night of destruction in which man's voice and man's existence—and they are one and the same—finally and inexorably perish.

The revocation of the voice, the cancellation of the word as the lowest point of human despair: this is the meaning of *Dr. Fausti Lamentation*. And this obliteration of man's traces, this undoing of the creation seems to have a striking parallel in Hermann Broch's *Tod des Vergil*. Here again the dying poet insists on making the silence absolute by his desire to burn the great epic poem in which he had celebrated and glorified the past and present of his world. The artist as the sacrificial lamb, carrying upon his shoulders the sins and imperfections of all mankind, willing to atone for them by effacing himself as the witness of this world, by smothering his own voice and drawing the shroud of silence over the creation—this nihilistic heroism is Virgil's no less than Adrian Leverkühn's. And quite logically Broch's monumental work culminates, or almost culminates, in the undoing of God's creation, in the reversal of the seven days of divine labor, the re-establishment of that *tohu-bohu* which precedes all existence. This relapse into nothingness, averted only at the very last moment by an act of grace, marks indeed the aftermath of the apocalyptic horsemen, yet not conceived as a far remote eschatological vision, but recognized as the *signum* of our here and now. In his letter to Hermann J. Weigand, Broch explicitly states that Virgil's desperate and self-destructive plan had something to do with the whole historical and metaphysical character of his age, and by implication, of ours.

And is this longing for the absolute silence of nothingness not also the ultimate meaning of Kafka's ruthless last will to have his literary work, the trace of his existence, destroyed? Here again is the poet who cannot say "yes" to his own word because life proves to be unspeakable, because all hope for communication has to be abandoned so that even the voice that brought the message of despair has to strangle itself. Is not all of Kafka's work the heroic and desperate attempt at starting a dialogue, and by doing so, establishing oneself in the community of the living, an attempt which unfailingly ends in the breakdown of the voice, in the utter hopelessness of ever piercing through the silence which surrounds man like a wall? Kafka's world is, to paraphrase Thomas Mann's thought, a world without echo in which the word, yes even the cry, dries up like a rivulet in the desert. So the hero of *Der Prozess* dies like a dog, wordlessly crushed and pushed aside, and it is most likely for this reason, too, that in Kafka's narratives the animal, the mute creature, plays such an important part. There is the pitiful vermin of *Die Verwandlung*, whose voice is distorted to the point of utter unintelligibility until it fails completely; there is the animal in *Der Bau*; there are the dogs, mice, and monkeys, this large field of the subhuman, but subhuman just for the very reason that in Kafka's universe the human voice can no longer assert itself. The borderline between the still just bearable and the utterly unbearable runs exactly where the voice is drowned in the sea of inexorable silence. In the little anecdote of Ulysses and the sirens, Kafka has conjured up the radical deadliness of silence. He gives a new twist to the old myth: the most horrible threat to the seafarer is not the singing of the sirens. Against their voices there is still protection, still hope for survival; only when they grow silent has the ultimate torment, the ultimate deadly paralyzation, become reality.

Yet at the moment when man has probed the bottomless abyss of despair, when even the very last word has faded out —in this moment the miracle may happen, the hope which is beyond all belief, may be fulfilled. And the greatest witness of this miracle is Rainer Maria Rilke. More than any other poet of our century he has known the agonizing curse of silence. Not by chance has the word "unsäglich" become a personal property of Rilke, occurring in his work with tormenting frequency. Thrown into the rocky loneliness of existence, "ausgesetzt auf den Bergen des Herzens" as he puts it in one of his late poems, man is surrounded by the chilly power of silence.

> Aber der Wissende? Ach, der zu wissen begann,
> und schweigt nun, ausgesetzt auf den Bergen des Herzens.

But here, in this last desolation and extremity of the landscape of man's soul, in this stone quarry where no word blossoms, here the newborn word breaks through, the flower gentian, as it is called in the Ninth Duino Elegy, "ein erworbenes Wort" which the traveler brings home from the barren mountain slope and which bestows life upon the earth, "die allen unsägliche."

> Bringt doch der Wanderer auch vom Hange des Bergrands
> nicht eine Hand von Erde ins Tal, die allen unsägliche, sondern
> ein erworbenes Wort, reines, den gelben und blaun
> Enzian.

When the last silence, the blackest vacuity of muteness is crossed, then man has regained the power of the word, then the poet is reborn who can now speak and call, and by speaking and calling resuscitate the petrified world. When the word faded out, the world turned into a desert, its forms at the mercy of the corrosiveness of time and doomed to mere temporality. Now that the poet has brought back from the barren rocks "ein erworbenes Wort," he has redeemed the world and made it a present to us, to him, and to itself. This is the meaning of the Ninth Elegy: the mission of the poet and of his word, of his holy act of speaking which creates the everlasting realm of invisible forms, and which transfigures the ineffable reality of our earth into the yellow and blue gentian of the spoken word.

> Sind wir vielleicht hier um zu sagen: Haus,
> Brücke, Brunnen, Tor, Krug, Obstbaum, Fenster—
> höchstens: Säule, Turm . . . aber zu sagen, verstehs,
> o zu sagen so, wie selber die Dinge niemals
> innig meinten zu sein . . .
>
> ----
>
> Hier ist des Säglichen Zeit, hier seine Heimat,
> sprich und bekenn.

The voice which returned from the yonder shore of silence can now weather the most excruciating extremities. The poet has again become the mouthpiece of the world, the voice through which alone our earth can find significance and value. Therefore his highest office is speaking, calling out, clamoring—and clamoring is in the German language the original and basic meaning of the word "rühmen." Whosoever speaks praises. And whosoever praises has forever dispelled the curse of silence. "Rühmen, das ists!"—so begins the Seventh Sonnet to Orpheus, and in the act of "rühmen" the poet has found his indestructible and world-redeeming victory.

> O sage, Dichter, was du tust!—Ich rühme.
> Aber das Tödliche und Ungetüme,
> wie hältst du's aus, wie nimmst du's hin?—Ich rühme.
> Aber das Namenlose, Anonyme,
> wie rufst du's, Dichter, dennoch an?—Ich rühme.
> Woher dein Recht, in jeglichem Kostüme,
> in jeder Maske wahr zu sein?—Ich rühme.
> Und dass das Stille und das Ungestüme
> wie Stern und Sturm dich kennen?:—weil ich rühme.

# THE ORESTEIA TODAY:
# A MYTH DEHUMANIZED

In the novel of his old age, *Wilhelm Meister, Journeyman*, Goethe writes: "All worthwhile thoughts have already been thought; we must only try to think them anew." It may be permissible in an essay which is informed by the spirit of comparison, analogy and interrelationship, to begin with a paraphrase of Goethe's dictum so that it will come to read: All worthwhile stories have already been told; the poets only try to tell them anew. Indeed, the story with which I shall deal has been retold dozens of times. And as in the past, it seems to serve today as a vehicle for our most pressing problems, an articulation of our plight and misery, a veiled but concise statement of man's fate in our age. It is a cruel and violent story—and could it be that its very cruelty and violence have recommended it so strongly to a number of writers in our century?—: King Agamemnon sacrificing his daughter Iphigenia on the altar of the goddess Artemis to buy favorable winds for the Greeks' campaign against Troy; slain, upon his return from the wars, by his wife Clytemnestra; she, in turn, slaughtered by her own son Orestes, who is driven to the frightful revenge by the order of the god and the impassioned prodding of his sister Electra; then, after the dreadful deed, a prey of the Furies, who will pursue him mercilessly until the curse is lifted from him by his bringing back to Greece from the Barbarian land of Tauris the statue of the goddess Artemis, and with it his sister, the Artemis priestess Iphigenia, whom the goddess had secretly removed to the faraway shore when she was about to die the sacrificial death on the altar. A hopelessly remote story, we might say; yet it has come back to us, through the hands of contemporary authors, as our very own, as the mirror in which we are to recognize our face, even and especially if this face should dangerously resemble a grimace.

More or less at random I have chosen three recent versions of the old myth, or of certain parts of this myth: A German dramatic tetralogy, a French play, and an American poem with dialogic interludes, works which at first glance would seem very different, grown on different soils, under different circumstances, written by men who were scarcely aware of one another. It is unlikely that the French author Jean-Paul Sartre, whose, play *The Flies* we intend to consider, knows much about the German dramatist Gerhart Hauptmann who, at the end of his life, as an octogenarian, once more mustered his creative strength to write a sequence of four tragedies: *Iphigenia in Aulis, Agamemnon's Death, Electra,* and *Iphigenia in Delphi.* And I am sure neither of them had heard of the American poet Robinson Jeffers who, some twenty years earlier, in the wake of the First World War, had written *his* Oresteia, "The Tower beyond Tragedy." Yet, the very unconnectedness of the three works may make it rewarding to connect them, to search underneath their dissimilar individualities for the general and symptomatic, to find that hidden element which attracted the three different authors to the old story, and made the old story serviceable to convey the new meaning, to reflect the existential condition of our generation. What happened to the familiar legend I have already indicated in the title: the dehumanization of the myth, a process from which we can read, as from a fever chart, the afflictions and inflictions, the affections and infections of our age.

At this point we must remember that there was a time in our intellectual history, not more than 170 years ago, when one phase of this very same myth was capable of becoming the expression of the loftiest humanitarian creed, the affirmation of faith in man, of the hopeful message that, no matter how dark the curse under which we are living, no matter how dreadful the crime we have committed, the strength of a pure and noble human heart will find the road to redemption, will heal the wounds and self-destructive impulses of the lacerated soul. It is Goethe's *Iphigenia in Tauris,* the song of songs in praise of the eternal sister, who by her refusal to be tainted by deceit, disloyalty and fear saves her brother and her house, but far beyond this immediate task redeems a doomed world and blunts the sword, whose shadow falls upon the destinies of man. Goethe's *Iphigenia* is the glorious humanization of an old story spilling over with human sacrifice, murder and bloody revenge; it is, in the history of the European soul, the great moment when man's heart has become the incorruptible vessel of the divine, of everything good, true, and beautiful, and when the divine recognizes itself as divine only in and through the voice of the human heart. We shall keep this blessed moment in the back of our minds, as a yardstick, so to speak, by which we can measure the road humanity has traveled, the mutations in the bloodstream of our civilization.

Can it be a mere accident that in the three contemporary Oresteias (and in others, too, for instance in Eugene O'Neill's and Hugo von Hofmannsthal's Electra tragedies) the phase of the legend which Goethe treated is completely lacking: Orestes' reunion with Iphigenia, the moment when the long period of atonement for his dastardly crime is ended and the curse is lifted from his head? The Orestes of Sartre and Robinson Jeffers disappears from the scene, his hands still dripping with his mother's blood, clutching his desperate deed as the only possession left him, with no hope, indeed with no willingness ever to re-enter his father's house. Where Goethe's *Iphigenia* culminates in the blissful vision of return and home-coming, the modern matricides face the flight into emptiness, into the nowhere, which does not become less desolate and frightening for the fact that Sartre and Jeffers try to convince themselves that this flight into the nowhere is a march into freedom. They are thrown into nothingness, not, as is Goethe's Orestes, restored to humanity and his own identity. He had, so says Jeffers of his Orestes in the last line of his poem, "climbed the Tower beyond time, consciously, and cast humanity, entered the earlier fountain." This "and cast humanity," this desperate triumph or triumphant despair, is the last vision with which Sartre and Jeffers leave us. And it is, fundamentally, Gerhart Hauptmann's last vision, too. To be sure, in the concluding part of his cycle, in *Iphigenia in Delphi*, he does tell of Orestes' and Iphigenia's home-coming, of the matricide's final purification and absolution in the temple of Apollo. But we must not forget that the true protagonist of this last tragedy is not Orestes but Iphigenia, that she and her fate overshadow her brother's redemption. And what is her fate? While the people are preparing for the announcement and celebration of the good tidings of Orestes' absolution and of the arrival of the Taurian Artemis statue on Greek soil, the high priestess whose identity is unknown to anyone but Electra throws herself into the rocky gorge before the city gates, buries herself, a stone among stones. In vain Electra had pleaded with her to show her sisterly face again, to return home, to the community of the living: this Iphigenia, too, has "cast humanity" and returns to the earlier fountain. Or rather she has been cast out of humanity, the imploring voice of her sister cannot reach the stony deadness of her heart; for "you must know," so she informs Electra, "my dwelling is below in Persephoneia's realm." At the end of the play the high priest of Apollo pronounces the terrible truth:

> Yet who was once chosen by a god to be a victim,
> And may it seem a hundred times that he escaped the horrible decree
> The eyes of fate will rest upon him and bring him back,
> Wherever he may hide, to the predestined altar.

Home and shelter are lost for ever, man has reached the point of no return; be it the tower beyond time which Jeffers' Orestes has climbed; be it the kingdom "without land and subjects," of which Sartre's Orestes speaks when leaving the place of his crime, accompanied by no one but the consciousness of his deed and the cloud of flies, the furies, those terrible reminders of what he has done; be it the roadless wilderness of the rocky gorge where Iphigenia finds what she has carried in her breast all the time: death.

If we consider more closely the fate of Hauptmann's Iphigenia we shall see that what in Goethe, yes what even in the original Greek myth was a message of hope has turned into a lament at our despair. Whatever else the story of King Agamemnon and his children may have meant, one phase of it, the sacrifice of Iphigenia on the altar of Artemis, clearly indicates that man had extricated himself from the archaic ritual of blood shedding and brutal destruction. The intervention of the goddess who, at the last moment, substitutes an animal for the offered human victim is the symbolic presentation of that proud moment in man's history when he realizes that the gods do not want him to bleed at the altar, the same humanization of religion which shines through the story of Abraham whose hand is stayed by God when he is about to kill his only son Isaac as a sacrificial offering. Although the cloud of death hovers closely over man's head, God wants him to live, to preserve him for future life. This preservation for life even though, or perhaps because, the wing of death has grazed us, seems to me the very core of Goethe's *Iphigenia*. She is, indeed, the embodiment of the vital and revitalizing impulse; touching her, the broken soul of her murderous brother returns to life, living near her changes the barbarian Taurian king Thoas into a benevolent, life-protecting ruler. Although removed to the distant island, although thrown into the loneliness and isolation of a shadowy existence, she waits undaunted for the message that will link her again with her fatherland, her family; for she knows that the miracle in Aulis, her preservation at the moment when death already stood at her side, cannot have been in vain.

For Hauptmann's Iphigenia it was utterly in vain. In fact, something entirely different happened to her on the altar in Aulis. As she will proclaim later: "at this moment I died into the state of divineness"; world, life, humanity will no longer touch her since she has become the merciless servant of a merciless goddess, she, once a victim, now spilling the blood of innumerable victims, spreading incessantly the germ of death which was planted in her on the altar of the goddess. It is here that Hauptmann casts the story into an entirely different mold. He revives an archaic form of the myth, cancels, so to speak, the historical moment for which the thwarted sacrifice of Iphigenia symbolically stands. For his Artemis is no more, or rather not yet, the Artemis as we know her in her last evolution: the tender protectress of the hunted deer; she is what she once was before her face was humanized, the inexorable hunter, not the soft moon-goddess who, in Goethe's vision, spreads the balmy light over the dread blackness of the night, but the cold star under whose chilly gaze no life can flourish. It is for this reason that Hauptmann changed her name, or rather reinstated her old and frightening name: Hecate, the goddess of death, surrounded by the howling hounds itching to dig their fangs into their victim's flesh.

Even if we did not know that Hauptmann's great dramatic cycle originated between 1940 and 1944, his picture of a world under the rule of the death goddess, under the scourge of slaughter unrelieved would clearly date his Oresteia as the story of our generation. To make it quite explicit what and whom he meant, the brave old poet sketched in the portrait of the devil incarnate who, frothing at the mouth, whips his people into the frenzy of war, the "power-drunk villain," as he is called, who claims to be the mouthpiece of the gods, the ruthless spellbinder who cries for the blood of the innocent victim so that the war can get under way. His name in the play is Calchas, the High Priest; but when we hear his hoarse and frenzied voice, we know what his real name was. The great mythological cycle is not only Hauptmann's own swan song; it is his heart-breaking farewell to a humane humanity, his great lament at a world which has become deaf to the voice of Iphigenia, Goethe's Iphigenia, and which instead chose to follow the path of brutality, destruction and death. The curtain has fallen over the glory that was Greece, and it is Menelaos who calls out in Hauptmann's play:

> Once was a country, and we called it Greece.
> It is no more; for where lives still a single Greek?

In Sartre's play the molding of the old story into a mirror of contemporary events may not be quite so obvious. But no less than in Hauptmann's tragic cycle Sartre's world is ruled by death, filled with the stench of corpses. The stage direction to the first act simply reads: "A square in the city of Argos. A statue of Jupiter, god of the flies and of death. White eyes, blood-smeared face." It is the shadow of this horrible sanctuary that has fallen upon and crushed down the citizens of Argos. To be sure, it is not a world ravaged by war, but its deadness and deadliness are even worse. Death is not only all about these men and women of Argos, it has crept under their skin, eaten its way into their marrow, sapped their strength and vitality from within, sucked their lifeblood like vampires or, to use Sartre's horrifying symbol, like flies who cluster all over them, in their eyes, their nostrils, the corners of their mouths. Once a year, at their most solemn festival, the high priest removes the huge stone that blocks the entrance to the cavern before the city gates, and then the dead come swarming out from the underworld to live for twenty-four hours with the people, to sit at their tables, sleep in their beds, torturing them with their all-pervading, yet invisible presence. They live—if life it can be called—in permanent fear, in their hearts like a festering wound the memory of the great crime which was once committed in their midst, the slaying of their king Agamemnon by the hands of Clytemnestra, the original sin, if we are permitted to shift the symbol to the level of Christian theology. And all this, the original crime and the ensuing self-mortification of the people, is the vicious handiwork of Jupiter, of a God whose authority and order can be maintained only as long as man trembles in fear, castigates himself by remorse in the bondage of his own contrition and, by renouncing decision and action, becomes the obedient slave of the secular and divine overlord. As Jupiter puts it in his first conversation with Orestes: "They (the people) have a bad conscience, they have fear—and fear, bad conscience are a delicious incense in the nostrils of the gods. Truly, they please the gods, these pitiful souls." It will be Orestes' mission to deliver the people from this god of the flies and of death, to do the deed which, in

## THE ORESTEIA TODAY 243

Sartre's perverse scale of values, will present itself as an act of liberation and the abolition of the godhead.

Godhead? We must retract the word. For a world from which the humane has been drained is, of necessity, a world without gods. It is futile and only leading into the labyrinth of the unspeakable to ask what here is cause, and what is effect. All we can say is that man was created in God's image, and this implies intrinsically that, if man can find in his face only the features of barbarism and brutality, the likeness of god which he erects in the city square of Argos will have white eyes and a blood-smeared face. Again, it is Goethe's *Iphigenia* which movingly and tellingly impresses upon us that the process of the humanization of man is the process of the divinization of God. At the moment of her deepest despair, when all seems lost and no hope left, she implores the gods: "Save me, and save your image in my soul!" Actually, in Goethe's view, the preservation of man in his humaneness coincides with the self-preservation of God in his divineness. Goethe's Iphigenia goes one step farther—and here is Goethe's most daring and most startling departure from the old story—she forces the gods ahead on the road to supreme divineness. Euripides in his *Iphigenia in Tauris* had transmitted the original version: that Orestes has to travel to the Barbarian island to steal and bring home the statue of the goddess Artemis: this was the order of Apollo. But Goethe's Iphigenia counteracts this very command of the god; at the last moment she will foil the execution of the plan, because to her it is unthinkable that the god could require a deed which involves trickery, disingenuousness and theft. The true greatness of the god is, so to speak, established only by her incorruptible humaneness; and the end of Goethe's play seems to be bathed in the amazed smile of Apollo at the pure beauty of a human heart which taught him, the god, how to be really godlike.

There is no Apollonian smile in our modern Oresteias. There is Hecate's inexorable rule in Hauptmann's tragic cycle; not only man, but also the gods are helpless against her immutable thirst for annihilation. Before her stony face all the other Olympian powers are eclipsed, and, as the high priest states,

> Pythos' strict decree
> Even the goddess was unable to remove,
> Apollo's pale-faced sister Artemis.

There is no god at all in Sartre's play, although this is the only one of the three where a character by the name of Jupiter actually appears on the stage. Yet he is the instigator of everything evil; having pushed Clytemnestra to commit the murder of her husband so that he could unleash the swarm of flies, fear and trembling on the citizens of Argos, he now tries to induce Aegisthus, Clytemnestra's accomplice and second husband, to do away with Orestes. For the murder which Orestes contemplates and is almost ready to commit is the one which Jupiter wants to prevent. And he tells Aegisthus why. "I love the crimes that pay . . . But what am I to do with a murder without remorse, with an insolent murder, with a murder pregnant with peace, and light like air in the murderer's soul?" And there are, in Jeffers' long poem, only two gods fleetingly alluded to in Cassandra's violent curse on life: the one who ravished her and gave her, as a horrid wedding present, the gift of prophecy, and the other one for whom she yearns because he will forever extinguish all visions in her:

> I have known one godhead to my sore hurt: I am growing to
>    come to another. O grave and kindly
> Last of the lords of the earth . . . Death.

But such a godless world and humanity are bound to fall prey to the forces of the demonic, of the nether regions, of the unclean spirits which the Greeks, in contrast to their gods, called the *kakodaimon*. What the modern authors present to our view is indeed a world possessed, primitive and archaic, as if it had not yet arisen from the primordial slime that was before the creation of distinct and distinguishable forms. Again and again, we seem to witness a witches' sabbath, the eruption of the subhuman, the indecent mingling of the upper and nether regions. Man is no longer planted on *terra firma*, but the earth on which he moves is full of cracks and crevices exuding the miasmic and dimming fumes of the underworld. It is in such a crevice filled with the steam of a well surging up from the center of the earth that Hauptmann's Clytemnestra buries the axe in her husband's skull, and in the same grotto the same axe, swung by her son Orestes, will slay her. There is in Sartre's play the cavern in the mountain which is unsealed once a year and from which the pestilential swarm of the dead burst forth, the same pestilential swarm which, all the year round, infests the air of Argos in the shape of flies. This is no longer Greece, the sun-flooded land of measure and form which through the centuries the European soul has created again and again as the locale and ambiance of a self-possessed

THE ORESTEIA TODAY 245

and self-controlled humanity; it is a world writhing in convulsions, possessed by demons and evil spirits, a pandemonium reminding us of the violent rites of primitive tribes: exorcisms, incantations, magic spells, witchcraft, madness. There is, in Hauptmann's *Iphigenia in Aulis*, the old nurse Peitho (could it be just accidental that her name sounds so much like that of the convulsive priestess Pythia?) who belongs to the underworld and whose dark sibyllic utterances are a strange mixture of lunacy and prophecy. There is in Jeffers' "Tower beyond Tragedy" the most horrid act of voodoo imaginable: Cassandra being possessed by the ghost of Agamemnon, the dead king entering her body, forcing himself into her while her every limb is twitching in an epileptic fit, until the king-man has overpowered her and his croaking voice is sputtering forth from her mouth. While in this case we witness a demoniacal re-incarnation and re-animation, Jeffers presents us in another episode with an equally frightening and subhuman case of de-animation and paralysis brought about by voodooistic frenzy. Clytemnestra, threateningly surrounded by Agamemnon's soldiers after she has told them about the murder she has just committed, literally turns into a witch, paralyzing the outraged men by the hypnotic spell of her glance, and when this spell seems to wane, tearing her dress off to hold them subjugated in the stupor of an exhibitionist orgy. Sartre does not drive the ghoulish bedlam quite to the same extremes, yet in his world the ghosts and subterranean demons are no less on the loose. No less macabre and infernal is the scene in front of the cavern before the dead are unleashed upon the citizens of Argos, upon those men stupefied by terror and rolling their eyes in madness, those women screaming in anticipation of the horror to come, and falling in spasms to the ground. Bewitchment and trance have in our modern Oresteias broken down the dikes of sanity without whose protection human existence and civilization are impossible. Here indeed is chaos, the rule of the night, a world which has not yet heard the command of the first day of creation: Let there be light! In this chaos man is a creature of the twilight zone, not resting secure in his clearly delineated consciousness, but communicating with the subhuman and superhuman host, falling again and again into a state of ecstasy—ecstasy in the literal sense of being beyond, being outside of oneself: Iphigenia in Aulis, a somnambulist walking ecstatically toward her consummation on the altar, breaking out in hysterical cries ("demonically screaming" the stage direction reads); Jeffers' Cassandra with her mad prophetic ravings; Sartre's Electra in her wild ecstatic dance which belongs very much to her, even if Sartre may have borrowed the scene from Hofmannsthal's *Elektra*: a world possessed, a humanity dehumanized.

Whether we like it or not, this is the brutal mirror which three contemporary writers hold up so that we may recognize ourselves. But what do they offer us as an answer, what is to be done to relieve the agony of our existence? It seems to me profoundly and touchingly paradoxical that of the three, it is the German poet, literally seeing his country, his world falling to a shambles all around him, who offers beyond the darkness of despair at least a ray of hope, the timid faith that, as the high priest announces at the end, "the cycle is completed," that Iphigenia's self-destruction may be accepted by the gods as a sacrificial offering which will ransom mankind from its cruel fate. This is a far cry from Goethe's message that it is the noble human deed, or rather the faithful listening to the voice of the noble human heart, which breaks the curse to which we are chained. The message that Hauptmann brings is no more than the faint hope that the gods may relent after they have exacted the last ounce of blood. All we can do is to wait in submission and trust, mindful of the last words of the tetralogy spoken by the priest to his young acolytes:

> And so, young friends, abide in the devotion
> And in the awe of god.

Yet this is still an admonition to human courage, to suffer, bravely, what is in store for us. Jeffers' answer is clearly inhuman, a violent abdication of man as man, the reduction of existence to nothingness. His horribly blissful vision is the end of all conscious life, the tower beyond tragedy, that stage of numb aloofness and immobility where nothing will touch us any more, where we are, indeed, beyond tragedy and time, because we are no longer man. I know in all literature hardly a more frightening embracing of deranged nihilism than Cassandra's prayer:

> I pray you, lead my substance
> Speedily into another shape, make me grass, Death, make me stone,
> Make me air to wander free between the stars and the peaks,
> But cut humanity out of my being,
> That is the wound that festers in me.

Grass and stone and air: this is the end; man craving to become

## The Oresteia Today

soulless matter: this is the cancellation of the last day of creation, not only the dehumanization of a myth, but the withdrawal of man from the universe. In his last speech Jeffers' Orestes will exclaim: "I have fallen in love outward,"—but "outward" means beyond the pale of human existence, the nothingness and nowhere into which Jeffers' Orestes vanishes.

And what is Sartre's answer? It is clearly not the fatalistic submission and faint hopefulness of Hauptmann's, it is even less Jeffers' prayer for complete extinction, for the transformation into grass, stone and air; but it seems to me no less inhuman, probably even more dangerously so, since it pretends to be a new and higher form of humanism. We must not forget that, shortly after he had written *The Flies*, he proudly proclaimed in the title of a public lecture that "Existentialism Is a Humanism." Orestes, then, is clearly Sartre's *homo novus*, his deeds and declarations the manifestation and program of French existentialism. If we can trust Sartre, Orestes is man who fought himself free, and by this fight set the great example for his countrymen to become free themselves—free from the paralyzing grip of fear, of being haunted by the shades and memories of the dead, free from the yoke of God who holds mankind in submission by the plague of flies, those vampires which are nothing else but the materialization of our own feeling of guilt. It is this bad conscience that has made man impotent, incapable of living, a plaything in the hands of those who use man's paralysis to maintain the sterile and corrupt order of the world. The cure the existentialist has to offer is simple, horribly simple: instead of just passively being in the world, being thrown into an overpowering set of circumstances, man has to engage himself consciously in life by an act of decision, by a deed which is unmistakably his own, no matter what sort of a deed, as long as it is his, freely and gratuitously chosen, not denied and revoked later by remorse and bad conscience. This is the deed Sartre's Orestes commits, the murder of his mother, perpetrated in cold blood and not to be regretted afterwards. Here is a short passage from the dialogue between Jupiter and Orestes after the horrid deed has been done:

JUP.: Stop this proud tone. It is not fitting for a culprit who is just about to expiate his crime.

ORE: I'm not a culprit, and you will not make me expiate what I do not recognize as a crime.

JUP: Perhaps you are mistaken, but patience: I shall not leave you long in your error.

ORE: Torture me as much as you want to. I do not regret anything.

And a little later, after Jupiter has tried in vain to make him repent, to lead him back to the law of god, the law of nature which Orestes has broken by his unnatural crime:

ORE: I shall not return under your law. I am condemned to have no other law but my own. I shall not return to your nature; in her a thousand roads are traced which lead toward you, but I can follow only my own road. For I am a human being, Jupiter, and each human being must invent his road.

Clearly then, man creates himself out of nothing, there is no model, no pattern which he can and will follow, no authority which prescribes, no prefigurative image which he may realize. In short, it is a world and a life without order, order being the realization of a pattern which is accepted as regulative and binding. What Sartre announces through his Orestes is rebellion in permanence, anarchy unadulterated; for Orestes' admission, "I am condemned to have no other law but my own," is the proclamation of absolute lawlessness, of unrestricted arbitrariness from which only one type of deed can spring: a deed which is prompted by my own unjustifiable will to do a deed. Yet such a deed, no matter what it is, is bound to be a deed without responsibility, responsibility meaning that we respond to something that faces us, something that is outside of the act itself: a demand, a challenge, a question. But Sartre's Orestes does not respond: his act is done in cold blood, and since no authority is accepted, neither divine, nor natural, nor human, the act cannot be made to answer before any tribunal whatsoever, least of all before the tribunal of one's own conscience, which has been done away with if the individual does not acknowledge any norm and order except his free will. It is highly significant that Sartre hardly alludes to the objective, legal motivation which in the old myth forced Orestes to commit the atrocious act: his obligation to revenge his father's murder. The deed of Sartre's Orestes is a deed for the deed's sake, making no other sense than to prove that man can will and do, and by willing and doing feel alive. *What* he wills and *what* he does, *what* he ought to will and ought to do, is for the existentialist an unanswerable question, because for him there is no pre-existent norm, rule or design which could establish what man is, or what he ought to be. Man, so Sartre contends, is not created in anyone's image, but he creates himself only in and through his act: existence precedes essence, so the existentialist slogan runs. The trouble is only that, if we do not know what man's essence is, we cannot possibly know which of his acts are human, and which are not.

Sartre, of course, does not know. And so it is only logical that he presents a murder most foul, a horribly unnatural crime as an act of liberation, as the means by which a hollow man becomes a man, by which someone too light, too unattached engages himself in life. We are to assume that lacerating the womb that gave us birth, the hideous revolt against nature, is the act by which we break through to true self-realization and existence. Indeed, the myth has come full circle. In Goethe's truly human symbolism, Orestes' baneful act had exactly the opposite meaning. By striking his mother, he struck at the roots of his own life, threw himself headlong—and so we meet him at the beginning—on the road to insanity and extinction. His disease is his craving for extinction, his refusal to live, to be man—and this is what the crime he committed symbolically stands for. He wants, as he tells us, to throw off "life's fitful fever," to become unborn again, to join the shadows or, to use Jeffers' words, climb the tower beyond time and tragedy, that impenetrable enclosure where nothing stirs any more. Yet if we want to be human and not grass and stone and air, this craving has to be stopped. An Iphigenia has to appear to heal by hope, faith, and love the suicidal wound which we have inflicted upon ourselves by wounding the mother. The claim which Sartre wants us to share, namely that wounding the mother is to engage oneself in life, is as inhuman as it is mad.

But the end is not yet. Not only are we to believe that Orestes frees himself by his hideous deed and turns from a faceless and fateless onlooker into a man committed and heavy with destiny, but Sartre also suggests that Orestes, by committing his crime, has actually ransomed the crimes of his people. "Your faults and your remorse," he tells the citizens of Argos before leaving his city for ever, "your anguish and your nightmares, the crime of Aegisthus, all is mine, I take all of it upon me." The matricide as the savior—there can be no doubt about it! And this is the most scandalous dehumanization and brutalization of the myth. In all of man's history, as far back as we can see, there is a clear ritual pattern which prescribes how man can be redeemed from his flaws, how he can resurrect himself and cleanse, together with himself, the impurity and deadness of the world in which he lives. This ritual is the sacrifice. The pure animal that bleeds on the altar dies for us and washes away with its blood the sins and imperfections of our blood. Nowhere has this ritual pattern found a more hallowed realization than in the core of Christian theology: God, who is the son of man, taking all human guilt upon himself, and by bleeding to death on the cross buying for us eternal life. But the charisma of resurrection and salvation is not brought about by the arm that strikes, but by the immaculate lamb that lets itself be struck for us. Only in an inhuman vision—in Sartre's—the killer with his hands still dripping with his mother's blood, the one who admits "my crime is my reason for living and my pride", can proclaim himself the savior and redeemer of his fellow man.

Again it is Goethe's *Iphigenia* who ideally fulfills the human vision. At the end of the play it seems as if only brute force could settle the issue: Orestes wielding his sword to hack for Iphigenia, himself and his friend a path to the ship in the cove waiting to take them home to Greece; Orestes threatening the king, challenging him to a fight that is to decide their fate. Yet Iphigenia knows that the arm raised, the blow struck, cannot bring about the beginning of a new life, a life free from the curse of the unbroken chain of crime and guilt, revenge and remorse. The chain has to be broken, and it is she who breaks it by inducing the brother to drop the raised arm, and by delivering herself, as a sacrificial offering if need be, into the hands of the king. After she has apprised the king of the treacherous act which—with her connivance—is being perpetrated against him, she ends with the following words:

> I have surrendered now into thy hands
> The remnants of the house of Tantalus.
> Destroy us if thou canst.

Of course, he cannot. For in the human vision self-delivery, dedicated offering, are the seal and promise of salvation. Iphigenia's self-surrender can and will solve and absolve; the rebellious deed of Sartre's Orestes, born of the ruthless will for self-creation and self-insistence, can never work the miracle of resurrection and revival which leads through the act of sacrifice and self-abandonment.

Iphigenia's words, "I have surrendered now into thy hands the remnants of the house of Tantalus," may lead us to the core of our problem, of the painful and perturbing question why in

THE ORESTEIA TODAY 251

the hands of three contemporary authors the old myth has become dehumanized, why in the mirror of their work we see the human face, our face, as a frightening and petrifying grimace. Iphigenia's words indicate that she is ready and willing to stand judgment, to have her deeds, her life, her whole being weighed and measured so that the meaning of it all can be distilled and pronounced. Judgment is the moment of accounting, the moment when the doer meets the deed he has done, when man, so to speak, steps out of his own existence in order to look at himself from the outside, when, transcending the immediacy of his acting and living, he encounters his acts and life, sees the pattern which he lives, his meaning and his being-meant-for, in short, his destiny. It is the moment of recognition. This gift to stand face to face with ourselves, to recognize the pattern and the meaning, is the source of all misery, but it is equally the source of all glory, the very feature that distinguishes us from the rest of creation, and makes this being, and only this being, man. This very feature seems to be lacking in the new Oresteias; and this lack may well account for the basically dehumanized turn the old myth has taken. The answers which the three authors give to the question of human existence all seem to avoid the moment of terror and hope when man opens his eyes and exclaims, "I see." Hauptmann ends on the note of blind submission, tempered by the vague hope that destiny, inscrutable as it is, may hold in its cloak something else but slaughter and destruction. In Jeffers' "Tower beyond Tragedy" there is no eye to see, and no deed that can be seen, but only dead eternity which obliterates all, action as well as recognition. And the deed of Sartres' Orestes is a blind deed, refusing to be weighed and measured, an act of wilful and violent engagement; but recognition can only be the fruit of dis-engagement, of detaching oneself from one's own involvement in the maelstrom of life.

On Apollo's temple in Delphi there was inscribed the command: Learn to Know Thyself. This was assigned by the god as man's highest task, the highest because it is the uniquely and exclusively human task. I think that it is for this reason that the scene of recognition in Greek tragedy (*anagnorisis*, the Greeks called it), assumes a truly religious impact and importance. When Oedipus learns what he has done, when Electra recognizes Orestes, when Iphigenia realizes that the man standing before her is her brother, then it seems as if Tyche, the goddess of destiny, had descended from her hidden abode and appeared visibly on the scene. This is the moment when man virtually sees his fate in front of himself, when his acts, his life, his very being, shrouded in darkness and unawareness, suddenly are thrown into the light, when he realizes that his life has a meaning, and what sort of meaning it has. This revelation may become, as it does in the case of Oedipus, the most horrible agony man has to endure; but that he endures it, that he is capable of meeting himself and of facing his own fate, is his dignity and the proof of his being human. It seems very characteristic to me that in the modern Oresteias the scene of recognition, around which so much of Greek tragedy revolves, hardly plays a part at all. Or at least not a central part. It is completely absent in Jeffers' poem, and it has to be, since his work is the wild protest against the agony which is, indeed, part and parcel of recognition, awareness, consciousness. In Sartre's play *anagnorisis* is only superficially present. To be sure, Electra does recognize Orestes, but significantly enough only in and by his determination to do the frightful deed. Recognition is here not the suspended moment of revelation, not the flash in whose light the twists and turns of destiny become suddenly transparent, but it is the fleeting by-product of the decision to act. Fleeting, indeed: at the moment the deed is done, recognition is lost again. It seems to me highly characteristic that, in Sartre's play, on the morning after the crime, when Electra awakes from sleep at her brother's side, her first words addressed to Orestes are: "Who are you, you?"; and that, toward the end, when she turns away from him and his deed in horror and disgust, she calls out: "You were my brother, the head of our family"—"you were," in the past tense, for he is no more; recognition, born only from the commitment to act, is devoured again by the act committed. Yet nothing compares to the heart-rending struggle for recognition as Hauptmann presents it in his last play *Iphigenia in Delphi*. It is as if the poet knew that, if *anagnorisis* were only possible, firm ground, human ground, could be won again. Most of the play is a nerve-racking attempt of the characters at recognizing each other, all of them laboring as if in the throes of childbirth to bring forth the answer to the question: Who are you? Electra and Orestes locked in a tormenting battle to recognize each other, Electra assailing the immovable priestess of Artemis to give her a sign that she is Iphigenia, the lost sister. But the answer dies before it reaches the lips; for the fraction of a moment the veil seems to lift, but then it drops again; Iphigenia disappears among the rocks, unknown, unrecognized. The rest is silence—and no Fortinbras to blow the trumpet of recognition.

A last glance back at Goethe's *Iphigenia*. If, within the store of immortal documents of the European soul, this work of Goethe's has become the triumphant gospel of humanism, it is for the reason that it celebrates the redemptive power of recognition. Exactly in the middle of the play, in its very center— and center is here not only an indication of place—Orestes facing the unknown Artemis priestess who, in turn, does not know him either, exclaims: "Between us twain be truth. I am Orestes." It is an agonizing confession, because by naming himself he names and confesses to his unspeakable crime. But it is this confession, this making himself known, which is the beginning of his recovery, of his liberation from the suffocating grip of guilt and corrosion. "Between us twain be truth"— Iphigenia could repeat these very same words when she faces king Thoas and informs him of the deceitful stratagem which —with her consent—has been hatched against him: the theft of the Artemis statue and the surreptitious flight of the three Greeks. It is a confession fraught with mortal danger—and Iphigenia is fully aware of it—because the irate king may easily destroy her, her brother, and his friend. But it is the truth that has to be risked if man's relationship to his fellow man is to be more than an impenetrable jungle of fraud, selfishness and exploitation. There is a third moment of recognition: Thoas realizing that the foreigner who wants to rob him of his most precious possession is Iphigenia's brother, and that he has a claim on her to which he, the king, has to bow. It is a recognition involving the most painful suffering of renunciation, because with Iphigenia's loss the king will lose the one being whom he loves most. But, at whatever expense, the truth has to be accepted if the new millennium of friendship, peace, and mutual understanding is to be ushered in. Know thyself, make thyself known, the moment and act of recognition, self-accusing, dangerous, bitterly painful as it may be, is the signum of true humanity. Once, in Goethe's hands, the Oresteia was aglow with it. In today's Oresteia the command inscribed on the temple of Apollo has become mute.

Yet, even if it may have become muted in the works of the

three contemporary authors, these very works are but an echo of the admonition of the Delphian godhead. The picture in the mirror which they hold up before us may be frightening and inhuman, desperate, and deceptive in the arrangement of perspectives which seem to open up roads where there is none. But still it is a picture in a mirror in which we are to recognize ourselves. This is the miracle of art that even the poet crying out in despair and wishing to cut humanity out of the human being like a festering wound, calls us back, shocks us back, by his cries and his despair, into the recognition of our human condition. As long as the poet speaks, no matter from what abyss of bleakness and desolation, there is for us, the listeners, a bridge on which the abyss can be crossed. Even the dehumanized myth can, if we wish it, on the very strength of its dehumanization, become a guidepost on the road to a new humanization. The knowledge about ourselves and the world we made which the poet imparts to us may be frightening and crushing, but, being knowledge, it contains the seed of regeneration. In his poem "Gerontion" T. S. Eliot asks the question: "After such knowledge, what forgiveness?" Can it be, may we at least dare hope, that the knowledge itself is already the beginning of forgiveness?